Pedagogy of Demo

Pedagogy of Democracy

*Feminism and the Cold War
in the U.S. Occupation of Japan*

MIRE KOIKARI

TEMPLE UNIVERSITY PRESS
Philadelphia

Mire Koikari is an Associate Professor in the Women's Studies Program at the University of Hawai'i at Manoa.

TEMPLE UNIVERSITY PRESS
Philadelphia PA 19122
www.temple.edu/tempress

Library of Congress Cataloging-in-Publication Data

Koikari, Mire, 1965–
    Pedagogy of democracy : feminism and the Cold War in the U.S. occupation
of Japan / Mire Koikari.
        p. cm.
    Includes bibliographical references and index.
    ISBN-13: 978-1-59213-700-8 (cloth : alk. paper)
    ISBN-13: 978-1-59213-701-5 (paper : alk. paper)
    1. Women—Japan—Social conditions.   2. Women—Violence against—
Japan—History.   3. Japan—History—Allied occupation, 1945–1952.
4. United States—Foreign relations—Japan.   5. Japan—Foreign relations—
United States.   6. Postcolonialism.   7. Feminist theory.   8. Cold War.
I. Title.
    HQ1762.K5658 2008
    305.48'8956009044—dc22
    2007049494

091312P

For my parents, Koikari Yūji and Michiko

Contents

Acknowledgments

In the course of researching and writing this book, I have accumulated debts to many individuals and institutions. At the University of Wisconsin at Madison, I benefited from criticism, support, and encouragement generously offered by Charles Camic. As dissertation advisor, he provided solid guidance at the earliest stage of the project, without which this book would never have happened. Elaine Marks, Mary Layoun, Gay Seidman, Jane Collins, and Ann Orloff each helped me think about gender from critical feminist perspectives and sparked my interest in rethinking the meanings of the U.S. occupation of Japan. At the University of Hawai'i at Manoa, Kathy Ferguson and Ruth Dawson have sustained the project by reading and commenting on different versions of the manuscript, offering advice and suggestions in publishing, and always believing in the significance of the book. Colleagues at other institutions have also provided the kind of support that I could not do without. Jan Bardsley has always been more than generous in expressing enthusiasm about the project and offering help whenever I need it. Elyssa Faison, Tsuchiya Yuka, and Kinukawa Tomomi continue to be my source of inspiration; their commitment to critical pedagogy, keen insights into the history of U.S.–Japan relations, and wisdom and tenacity with which they navigate through American and Japanese academia have taught me more than they ever realized.

Since the beginning of this project I have heavily relied on the assistance of librarians and archivists in the United States and Japan. James

Zobel at the MacArthur Memorial, Library, and Archives in Norfolk, Virginia, has been of tremendous help since my initial visit to the archives many years ago. The staff members at the following libraries and archives have also been indispensable in carrying out my research: in the United States, the National Records Center in Suitland, Maryland, and the Sophia Smith Collection at Smith College in Northampton, Massachusetts; and in Japan, the National Diet Library and the Tokyo Women's Plaza in Tokyo, and the Kanagawa Josei Sentā in Fujisawa, Kanagawa.

At Temple University Press, my editor, Mick Gusinde-Duffy, has skillfully guided me through the process of turning a manuscript into a book, always providing quick, useful, and concise advice along the way. Anonymous reviewers at the Press have helped me refine and strengthen various arguments in the book and keep in mind the multidisciplinary nature of its (potential) readers. Gary Kramer, Carey Nershi, Marianna Vertullo, and Teresa Horton have also provided assistance indispensable in the completion and publication of the book.

Parts of an earlier version of the book are published as "Rethinking Gender and Power in the U.S. Occupation of Japan, 1945–1952," *Gender and History*, vol. 11, no. 2 (1999), Blackwell Publishers, and "Exporting Democracy?: American Women, 'Feminist Reforms,' and Politics of Imperialism in the U.S. Occupation of Japan," *Frontiers: A Journal of Women Studies*, vol. 23, no. 1 (2002), University of Nebraska Press. Permission to reprint is greatly appreciated.

This book would not have been possible without the help and support of my parents, Koikari Yūji and Michiko, who went through the turbulent years of wartime and postwar Japan and experienced consequences of war, defeat, and foreign occupation in their own lives. As a child growing up in the midst of postwar affluence, I heard various stories of "Japan" that were often hard to imagine from my parents. These stories have stayed with me, informing my sense of Japan and its past and leading to this project. For planting a seed of historical inquiry into the fascinating topic of Japanese feminism, nation, and empire, I dedicate this book to my parents.

Note on Japanese Names

In accordance with Japanese convention, all the Japanese names are given with the family names first followed by the given names, except in the cases of identifying Japanese authors who have published in English, whose names then are given in the reverse (that is, Western) order.

Pedagogy of Democracy

1

Introduction

Recasting Women in the U.S. Occupation of Japan

> *Our experience in the Philippines and in the more recent reformation of Japanese life, where in reshaping the lives of others we have been guided by the same pattern from which is taken the design of our own lives, offers unmistakable proof that while American in origin and American in concept, these tenets underlying a truly free society are no less designed to secure, preserve and advance the well-being of one race than of another. . . . The lesson from past and contemporary events is that they are no longer peculiarly American, but now belong to the entire human race.*
>> —FOURTH OF JULY MESSAGE, GENERAL DOUGLAS MACARTHUR, SUPREME COMMANDER IN OCCUPIED JAPAN[1]

> *This occupation has had no historical guide. Its approach is an out-growth of the slowly rising tide of humanism in the West. . . . The goodwill, the desire to be helpful to the Japanese as a people and as a nation is found, by and large, at all levels and seems to stem from the genuine altruism and enlightened concept of the United States interests of General MacArthur and many members of the Occupation. One needs only to recall the colonization policies in the East of the Western world in the last centuries to realize the colossal differences in points of view.*
>> —DR. FLORENCE POWDERMAKER, VISITING EXPERT[2]

> *The remarkable progress of Japanese women as they pull themselves up by their geta straps to pioneer in democratic procedures provides an inspiring record of world history. Only by comparison with their previous subjugation under feudalistic tradition little more than one year ago can the full significance of their achievements be realized.*
>> —LT. ETHEL WEED, WOMEN'S AFFAIRS BRANCH OF THE CIVIL INFORMATION AND EDUCATION SECTION[3]

On August 15, 1945, World War II came to an end with Japan's unconditional surrender. General Douglas MacArthur, Supreme Commander for the Allied Powers (SCAP), flew from the Philippines to Japan with a mission to occupy and demilitarize the defeated nation. The place and manner of MacArthur's arrival seemed to signal the victor's absolute confidence and unquestioned authority over its vanquished enemy. MacArthur—the embodiment of U.S. military power and a consummate actor well known for his grand performances—landed at the Atsugi Airfield, previously a training field for Japanese *kamikaze* fighters, with a handful of Allied troops. MacArthur himself was armed only with a corncob pipe. Despite his staff's concern about possible attacks by enemy soldiers not yet disarmed, MacArthur's triumphant landing was followed by a smooth procession to the New Grand Hotel in Yokohama, and later an entry into Tokyo where he established the General Headquarters (GHQ) of SCAP. A new chapter of postwar U.S.–Japan relations thus opened with richly gendered and racialized symbolism: the United States' imposition of its white masculine military authority over Japan, now a defeated and subjugated nation in the Far East.

Following the ferocious belligerence between the enemies in World War II, many Japanese feared that the objective of the occupation was to punish Japan. Yet, MacArthur declared that his intention was benign and noble: to "reorient" and "rehabilitate" Japan into a modern, democratic, and enlightened nation. While he perceived the Japanese as "an alien race of spiritual growth stunted by long tenure under the physical, mental and cultural strictures of feudal precepts," he had supreme confidence in his ability to transplant the American ideal to Japan and civilize its subjects.[4] He had what he considered evidence to support his conviction: U.S. governance in the Philippines had demonstrated America's capacity to "civilize" an alien and inferior race, and establish "democracy" abroad. Just as the U.S. policy of "benign assimilation" in the Philippines had uplifted its subjects from a state of ignorance and savagery, so would the U.S. occupation give the Japanese an unprecedented opportunity for civilization and enlightenment.

As MacArthur frequently argued, U.S. intervention in Asia was distinctly different from the European colonialism that preceded it, a sentiment clearly shared by Dr. Florence Powdermaker, a "visiting expert" who reported on the occupation's effects on the Japanese. This belief in the exploitative and oppressive nature of European colonialism was widespread among Americans involved in the occupation, who believed that U.S. overseas operations were driven by superior "humanitarian" objectives. Thus, MacArthur and Powdermaker articulated—in extraordinarily universalizing and expansionist terms—the new mission the Americans were to perform in the postwar world: the dissemination of American tenets of freedom and democracy that were "no longer peculiarly American, but now belong to the entire human race."

It was in this context of the American project to civilize and democratize a racially inferior other that Japanese women as gendered subjects emerged as centrally important figures. Seen as victimized for centuries by "Oriental male chauvinism," Japanese women embodied for the Americans feudal tradition, backwardness, and lack of civilization. As oppressed and helpless women of color, they became ideal candidates for Western salvation and emancipation. The occupiers' zeal for liberating Japanese women from indigenous male domination was all-consuming and multifaceted. MacArthur granted suffrage to Japanese women and praised their "progress" under U.S. tutelage as setting an example for the world,[5] while other male occupiers "emancipated" Japanese women by initiating various constitutional and legal changes and policies.

Following a familiar colonial trope of heterosexual romance between Western men and non-Western women, American men involved in the occupation expressed their desire to save Japanese women in various ways. Earnest Hoberecht, a correspondent for United Press International, advocated kissing as a path to liberation.[6] Kissing, of course, was often only a prelude. Many occupiers believed that fraternization and marriage were ways to save Japanese women. Based on a James Michener novel, the popular film *Sayonara* portrayed a sexual encounter between a U.S. soldier and a Japanese woman as an analogy of the U.S. occupation of Japan. Romance provided the woman with a means of escaping from restrictive social systems in Japan, allowing her to achieve individual fulfillment and freedom. As if to enact the script of *Sayonara*, Raymond Higgins, the military governor stationed in Hiroshima, married his Japanese maid, "saving" her from the aftermath of the atomic bomb and her abusive husband. Their union symbolized a new, heterosexual, familial coalition between the two nations in the postwar world.[7]

The postwar U.S.—Japan encounter also involved dynamics that exceeded the colonial trope of heterosexual romance, however. No less earnest in their attempts to emancipate and transform Japanese women were women reformers in the occupation forces, and especially Beate Sirota Gordon, a European Jewish woman who had acquired American citizenship just a few years prior to her enlistment in the occupation. Although she had lived in Japan before the war and possessed Japanese language skills, she had absolutely no legal expertise. Nevertheless, the twenty-two-year-old college graduate was placed on the all-American—and almost all-male—constitutional revision team, and assigned to draft articles for Japanese women's civil rights. She thus came to play a critical role in pushing for a constitutional guarantee of gender equality, a guarantee nonexistent in the United States.

The ideal of gender equality proclaimed in the new constitution was to be implemented by a group of American women occupiers led by Ethel Weed. Their passion for gender reform was all the more remarkable, as they were utterly unfamiliar with Japan, had no language skills, and received no extensive training for their job in occupied Japan. Low ranking within the predominantly male occupation bureaucracy, these women nonetheless worked tirelessly to emancipate and transform Japanese women. Despite rhetoric to the contrary about its importance, gender reform efforts were frequently left to individual women occupiers' ingenuity and commitment. Many other, "more important," reforms originated from blueprints created prior to the occupation, or from MacArthur's directives, and involved higher ranking personnel in the U.S. government or the headquarters in Tokyo.[8] Ironically, this gave women occupiers some autonomy and allowed them to devise and implement—often from scratch—their own visions of gender democracy in Japan. Many Japanese women enthusiastically welcomed American women occupiers and their efforts to democratize Japan, and tapped into shared discursive repertoires of gender equality and democracy to articulate their own visions of postwar womanhood.

As the occupiers' memoirs and autobiographical writings indicate, the occupation offered many American women the best and most memorable years of their lives. As citizens of a nation founded on principles of democracy, and confident about their qualifications and effectiveness as educator-reformers, they believed that American women were the ideal teachers for Japanese women. Ethel Weed's epigraph at the beginning of this chapter demonstrates her conviction that the arrival of Americans ended centuries of oppression of Japanese women. During the occupation, American women were given a rare chance to engage in a mission of national, indeed global, significance. By disseminating freedom, equality, and democracy in postwar Japan, they were supporting American Cold War struggles against communist totalitarianism.

Over the past five decades, belief in the successful transformation of Japanese women's lives provided many occupiers and subsequent generations of Americans with "unquestionable" evidence that U.S. interventions in Japan were benign, and indeed beneficent. The picture of Japanese women being liberated from male domination and gaining new rights under U.S. tutelage is also etched in the minds of many Japanese, and is understood as a turning point in the history of Japan. This view of the occupation as a remarkably generous effort by the victor to "democratize" Japan and especially its women has constituted an extraordinarily powerful historical account shaping American and Japanese self-understandings. For Americans, the narrative of Japanese women's emancipation has solidified the image of the United States as the leader of freedom and democracy, justifying and promoting its pursuit of imperial hegemony in the post–World War II world. For Japanese, the celebration of the occupation as Japan's new beginning, its rebirth as a democratic and peace-loving nation, has resulted in historical amnesia about its colonial violence prior to the occupation and subsequent involvement in the Cold War. In crucial though often unacknowledged ways, the gendered narrative of occupation has effected a cleansing of the images of two imperial nations with violent pasts.

Rethinking the Occupation:
Gender and Cold War Imperial Feminism

Pedagogy of Democracy: Feminism and the Cold War in the U.S. Occupation of Japan is an attempt to intervene in the triumphal narrative of the occupation, women, and democracy from a critical feminist perspective.[9] I argue in this book that rather than an unprecedented moment of liberation for Japanese women, gender reform in occupied Japan was intimately connected on the one hand to prewar nationalist and imperialist politics, and on the other to emerging Cold War cultural dynamics. By resituating the U.S. occupation and its feminist interventions in larger geopolitical and cultural contexts, I examine it as an extraordinarily complex and problematic instance of Cold War imperial feminism in the Far East.

In critiquing the existing narrative of the occupation, I do not simply replace the "occupiers as liberators" model with that of "occupiers as oppressors," but offer a far more nuanced and multilayered analysis. During the occupation, as I show, American women simultaneously promoted and undermined the U.S. pursuit of Cold War hegemony. At one level, they clearly participated in U.S. imperialism by disseminating Cold War discourses of femininity and domesticity and promoting the Americanization of postwar Japan in the name of women's emancipation. Their project of emancipating Japanese women was inspired by, and in turn promoted and justified, U.S. imperial expansionism in the early postwar years. At the same time, American women also subverted the dominant structure of power, as their participation in gender reform visibly contradicted the Cold War notions of women and domestic containment. Japanese women's participation in the occupation had equally or more complex consequences. On the one hand, Japanese middle-class women enthusiastically welcomed the occupiers' reform project and embraced American discourses of democracy and gender equality. On the other hand, however, they also developed a close personal bond with American women reformers, deviating from the Cold War tenet of heterosexual normativity by creating a female homosocial sphere and causing anxiety among American male occupiers. Even Japanese women's resistance often resulted in ambiguous and unpredictable outcomes. Women unionists openly defied the American authorities by participating in communist-led labor protests and praising gender policies in the Soviet Union and China as the ideal. However, they also insisted on the Cold War ideals of domesticity and heterosexuality and stigmatized poor, economically displaced women who earned their means as prostitutes. In U.S.-occupied Japan, then, American and Japanese women were constantly stepping in and out of the dominant apparatus of power, sometimes reinforcing and at other times undermining an emerging structure of hegemony. Recast from a critical feminist perspective, the U.S. occupation of Japan becomes an extraordinarily dynamic and multifaceted story about women's negotiations with power. Simultaneous tenacity and instability of hegemony, and unpredictable and ironic outcomes of feminist political mobilization, constitute the major themes of this book.

In analyzing the occupation as a case of Cold War imperial feminism, I create an interdisciplinary dialogue among occupation studies, Cold War cultural studies, and feminist colonial and postcolonial studies. This multi-disciplinary dialogue not only results in richer analysis of the occupation itself; it also challenges each discipline to reconsider some of its preexisting analytical and empirical assumptions.

Occupation Studies

The task of documenting and evaluating the U.S. occupation of Japan has generated numerous and contentious debates among scholars and nonscholars in Japan and the United States, resulting in a large body of work collectively referred to as occupation studies, or *senryō kenkyū*. Often at stake in these debates are national self-understandings of each country. Review essays by John Dower and Carole Gluck illuminate this aspect of occupation studies.[10] During the 1950s and 1960s, American scholars had a strong tendency to define the occupation as an example of beneficent American rule, which liberated and democratized the Japanese. Americans thus focused on demilitarization and democratization, but largely ignored the antilabor and anticommunist measures that accompanied economic recovery and Cold War containment policies. Japanese scholars during the same period were highly critical of U.S. operations, focusing on the occupation's "reverse course" and its repressive and antidemocratic measures. The reverse course refers to a major shift in U.S. policies in Japan around 1947, when the agenda of democratization was replaced by one of rebuilding Japan as an economic and military ally for the United States in the emerging Cold War. Strongly influenced by Marxist class analysis, Japanese scholarship thus focused on the occupation's repressive measures toward leftist labor and other popular movements, and the resurgence of prewar Japanese conservative forces and the economic structures.

Spearheaded by John Dower in the United States and Takemae Eiji in Japan, since the 1970s, these scholarly communities have modified their clearly opposing views, and begun a dialogue and even collaborative research. As Carol Gluck succinctly notes, while earlier studies focused on "what the well-intentioned United States had done for Japan in political and social reform" revisionist scholarship questioned "what the United States had, for its own ideological and security interests, done to Japan in the way of economic and military involvement."[11] Revisionist historians began to pay more attention to the operation of power at various levels in the U.S. occupation and to Japanese dynamics, as well as to the larger geopolitics of the Cold War. On the Japanese side, Takemae and other revisionist historians have refrained from overarching generalizations regarding U.S. interventions, examining instead individual policies and decision-making processes, in particular pertaining to land reforms, labor policies, and the imperial throne, and tracing the motives and intentions of individual occupiers and Japanese responses to them. Since the onset of this revisionist historiography, American and Japanese scholars have collaborated in joint conferences, most notably a series of symposia involving scholars and ex-occupiers held at the MacArthur Memorial, Archives, and Library in Norfolk, Virginia, from 1975 to 1991.

These studies have provided an important foundation for subsequent scholarship by identifying the occupation's general trend, organizational structures, and major policies. Started as the Allied occupation of Japan at the end of World War II, the occupation was almost from the very beginning exclusively controlled by the United States, which evaded interference from other Allied powers such as Britain, the Soviet Union, China, and Australia. Under the command of General Douglas MacArthur, who as SCAP upheld demilitarization and democratization as the twin agenda in postwar Japan, American occupiers set up general headquarters, GHQ SCAP, in Tokyo and proceeded to administer indirect rule of mainland Japan by executing reform through the existing Japanese government. While General MacArthur stood as the head of SCAP, the bulk of reform efforts was carried out by American military and civilian bureaucrats in staff sections of Tokyo headquarters, including Government Section, Public Health and Welfare Section, Civil Information and Education Section, and Economic and Scientific Section, among others. Literally thousands of directives, memoranda, and verbal orders were issued by these sections in areas ranging from reform of the Imperial Throne to economic reconstruction to educational liberalization. To assist GHQ SCAP, local military government teams were set up throughout Japan, with American occupiers transmitting orders and directives from GHQ to local Japanese officials and monitoring the progress of democratization. Built in extreme haste, the occupation's organizational structure suffered from numerous conflicts and disagreements among sections and poor communications between Tokyo headquarters and local military teams. Furthermore, despite their zeal and self-understanding as democratizers, many of the occupiers had little knowledge of Japan and lacked qualification and experience as reformers. These factors contributed to the occupation dynamics that were frequently contradictory and unpredictable, even haphazard and chaotic.

By now, it is commonplace among scholars to characterize the occupation as consisting of at least two different phases, with the so-called reverse course causing a major shift in occupation policies somewhere between 1947 and 1949. The initial phase of the occupation witnessed strong idealism among American occupiers who went on to initiate a series of radical reforms aimed at demilitarization and democratization. They include constitutional revisions that upheld popular sovereignty and pacifism; purges of wartime collaborators from public offices and trials of war criminals at military tribunals, the most famous of which was the International Military Tribunal for the Far East; liberalization of politics that released prewar political prisoners, legalized the Japan Communist Party, and enfranchised women; economic reform that dissolved *zaibatsu* (industrial conglomerates) and abolished the exploitative system of rural landlordism and tenancy; protection of workers' rights through such laws as the Trade Union Law that encouraged unionization and the Labor Standards Law that set the standard for working conditions; and educational reform that promoted coeducation and emphasized propagation of democracy, peace, and freedom.

With the emergence of the Cold War, scholars argue, the occupation entered a conservative, retrenchment period characterized by increasingly repressive measures of remilitarization, economic recovery, and political containment of the left. While SCAP's intervention in a nationwide general strike scheduled for February 1, 1947 is commonly considered the beginning of reverse course, there are other events and policies that indicate an increasing "reversal" of the occupation policies. Those who had been purged at the beginning of the occupation were now depurged, and the "Red Purge" began to target Communist Party members and the left-labor front activists and workers. The policy of demilitarization was replaced by that of remilitarization, leading to an increasing pressure toward constitutional revision and Japanese rearmament, industrial remilitarization geared toward defense production, and a projection for long-term installation and expansion of U.S. military forces in Japan. Propagation of democracy, freedom, and equality gave way to anticommunist education, which emphasized the danger of communist infiltration and the importance of defending (American) democracy.

Clearly the occupation went through a shift halfway through its course. However, it is too simplistic to characterize the occupation as consisting of two distinctly different and contrasting phases, with the initial democratic and liberatory (thus positive) period replaced by the later antidemocratic and repressive (thus negative) period. As the subsequent discussions show, American democratic reform in Japan, especially its feminist intervention, was from the very beginning deeply informed by American racism, sexism, and imperialism. Even those seemingly positive reform efforts in the early days of the occupation such as inclusion of gender equality in the new constitution, enfranchisement of women, and grassroots educational efforts originated from and fed back into American assertion of imperial hegemony and racial and national superiority. As the Cold War increased its saliency, feminist reform discourses and practices got progressively entrenched in the politics of anticommunist containment, but the intertwining of feminism and imperialism had been a defining feature since before the onset of reverse course. Thus, instead of arguing for the drastic reversal of the occupation, this book examines how preexisting, and already problematic, imperial feminist discourses and practices were gradually revised and refitted to inform Cold War containment politics of gender, race, class, and sexuality.

In recent years occupation scholarship has witnessed a number of studies that challenge and expand empirical and analytical scopes of previous scholarship. Pushing the disciplinary boundaries of Japanese studies and occupation studies and drawing on critical scholarship on race, culture, and empire, studies such as John Dower's *War Without Mercy: Race & Power in the Pacific War* and *Embracing Defeat: Japan in the Wake of World War II* and Yukiko Koshiro's *Trans-Pacific Racisms and the U.S. Occupation of Japan* illuminate the significance of race in the occupation dynamics.

Focusing on the parallel and mutually reinforcing development of American and Japanese racism and imperialism, Yukiko Koshiro argues that race constituted a common discursive ground where the two former enemies came to affirm each other's standing in international hierarchies, which led to "successful" and indeed "smooth" Cold War alliance making. Adopting Western imperial discourses of racial and national hierarchies (i.e., the superiority of self and the inferiority of others) to engineer its own colonial expansionism in Asia, Imperial Japan had constructed itself as an "honorary white," a nation capable of assimilating into superior Western culture and civilization while standing apart from and above other inferior Asians. Despite its challenge to Western imperialism during the war, Japan had affirmed and reinforced Western imperial understanding of white supremacy, and Western nations in turn had accepted to an extent Japan's sense of superiority to Asia and proximity to the West. This mutual dependency of Western and Japanese racism continued into the postwar years. After a short period of time during which race was used as a punitive tool to put Japan back into its "proper place," the United States actively cultivated and even manipulated Japan's admiration toward the West and its distance from the rest of Asia to turn the former enemy into an effective Cold War ally. As Koshiro argues, race and racism functioned as a source of productive power during the occupation.[12]

Echoing Edward Said's thesis on Orientalism, John Dower's studies situate the occupation within the larger context of imperial culture, history, and politics and provide a genealogical perspective on race and racism that covers a longer span of time. Observing American racism toward Japan during the war and the postwar occupation, he argues that American understanding of self as civilized and superior and Japan as uncivilized and inferior traces back not only to "racial stereotypes that Europeans and Americans had applied to nonwhites for centuries: during the conquest of the New World, the slave trade, the Indian Wars in the United States, the agitation against Chinese immigrants in America, the colonization of Asia and Africa, the U.S. conquest of the Philippines at the turn of the century," but more generally to the long-standing Western colonial vocabularies of the superior West and the inferior Orient/Other.[13] Defining the occupation as an instance of "imperial democracy" driven by the notion of white supremacy, he argues that "[f]or all its uniqueness of time, place, and circumstance—all its peculiarly 'American' iconoclasm—the occupation was . . . but a new manifestation of the old racial paternalism that historically accompanied the global expansion of the Western powers."[14] Dower goes on to illuminate how within the context of American imperial democracy and racism Japanese actively engaged in a diverse range of political negotiations with the occupiers—from collaboration to manipulation to resistance—at the grassroots and intergovernmental levels. Both Koshiro and Dower shed light on the significance of race as an analytical category that merits careful attention in studies of the occupation.

Despite the enormous contributions that have been made in the past decades, in particular excellent analytical and empirical insights offered by Dower and Koshiro, occupation historiography—revisionist or not—has been primarily "masculine" scholarship. The voluminous scholarship of the last five decades offers little information and analysis pertaining to women during the occupation, and equally or more problematically, fails to see the occupation itself as a gendered and gendering process that is also informed by other vectors of power such as race, class, and sexuality.

Influenced by the increasing saliency of a women's studies approach, women scholars in the United States and Japan have undoubtedly intervened in this trend by focusing on women who had hitherto been ignored in occupation studies. Defining the occupation as an instance of "women's liberation," however, the predominant focus has been on the positive effects the occupiers allegedly brought to Japanese women. Susan Pharr's influential work, "The Politics of Women's Rights," is a prime example. She analyzes the policymaking processes in which American women occupiers formed "an alliance for liberation" with middle- and upper-class Japanese women leaders to achieve Japanese women's rights, despite patriarchal resistance from both Japanese and American men. The occupation, Pharr argues, was "the world's most radical experiment with women's rights," resulting in successful "feminist reform": "The marriage of democracy and women's rights in the minds of most Occupation personnel heightened the significance of their contribution."[15]

To a surprising degree, Japanese scholars share Pharr's perspective. Citing Pharr, they argue that the occupation's gender reform—constitutional and civil code reforms, women's suffrage, the establishment of the Women's and Minors' Bureau, grassroots educational programs, and so on—provides overwhelming evidence of the positive role that the United States, and especially its women occupiers, played for Japanese women. Even though U.S. gender interventions might not have been thorough or sufficient, the occupation was a positive event for Japanese women.[16] It is important to note, however, that the studies by these Japanese women scholars are significantly more nuanced than Pharr's, generally mentioning the limitations inherent in any effort to instill "foreign" notions of "democracy" and "gender equality." Uemura Chikako, for example, points out that U.S. gender policies were based on a U.S. middle-class ideology, and thus were not as radical as they might seem at first sight. Japanese women scholars are also aware of the reverse course and thus acknowledge the less than democratic nature of occupation interventions. Yet these observations do not lead them to a more critical reevaluation of U.S. gender reforms per se, nor of the meanings and implications of such reforms within the context of the occupation or of Cold War imperialism. They rarely question what they perceive as the genuinely liberatory motives and intentions of American women occupiers, and ignore racism, sexism, classism, and imperialism that informed these women's discourses and practices. As a result, they repeat a pattern well observed in other studies of women and imperialism: A feminist project of bringing women to the center stage of historical analysis of empire sustains and promotes, rather than challenges, Western imperial hegemony. Women's studies scholarship has played a salient role in reproducing a problematic connection between imperialism and feminism.

In the recent shift women's studies has caused in occupation studies, former women occupiers have played a salient role. Beginning with Susan Pharr's interviews with Beate Sirota Gordon in the 1970s, scholars and media have sought witness accounts from women who served in the occupation. As a result, Gordon, an author of the gender equality articles in the postwar constitution, and Carmen Johnson, an officer in charge of grassroots democratization efforts, have achieved a certain celebrity status as feminist mother-liberators of Japanese women. Not only have they become women scholars' favorite interview subjects; their memoirs have been published, first in Japanese and later in English; documentaries depicting their efforts to emancipate Japanese women have been produced in Japan; and academic conferences and lectures both in the United States and Japan have provided forums for them to tell their occupation stories to a predominantly female audience.

Gordon's 1997 English-language autobiography, *The Only Woman in the Room*, was praised by a number of American celebrities.[17] On its back cover, Gloria Steinem states that "[Gordon's] personal story will enlighten all who question the importance of women's presence in the corridors of power"; Yo-Yo Ma describes the autobiography as "[t]he story of a remarkable life . . . Fascinating"; and Joanne Woodward describes Gordon as a "marvel of a woman," whose book "reflects her genuine love of people, the arts and life itself." On February 10, 1999, Gordon was interviewed by Ted Koppel on ABC's *Nightline* regarding her role in emancipating Japanese women.[18] On February 18, 2002, in the midst of the U.S.–Afghan war following the attacks on the World Trade Center, Gordon was interviewed by Jackie Judd on NPR's *Morning Edition,* where she discussed not only her role in bringing gender equality to women in postwar Japan, but explicitly referring to the task she had performed for Japanese women more than half a century ago, strongly urged Afghan women to insist on their desire for gender equality.[19] In both her retelling of the U.S. occupation of Japan and commentary on the U.S.–Afghan war, women of color become students who need to be prodded and encouraged by Gordon, the ultimate feminist teacher-liberator. With a women's studies approach as her vehicle, and women scholars as her interlocutors, Gordon has played a vital role in recirculating the gendered narrative of women, democracy, and imperial might.

The exhilarating narrative of American women emancipating Japanese women is not simply a product of American bias. For instance, Gordon's memoir, first published in Japanese, resulted from her collaboration with a Japanese female filmmaker, Hiraoka Mariko. As the postscript to the Japanese-language version titled *1945-nen no kurisumasu* indicates, the project of documenting Gordon's story started with Hiraoka. Initially, an all-female film crew, directed by Hiraoka, created a documentary about Gordon's involvement in the constitutional revision. The popularity of the film led to the publication of her autobiography, in which Hiraoka was again instrumental. Not only did she interview Gordon, who dictated her life story in Japanese. Hiraoka conducted archival research, and interviewed a number of Japanese and American individuals who had been involved in constitutional revision. Then Hiraoka transcribed the dictation, incorporated the archival materials, and turned them into a book-length manuscript. To ensure its accuracy, she then revisited Gordon in New York, and read aloud the entire manuscript to her. The Japanese-language version of Gordon's autobiography was thus created through Hiraoka's remarkable dedication. The publication of an English version followed. Hiraoka's contribution to making Gordon's story public is thus crucial, and well acknowledged by Gordon.

Clearly, Japanese women—Hiraoka and numerous others who enthusiastically embrace the story of their own emancipation by foreign women—share overlapping discursive spaces with their American counterparts, drawing on the same reservoir of ideas and assumptions about the occupation and its positive impacts on women. How do we explain Japanese and American women's collaboration in maintaining and circulating this understanding of the occupation? Crucially, the narrative of successful gender reform (dis)locates both women outside the purview of critical analysis of nation and empire. The narrative hinges on the long-standing Orientalist construction of Japanese women as helpless victims who, until the arrival of American women in 1945, had been incapable of any action. The image of Japanese women as victims without agency conceals, and indeed makes unimaginable, their willing participation in Japanese colonialism. The same narrative also relies on and reinforces the notion of progressive, emancipated, and thus "superior" American women who selflessly pursued the emancipation of other, inferior women. Driven by good intentions, they initiated a remarkable, indeed revolutionary, feminist reform project. With an emphasis on the occupation's emancipatory intents and successful outcomes, it becomes extremely difficult, if not impossible, to imagine how American women's discourses and practices were in fact informed by racism, nationalism, and imperialism. In sum, the congratulatory narrative of the occupation constructs both American and Japanese women as innocent bystanders to, rather than complicitous participants in, the problematic politics of race, nation, and empire in the twentieth century.

Like other historical narratives, however, the stories of women and the occupation are complex and contested. An entirely different interpretation, which actually predates the women's studies' analysis, focuses on the experiences of working-class women, and on the antilabor policies that the occupation authorities and the collaborationist Japanese government pursued. These studies conclude that the occupation was essentially oppressive and exploitative, resulting in the curtailment of working-class women's union activism and their economic and political rights, and denying Japanese women the opportunity to achieve genuine democratic social transformation.[20] According to this argument, the pledge to "democratize Japan" was a false promise, and the occupation hindered, rather than promoted, Japanese women's democratic emancipation. This more critical argument, however, has been overshadowed by the narrative of successful gender democratization, which as I have shown, has far more institutional support from women's studies, as well as the stamp of authenticity from the American women occupiers.

A suggestive, although not fully developed, perspective is offered in a short article by Yoda Seiichi, who argues that rather than genuine democratization, the major objectives of the occupation were the demilitarization, modernization, and transformation of Japan into an effective ally in the emerging Cold War. Instead of the occupation's gender reform accomplishing the liberation of Japanese women or radicalizing Japanese gender relations, the intention was actually to create Japanese women who would be enfranchised and conservative allies for the United States. Posing as the liberator of Japanese women is seen as a U.S. strategy to gain the allegiance of women in the occupied country. Yoda's work points to the need to examine *gendered* strategies of the occupiers, not simply women's experiences, in analyzing the U.S. occupation of Japan. It calls for a careful and systematic study of how the concept of gender (i.e., a binary opposition between the meanings associated with women or femininity and men or masculinity) was mobilized to inform the occupiers' discourses and practices.[21]

Yoda's insight concerning gendered dynamics of the occupation is further developed in a number of studies that examine U.S. Cold War cultural formation. Lisa Yoneyama's recent article analyzes U.S. media portrayals of the occupation's gender reform and argues that during the occupation a feminist discourse of Japanese women's emancipation and rehabilitation was mobilized to disseminate an image of new—feminized and pacified—Japan and to affirm and justify Cold War U.S. hegemony both domestically and internationally. Such understanding of the occupation also depended on and recirculated the feminist imperialist notion that Western, especially American, women were more emancipated, progressive, and thus superior. Far from the moment of women's liberation, she suggests, the U.S. occupation of Japan should be examined as an occasion where the figure of Japanese women was strategically deployed to articulate U.S. nationalism and imperialism in the Cold War context. Caroline Chung Simpson's *An Absent Presence: Japanese Americans in Postwar American Culture, 1945—1960*, Naoko Shibusawa's *America's Geisha Ally: Reimagining the Japanese Enemy*, and Christina Klein's *Cold War Orientalism: Asia in the Middlebrow Imagination, 1945—1961*, also show the significance of gender in American Cold War formation where American self was frequently imagined as masculine and others (i.e., Japanese Americans, Japanese, and Asians) as feminine. [22]

The studies on women and the U.S. occupation I have reviewed here provide important historical information, and often drastically different conclusions, but their analyses are insufficient, and even flawed, in a number of ways. Pharr and other scholars who define the occupation as a successful feminist reform implicitly rely on an essentialist assumption about women: American and Japanese women *naturally* shared, because of gender, the same political visions and interests—the fight against patriarchal domination, whether by the male-dominant Japanese state or the male-dominant U.S. occupation. Such an argument conceals a multitude of hierarchies, as well as complex negotiations, that existed between women of the victorious occupying nation and those of the defeated and occupied. Furthermore, both the studies that focus on middle-class women's experiences and the studies of their working-class counterparts each draw their conclusions about the occupation by wrongly generalizing class-specific experiences to the entire population of Japanese women. Both fail to consider the category of "Japanese women" as heterogeneous and diverse, segmented by class, race, and other workings of power. Similarly, their implicit assumption that the American occupiers were a coherent, homogeneous category results in a static understanding of the occupation. An enormous, bureaucratic ruling body assembled in extreme haste, the occupation forces in fact constituted a diverse, conflict-ridden, and often incoherent and disorderly governing authority.

Perhaps more fundamentally, the existing occupation studies fail to explore in a systematic and extensive manner the occupation as a gendered and gendering political process. As Joan Scott argues in *Gender and the Politics of History*, taking gender as a category of analysis goes far beyond simply uncovering information about women. Scott defines gender as a socially constructed binary opposition between the meanings associated with masculine and those with feminine. Gender as a meaning system constitutes "a primary way of signifying relationships of power" or "a primary field within which or by means of which power is articulated," and "structure(s) perception and the concrete and symbolic organization of all social life."[23] Thus incorporating gender as a category of analysis leads to a drastic shift in historical studies. As she points out, gender analysis

> provides a way to decode meaning and to understand the complex connections among various forms of human interactions. When historians look for the ways in which the concept of gender legitimizes and constructs social relationships, they develop insight into the reciprocal nature of gender and society and into the particular and contextually specific ways in which politics constructs gender and gender constructs politics.[24]

While I take seriously Scott's insight concerning gender as a centrally important category in historical analysis, I see the need to go beyond a study based on a single category of analysis. The recent important shifts in the feminist paradigm—from excavating women's stories, to incorporating gender as a category of analysis, and finally to examining the intersectionality of multiple categories of race, gender, class, sexuality, and so on—have placed studies of history on new terrain.[25]

Among numerous studies that examine multiple and intersecting vectors of power, I find Anne McClintock's study, *Imperial Leather: Race, Gender and Sexuality in the Colonial Context*, particularly useful for the analysis of the U.S. occupation of Japan, as she delineates the intricate and often convoluted workings of gender and power in imperial and colonial settings. McClintock points out that gender is always articulated in relation to other vectors of power, and insists on the importance of an analytical paradigm that takes into account more than one category, cautioning against "narratives that orient power around a single, originary scene":

> Race, gender and class are not distinct realms of experience, existing in splendid isolation from each other; nor can they be simply yoked together retrospectively like armatures of Lego. Rather, they come into existence in and through relation to each—if in contradictory and conflictual ways. In this sense, gender, race and class can be called articulated categories.

As she emphasizes, race, gender, class, and so on are not "reducible to, or identical with, each other; instead, they exist in intimate, reciprocal and contradictory relations." What she refers to as "a fantastic conflation of the themes of gender, race and class" is a distinctive feature of both Western colonialism and the U.S. occupation of Japan.[26]

As the subsequent chapters of this volume show, the analytical approach suggested by McClintock not only casts new light on American and Japanese women's discourses and practices during the occupation, it also leads to the observation that the occupation was an extraordinarily dynamic political process simultaneously animated by gender, race, class, and sexual dynamics. Throughout this book, I point out how a multivector analysis of the occupation and its gender reform provides a unique analytical framework that leads to different interpretations of a given event that often oppose those exclusively focused on race, gender, or class. The significance of this approach is pointed out by Dorinne Kondo, who succinctly argues that analysis that pays attention to a single category of power "forecloses the possibility of ruptures and interventions when other forces are considered."[27] I argue that the heterogeneous— and often disruptive, contradictory, and uneven—nature of the occupation and its gender reform can only be illuminated by attending to the intersection of multiple strands of power that sometimes work with, but other times against, each other. A multivector analysis of power allows us to examine, for example, how the occupiers' gender reform as an apparatus of domination was made all the more powerful as it was energized by the convergence of race, gender, and class dynamics. Gender reform relied on and reinscribed the racialized imperial notions of American superiority and Japanese inferiority on the one hand,

and on the other recruited Japanese women as a tool of class containment; that is, as conservative, anticommunist allies in the midst of increasingly volatile labor mobilization. Yet, gender, race, and class dynamics did not always so neatly line up. Gender reform also caused much instability and incoherence in the occupation, as Japanese middle- and working-class women forged a cross-class alliance in critiquing the "undemocratic" treatment of Japanese women in the occupiers' venereal disease control and reasserted their racial, sexual, and national respectability. A feminist analysis informed by McClintock's and Kondo's insights thus sheds light on the ubiquitous nature of hegemony, but equally or more importantly, allows us to recognize hegemony's inability to hold itself together, or its constant "leakage," in U.S.-occupied Japan.

Cultures of Imperialism and Cold War Studies

In this volume I argue that the U.S. occupation of Japan was an instance of imperialism, and that strong similarities and continuities exist between European and American imperialism. In the U.S. academy, the notion of U.S. imperialism is not always recognized or accepted. In *Cultures of United States Imperialism*, Amy Kaplan critiques the "absence of empire in the study of American culture." As she points out, U.S. scholarly communities share a strong compulsion to disassociate the United States from imperialism, and if anything, perceive the United States as inherently anti-imperial since the time of its independence from Britain. As a result, current discussions of colonialism and postcolonialism frequently neglect the fact that the United States has had strong ties to European colonialism, and furthermore, has been internally and externally a colonizing and imperial force on its own.[28] The same point is made by Anne McClintock. "Since the 1940s," she argues, "the U.S. imperialism-without-colonies has taken a number of distinct forms (military, political, economic, and cultural), some concealed, some half-concealed," but nonetheless it could and did "exert a coercive power as great as any colonial gunboat." Thus one needs to see "continuities in international imbalances in imperial power" between European dominance up to the mid-twentieth century, and subsequent "U.S. imperialism without colonies."[29]

Strong similarities and continuities between European and American imperial politics can be found in the significance assigned to "native women." As feminist colonial and postcolonial studies reveal, in Western colonial processes, the figure of "native women," a gendered and racialized construct, played a number of critical roles. The colonizers often analogized relations between colonizers and colonized to a male–female sexual encounter. In European male colonial fantasy, Africa, the Americas, Asia, and the Pacific were feminine, colored, and sexualized bodies, while European colonizing forces were white and masculine, invading, exploring, and conquering "virgin lands."[30] As well documented in recent and expanding scholarship on American imperialism, similarly gendered and racialized imaginaries have been mobilized to justify as well as facilitate America's encounter with Others.[31]

The figure of "native women" played another equally important role in imperial and colonial encounters. In the minds of Western colonizers, indigenous patriarchal domination over women was an indication of the uncivilized and racially inferior condition of colonized societies. In contrast, the colonizers perceived their own societies as gender egalitarian, or at least well ordered and proper, and as such, civilized and racially superior. Thus the hierarchical construction of the West and of the non-Western Other was significantly mediated by gendered and racialized discourses. European and American women, including feminists, often actively participated in and endorsed such a construction of superior West and inferior Other, although their own subordination to Western men made their location within the colonial project often ambiguous.[32]

In colonial encounters, constructions of "native women" did not remain simply rhetoric, but frequently led to interventions in the name of "civilizing" native women and indigenous gender relations. Indigenous women were often perceived as a good means of "infiltration," and singled out as important "entry points" for the Western civilization project, whose objective was tantamount to socializing indigenous women with Western values to create obedient and loyal colonial subjects. Gendered and racialized acculturation projects were further informed by class dynamics: They often focused on schooling indigenous elite women. Following such reeducation, Western values would "filter downward" to the rest of the indigenous population, destructuring the indigenous power structure.

In the U.S. occupation of Japan and its gender reform efforts, stunningly similar dynamics were observed: the American masculine gaze toward Japanese women, indeed to the Japanese nation as a whole; constructions of Japan as feudal, patriarchal, and thus racially inferior, in contrast to the modern, gender-egalitarian, and thus racially superior United States; the centrality of Japanese women's reform as an American civilizing and modernizing project, and American women leaders' participation in it; and American reformers' focus on Japanese middle- and upper-class women leaders as the target of indoctrination. At the same time, as McClintock suggests, it is important to analyze the distinct features of U.S. imperialism in the postwar years—of which the occupation of Japan was but one example. For one, in asserting its own imperial domination, the United States sought to distinguish itself from, and establish its legitimacy against, its predecessor and rival (i.e., the European imperial powers). This required the United States to perform, among other things, rhetorical maneuverings so that its foreign operations would be perceived as different from, and better than, European colonial rule. Furthermore, U.S. imperialism in the case of the occupation was significantly shaped by the nature of Japan itself. What Tani Barlow calls Japan's "double relation" to colonialism—Japan's own development as a colonial power in Asia since the late nineteenth century within the context of Western imperial and colonial domination—complexly shaped the postwar U.S. occupation of Japan.[33] Third, the occupation took place in the context of the emerging Cold War culture. The U.S. efforts to democratize Japanese women were inseparable from Cold War containment politics. As feminist scholars frequently point out, Cold War containment culture was not simply about anticommunist rhetoric and practice. It also produced historically specific understandings of gender, sexuality, domesticity, nation, and so on. The occupiers' gender reform efforts in postwar Japan were deeply intertwined with these emerging, and deeply gendered, cultural dynamics.

In examining U.S. involvement in Asia since the 1920s, Mark Bradley examines American efforts to distinguish its own imperial foreign policies from those of European nations. On the one hand, American policymakers often relied on European Orientalist discourses, thus rendering authority and authenticity to their own (i.e., American) Orientalist constructions of Asia. At the same time, however, the United States frequently criticized European colonial rule in Asia as a "failure," because it failed to train the natives for eventual self-governance. In American eyes, European colonialism was exploitative, oppressive, and therefore "bad." In contrast, American overseas interventions, aimed at educating and civilizing—in short, "training"—the natives, who would otherwise be unable to govern themselves, were not only more successful but morally superior. The occupiers' emphasis on "rehabilitating" and "reorienting" Japanese women was inseparable from this understanding of American intervention as training. Typically the Philippines was invoked to showcase America's benign rule, despite the blatantly oppressive and exploitative nature of the U.S. colonization there.[34] MacArthur's Fourth of July message echoes this sentiment, presenting both the U.S. occupation of Japan as well as the Philippines as instances of U.S. beneficence in Asia.

However, U.S. imperialism in the case of the occupation was also shaped by the nature of Japan itself. Although the duration does not compare with European colonialism, Japan had been a ferocious colonial power in the course of its modernity. While contending with Western colonial domination, Japan pursued its own imperial project by colonizing its neighboring nations in the name of creating the Greater East Asia Co-Prosperity Sphere. Japanese modern feminism emerged out of this context, sharing intimate and problematic ties with Japan's nationalist and colonial dynamics. Despite its unconditional surrender and enormous reduction in territory at the end of

World War II, many aspects of Japanese colonialism, including its gendered nationalist politics, survived after the summer of 1945. As John Dower clearly documents in *Embracing Defeat,* the existing Japanese ruling sector tenaciously negotiated with, and even covertly resisted, the U.S. authorities. Since the U.S. needed to remake Japan into its ally in the emerging Cold War context, MacArthur often compromised, and even collaborated, with the existing elites, which led not only to a retention of the Imperial Household but also to the emergence of a conservative, pro-American regime in postwar Japan. As I later demonstrate, this led to, among other things, the Japanese rearticulation during the occupation of its own hegemonic nationalist and imperial discourses concerning women, race, family, and nation. Japanese middle-class women leaders who were empowered under the guidance of American women occupiers participated in these political dynamics and rearticulated their own imperial feminism in postwar Japan.

Finally, U.S. imperialism in the case of the occupation was uniquely shaped by the emerging Cold War culture. As well analyzed by a number of scholars, the Cold War spawned several distinct political discourses and practices, as the United States utilized a number of cultural and political strategies to establish and maintain hegemony both domestically and internationally. In the context of Cold War divisions, the United States constructed itself as a champion of democracy, freedom, and gender equality against communist totalitarianism. Exporting democracy to Japan and other parts of the world constituted a particularly important rhetorical and material strategy the United States deployed in creating allies against the communist block and maintaining its legitimacy as the leader of the "free world."[35]

During the Cold War, a narrative of containment became a dominant trope in the United States. Containment of nuclear energy was often equated with containment of women, of racial others, of sexuality, of subversion, of degeneracy, of disease, of communism, and so on.[36] Domestic containment became a powerfully gendered and sexualized trope within this context. The white middle-class heterosexual familial sphere came to possess new political significance. It was simultaneously a means to personal and national security, a symbol of (American) democracy and freedom, and a bulwark against the danger of communist infiltration. Thus traditional heterosexual gender roles within the family came to be invested with new meaning and significance, resulting in the postwar cult of domesticity. Those who fell outside of this new familial sphere included not just "failed" wives and mothers, but leftist women, prostitutes, and homosexuals, among others. Perceived as uncontainable they became subjected to intense social surveillance as subversive elements, and even as communists.

U.S. Cold War strategies involved disseminating containment narratives involving women, family, and sexuality in postwar Japan and elsewhere. In occupied Japan, the project of gender reform became a salient site of Cold War cultural dissemination where American and Japanese middle-class women came to share overlapping discursive repertoires, drawing on the common reservoir of ideas, assumptions, and language practices to make sense of their world. American women occupiers worked tirelessly to make available the discursive repertoire of democracy and gender equality along with proper domestic life. For many Japanese middle-class women, that repertoire of sense-making practices was congenial, resulting in their willing participation in containment narratives. Yet, this gendered Cold War strategy did not go uncontested. Drawing from a different and competing universe of meanings, working-class unionized women upheld Soviet and Chinese gender orders as their ideal and denounced American democracy as a "sham," thereby coming under strict surveillance and discipline by the occupation authorities.

The centrality of the Cold War is also visible in the American women occupiers' reform techniques. In reeducating and democratizing Japanese women, the American women occupiers devised numerous skits and role plays with containment themes, and at training sessions, Japanese women were required, quite literally, to play a part, practicing their roles until their performance became flawless—proof that Japanese women were rehabilitated and reoriented. Through repetition, American women occupiers, and also many Japanese women, came to believe in the veracity of the American democratization of Japan and the desirability of the American way of life, a reform strategy that shared striking similarities to the U.S. civil defense program in the 1950s. In the Cold War United States, Guy Oakes and Laura McEnaney point out, the civil defense program also relied on "performance," in particular learning and mastering skills and procedures through repeated drills and exercises. The U.S. civil defense programs "identify the procedures essential to survival and teach the American people how to perform them," with the understanding that "a set of rules, if correctly followed, would produce the desired results." Had nuclear deterrence failed, it was argued, Americans could still protect themselves and survive nuclear attack by utilizing civil defense techniques and procedures. Survival in the nuclear age was thus "reduced to the performance of routines."[37]

In the Cold War United States, the acquisition of techniques and procedures also had moral and ethical implications. Civil defense was considered a means to build a national ethic, solidify morale, and ensure the survival of the American way of life. As planners argued, civil defense was "a moral obligation of every household," teaching "civic virtues indispensable to the American way of life in the nuclear age."[38]

The occupation period—from 1945 to 1952—took place in an early phase of the Cold War, where a multitude of political and cultural discourses and practices were beginning to be articulated through the narratives of containment. Within this context, occupied Japan became a highly charged theater for emerging Cold War culture, where containment discourses and practices, including mastery of skills and techniques through repeated exercises, proliferated. It was not simply that Cold War culture was being exported to and imposed on Japan. It would be more appropriate to argue that despite its geographical distance from the U.S. continent, Japan became a salient site for the articulation of Cold War containment culture, with a remarkable degree of willingness on the part of Japanese to participate in its performance. The occupiers' gender reform constituted one exemplary locus of such containment culture.

Feminist studies of the Cold War, such as *Homeward Bound: American Families in the Cold War Era* by Elaine Tyler May, and *Survival in the Doldrums* by Leila Rupp and Verta Taylor, frequently emphasize the conservative nature of the era. From this perspective, the Cold War spawned the postwar cult of domesticity, confining women within the sphere of home, eroding economic and other gains women had made during World War II, and commencing a downturn in feminist mobilization. However, an increasing number of scholars question this understanding of the Cold War and its impact on women. For instance, *Not June Cleaver: Women and Gender in Postwar America, 1945–1960* edited by Joanna Meyerowitz presents a far more heterogeneous and ambivalent picture. "While no serious historian can deny the conservatism of the postwar era or the myriad constraints that women encountered," Meyerowitz argues,

> an unrelenting focus on women's subordination erases much of the history of the postwar years. It tends to downplay women's agency and to portray women primarily as victims. It obscures the complexity of postwar culture and the significance of social and economic changes of the postwar era. Sometimes it also inadvertently bolsters the domestic stereotype. Especially in works on the 1950s, the sustained focus on a white middle-class domestic ideal and on suburban middle-class housewives sometimes renders other ideals and other women invisible.[39]

Indeed the Cold War United States witnessed numerous instances of contradiction, resistance, and challenge by women, as containment politics were far more ambivalent and unstable than previously understood. Laura McEnaney's study, *Civil Defense Begins at Home: Militarization Meets Everyday Life in the Fifties*, provides a fascinating example of ambivalent and contradictory dynamics of the Cold War which could never completely contain women. Her analysis builds on and expands Meyerowitz's insight by showing how Cold War tenets of femininity, domesticity, and anticommunism combined to provide an impetus to a version of feminism in the postwar United States. "[T]he postwar cult of domesticity," McEnaney writes, "was a malleable and widely applicable construction in the Cold War years," and American middle-class women leaders appropriated the discourses of motherhood, anticommunism, and Cold War nationalism to pursue their feminist political objectives.[40] These leaders saw in civil defense mobilization "an opportunity to expand their membership rolls and enhance their political influence," and "[t]hrough a peculiar fusion of militarism, maternalism, and feminism," collaborated with the postwar state to demonstrate "that women's full participation in the polity was still necessary even after World War II's demand for their labor had disappeared."[41] Arguing that "there were no predicable politics that unfolded from postwar domesticity," McEnaney calls for "a more complex view of the relationship among the Cold War, the feminine mystique, and women's political activism."[42]

As a case study illuminating the complex and often unpredictable relationship between the Cold War and women, the U.S. occupation of Japan reveals how the Cold War also facilitated, rather than suppressed, feminist mobilization of both American and Japanese women and opened up a new political and cultural space in which the women both bolstered and resisted the dominant structure of power. While often willing participants in the Cold War mobilization, neither American or Japanese women completely believed in the containment narratives and assigned different, often radically opposing meanings to the ideas of femininity, domesticity, and democracy. Armed with feminist discourse of women's liberation, American and Japanese women involved in gender reform refused to be contained within home and family and sought for autonomy, mobility, and empowerment. Although these women's transgression did not go unpunished, they continued to express their political agency in ways that often exceeded all expectations. Examining women's active and often subversive negotiations with the Cold War tenets of femininity, domesticity, and heteronormativity thus constitutes an important task in this book.

The unpredictability of women's agency McEnaney and Meyerowitz point out and this book will delineate has much to do with the ambivalent nature of Cold War culture itself. As existing studies on Cold War containment politics frequently point out, sexuality constituted a particularly significant source of this ambivalence, undermining the dominant narrative of white, middle-class, heterosexual domesticity as the bulwark against communism.[43] As exemplified in the national debates surrounding George/Christine Jorgensen, a World War II veteran who underwent a "sex change" operation in 1952, American male sexuality was at best an ambiguous, and often extremely unreliable, symbol of national strength and prowess. In the Cold War context where national security was frequently articulated in relation to sexuality, an ambivalent American masculinity became a source of much anxiety and insecurity.[44]

In postwar Japan, sexuality also constituted a site of ambivalence and instability. By relegating the task of gender reform to women, the occupation authorities inadvertently created a "women-only" sphere consisting of American and Japanese women reformers. While these women were ardent promoters of containment politics, they also developed close working relationships, and sometimes extremely strong and passionate bonds, with each other. In the Cold War context, where any sexual transgression was immediately associated with political subversion and thus a cause for suspicion, the existence of a female homosocial sphere in postwar Japan disturbed the occupation authorities. MacArthur and other male occupiers often warned against, and even expressed hostility toward, the formation of a "women's block" in gender reform.

Sexuality became a source of disturbance in another way as well. Fraternization between American soldiers and Japanese women, and the resulting widespread venereal disease infection, caused much controversy. Far from being compliant subjects of the occupation, Japanese women proved to be a source of "contamination," indeed "menace." Unruly and uncontainable, Japanese women's sexuality was endangering the very success of the occupation. Equally or more problematic, venereal disease was considered a sign of American soldiers' moral, spiritual, and physical degeneration. The American soldiers' lack of self discipline was jeopardizing the U.S. mission of defending democracy in postwar Japan.

Such observations challenge and complicate existing feminist understandings of imperial and colonial encounters. By now it has become commonplace to argue that sexuality provides a familiar trope for international domination and subordination. In the Western colonial imagination, the West's encounters with others were often analogized to male–female sexual relations. The significance of sexuality was not limited to its metaphorical power, as many imperial and colonial encounters actually entailed sexual subordination of indigenous women to Western men. An increasing number of scholars apply this insight to the occupation, arguing that the United States stands as a dominant, masculine figure with a mission to rescue subordinate and feminized Japan. Early postwar films, novels, and other cultural artifacts certainly attest to the power of this heterosexual metaphor for shaping American understanding of the occupation. Fraternization between American soldiers and Japanese women was a concrete manifestation of such hierarchical, gendered, and sexualized dynamics between the two nations.

Yet, a closer examination of the occupation reveals other political dynamics that do not easily fit this analytical framework and thereby points to a need for more complex analysis of women, gender, and sexuality in

U.S.–Japan relations. The crisis of American masculinity represented by venereal disease indicates the precariousness of the notion of America as masculine and powerful and Japan as feminine and docile. Lacking self-discipline and control, American soldiers were undermining, rather than promoting, U.S. hegemony. Uncontainable and menacing, Japanese women were posing a serious challenge to the occupation authority. The emergence of female-to-female bonds in the course of gender reform further challenges and complicates the argument that the occupation be read exclusively as a heterosexual narrative of white men dominating, possessing, and rescuing subjugated and docile women of color. Stepping into a postwar imperial project primarily defined in heterosexual and masculinist terms, American and Japanese women shifted, rather than simply replicated, these terms. A reform network consisting of American and Japanese women introduced a narrative of female homosociality into a Cold War project predicated on the erasure of homosexuality, thereby significantly unsettling containment politics. The current, almost exclusive emphasis on containment domesticity and heteronormativity in feminist analysis of the Cold War, and that of masculinization of America and feminization of Japan in gender analysis of U.S.–Japan relations, falsely construct Japan and its women as subjugated and without agency, and thus inadvertently reproduce the dominant orders of gender, sexuality, and nation without due attention to numerous examples of resistance, subversion, and contradictions that occurred during the occupation.

Feminist Colonial and Postcolonial Studies

Finally, in analyzing the U.S. occupation of Japan, this volume joins feminist postcolonial studies in pressing for new interpretations and formulations of feminism. My inquiry into the U.S. occupation of Japan and its feminist politics was sparked, and has been subsequently sustained, by analytical and political concerns emerging in this field. Gayatri Spivak, Chandra Mohanty, Inderpal Grewal, and Caren Kaplan, among others, have cast critical light on feminism, modernity, and colonialism, urging us to reconceptualize feminism and imperialism as two interrelated social formations. The meanings and consequences of feminism need to be reexamined as imperial and colonial formations that have significantly and problematically mediated the relations between Western and non-Western women. Critical feminist understandings of self and other demanded by feminist postcolonial scholars have serious implications not only for feminist scholarship, but also for feminist movement discourses and practices as a whole.

Feminist postcolonial studies have shown how modern Western feminism was enabled by the colonial construction of non-Western women as an embodiment of an oppressive and chauvinistic culture of others. In articulating a feminist vision of an emancipated self, for instance, foundational British feminist texts, such as *Jane Eyre* and *Vindication of the Right of Woman*, relied on, reproduced, and recirculated what Gayatri Spivak calls "the axioms of imperialism."[45] The emergence of the feminist subjectivity of the British woman, Spivak notes, crucially hinged on the simultaneous invocation and erasure of a non-Western, other woman. In showing that Western feminist writers frequently turned to images of oppressive, chauvinistic, and despotic "oriental life" to articulate their feminist visions of transformation of Western societies, Joyce Zonana traces similar dynamics in nineteenth-century British feminist texts: "[B]y figuring objectionable aspects of life in the West as 'Eastern,' these Western feminist writers rhetorically define their project as the removal of Eastern elements from Western life." Such "feminist orientalism" defined the project of feminist transformation of society as an attempt to "make the West more like itself"—more civilized, enlightened, and above all, gender egalitarian than the East.[46] In Western feminist articulations, then, non-Western women are treated as mute objects of oppressions, deprived of their political and historical agency, who nonetheless play crucial roles in the formation and maintenance of Western feminist subjectivity.

Silencing, indeed erasure, of non-Western women in Western feminist discourses is not limited to literary texts of the past. Erasure of other women continues to take place in Western feminist texts, be they literary or academic. In "Under Western Eyes: Feminist Scholarship and Colonial Discourses," Chandra Mohanty argues that similar discursive strategies continue to inform Western feminist scholars' analysis and result in binary understandings of emancipated and autonomous Western women and oppressed and victimized non-Western women.[47] Even though Mohanty's article has been widely read by feminist scholars by now, it continues to pose a challenge because her insights need to be situated in various and concrete historical settings to see how they work. In the case of occupation scholarship, Mohanty's arguments need to be complicated, as Japanese women have frequently collaborated with American women in maintaining a binary construction of emancipated American women and oppressed Japanese women, suggesting a more convoluted relationship among women, imperial politics, and production of knowledge.

These problematic dynamics have clearly shaped feminist movement discourses and practices. In *Burden's of History: British Feminists, Indian Women, and Imperial Culture, 1865–1915*, Antoinette Burton shows how these dynamics manifested themselves in British women's mobilization on behalf of their "Indian sisters" in Victorian and Edwardian England. British feminists frequently argued that Indian women were powerless victims of indigenous patriarchal culture, and that as "emancipated sisters," British women had a mission to help women in India. By presenting themselves as helpers of the colonized women, Burton points out, British women could effectively argue that they were performing a "womanly job" for the empire, thus establishing their own "imperial citizenship."

Despite numerous differences, American imperial feminism shares a number of recurrent threads and common opportunities for women with its British counterpart. In such works as Jane Hunter's *The Gospel of Gentility: American Women Missionaries in Turn of the Century China*, Ian Tyrrell's *Woman's World, Woman's Empire: The Woman's Christian Temperance Union in International Perspective, 1880–1930*, Leila Rupp's *Worlds of Women: The Making of an International Women's Movement*, and Tracey Jean Boisseau's *White Queen: May French-Sheldon and the Imperial Origins of American Feminist Identity*, the connection is made between U.S. imperial endeavors abroad and women's feminist articulations. Historically, in the late nineteenth and early twentieth centuries, with ideologies and practices underpinned by a "feminist" critique of male domination at home and an endorsement of an "international sisterhood" among Western and non-Western women, American women missionaries, moral reformers, and suffragists were often critical of U.S. imperial expansionism and European colonialism. Nevertheless, they often uncritically accepted and recirculated the notions of racially inferior, uncivilized, and oppressed non-Western women and civilized and emancipated Western women who were to save women of color. In practice, their work provided a critical means for U.S. imperial expansion abroad, lending force and justification (often in the name of feminism) to its pursuit of hegemony. The U.S. occupation of Japan reveals this same intimate connection between American imperialism and feminism as it unfolded in the Cold War context. Furthermore, one can trace tangible connections and continuities between European and American imperial feminism in the figure of Beate Sirota Gordon, a European Jewish woman who served on the occupation forces as an American member and played a central role in constitutional revision.

In *Scattered Hegemonies: Postmodernity and Transnational Feminist Practices*, Inderpal Grewal and Caren Kaplan explore the intimate—and problematic—relationship between feminism and imperialism:

> Our critiques of certain forms of feminism emerge from their willing participation in modernity with all its colonial discourses and hegemonic First World formations that wittingly or unwittingly lead to the oppression and exploitation of many women. In supporting the agendas of modernity, therefore, feminists misrecognize and fail to resist Western hegemonies.[48]

Their observations about feminism's "imbrication" with modernity and its related institutions, such as colonialism, racism, and nationalism, provide a crucial insight for analysis of Western feminist formation and its relation to other women. The question we need to ask is not simply whether Western feminists were imperialists or anti-imperialists. Rather we need to investigate when and how feminist discourses and practices inform and are in turn informed by politics of nation and empire.

In *Home and Harem: Nation, Gender, Empire, and the Cultures of Travel*, which examines British and Indian feminist formations, Inderpal Grewal offers analytical insights that are applicable to instances beyond British imperialism and that put not only Western women but also non-Western feminist formations under critical scrutiny:

> [M]any forms of feminisms existed through participating in certain dominant discourses so that the issue, then, is not a search for a transparent or transcendent feminism but a need to examine the conditions of possibility of these feminisms. . . . Rather than debate feminism's collusions or resistances, I argue that nationalism, imperialism, and colonial discourses shaped the contexts in which feminist subjects became possible *in both England and India*.[49]

Recognizing imperialism as an enabling condition—a condition that "provided possibilities and problematic" for feminism—is crucial.[50] Moreover, by showing colonized (in this instance, Indian) women's feminist formation as equally, although differently embedded in modernity, nationalism, and imperialism, Grewal challenges binary, oppositional notions of dominant and oppressed, or colonizers and colonized.

The feminist postcolonial critique already discussed, especially Grewal's nuanced understanding of imperialism and feminism, informs my analysis of the U.S. occupation of Japan. Like their European counterparts, American women's self-understandings have often hinged on the construction of unequal, racially inferior others, in this case Asian women. A primary signifier of otherness in American women's imaginations, Japanese women have been mobilized—discursively and materially—for white women's self-realization. A critical understanding of imperialism and feminism also needs to be applied to Japanese women, who in pursuing their own agendas, frequently utilized nationalist and colonial discourses that had survived defeat and surrender. Ironically it was the very presence of American women reformers that enabled Japanese women leaders to articulate postwar feminism in this manner. Through their collaboration with American women reformers, Japanese women were soon to participate in Cold War containment politics.

Indeed, in U.S.-occupied Japan, the Cold War provided an extraordinarily powerful context for all. Postwar understandings about women, family, sexuality, and democracy were deeply informed by containment narratives. To a remarkable degree, American and Japanese women proved to be willing participants, and even those who resisted the U.S. occupation were often so well informed by containment narratives that they were frequently recuperated back into the dominant social orders. At the same time, however, containment politics in postwar Japan were heterogeneous, and often disruptive, uneven, and unstable, and thus did not preclude possibilities of irony, subversion, and ambivalence. In sum, this volume reveals how the stories of the occupation subvert themselves in the process of their (re)tellings. In the name of democracy, empire extends its reach and tightens its grip; in the name of privatized domestic consumerism, women are mobilized into public, militarized activities; in pursuit of proper heteronormative families, women develop intense personal bonds with each other. As I show throughout the book, feminist discourses and practices that emerged out of these dynamics were fraught with ironies and contradictions.

Chapter Organization

The following chapters present a complex and multifaceted picture of Cold War imperial feminist discourses and practices in U.S.-occupied Japan. Chapter 2 examines the two major legal reforms initiated at the outset of the occupation: women's suffrage and constitutional revision. Long-standing symbols of Japan's postwar rebirth, these reforms were in fact deeply informed by preexisting American and Japanese dynamics involving gender, race, nation, and empire, and constituted central sites of Cold War articulations of domesticity, heteronormativity, and racial and national purity. The chapter especially focuses on Beate Sirota Gordon, author of women's rights articles in the new constitution, as an iconic figure who embodied both imperial hegemony and its instability. Clearly, her narratives about constitutional revision repeat, quite explicitly, a feminist imperial discourse about white, emancipated women endowed with a mission to liberate oppressed and victimized women of color. At the same time, Gordon, with her Russian Jewish background, disrupts the dominant narrative of the occupation by insisting on her difference from American occupiers and superiority of European and Soviet discourses of gender equality to the American counterparts. Tracing the complex historical dynamics that informed the occupation's gender reform, the chapter redefines women's suffrage and constitutional revision as a moment of women's reentry into, rather than emancipation from, ongoing nationalist and imperialist politics.

Chapter 3 analyzes the meanings and consequences of Cold War transnational feminist mobilization involving Japanese and American women. Following women's suffrage and constitutional reform, the occupiers attempted to disseminate the notions of democracy and gender equality among Japanese women. With the help of American women leaders back home, women occupiers initiated a series of grassroots educational efforts aimed at Cold War indoctrination of Japanese women. Japanese middle-class women, including its feminist leaders, enthusiastically responded to the occupiers' reform efforts and embraced containment tenets of domesticity and femininity. Ironically, however, the reform network of American and Japanese women soon became a source of instability and disruption. Not only did the network become a space where women would voice their critique of gender reform and point out the fallacy of American democracy. It turned into a female homosocial sphere where American and Japanese women reformers forged strong bonds with each other, subverting the Cold War tenet of heterosexual normativity. In U.S.-occupied Japan, women's complicity in a dominant system of power frequently gave way to subversion, undermining an emerging structure of hegemony from within. By focusing on the ambivalent and unpredictable role feminist mobilization played in the occupation, the chapter's analysis illuminates both the ubiquity of hegemony and its inability to sustain itself.

Following the analysis of women's complicity in hegemony, Chapter 4 explores the nature of "resistance" by examining the various ways in which women's attempt to challenge and undermine oppression gets reabsorbed back into the dominant system of power. In contrast to their middle-class counterparts, Japanese working-class women, especially women of the left-labor front, explicitly opposed the occupation's gender reform. Their oppositions to the United States were twofold, simultaneously informed by class and gender. On the one hand, they actively participated in the left-labor mobilization led by the newly legalized Japan Communist Party and contested the occupation's economic and labor policies. On the other hand, they also challenged the occupiers' gender reform by upholding the Soviet and Chinese gender systems as the model and forging connections with procommunist women's organizations abroad. In articulating their resistance, however, they also relied on containment narratives of heterosexual normativity, thereby failing to transcend the dominant orders of the time. Analyzing the dynamic interweaving of resistance and recuperation of leftist women, the chapter questions the notion of "pure" resistance and calls for a nuanced analysis of women's oppositional politics.

Chapter 5 brings together the themes of domination, resistance, subversion, and recuperation by focusing on controversies surrounding venereal disease infection among American soldiers. During the Cold War, venereal disease infection was equated with weakness and degeneracy of the (male) mind, susceptibility to communist manipulation, and a threat to democracy. In occupied Japan, poor, economically disenfranchised women who resorted to prostitution and allegedly infected the soldiers became a source of serious danger that threatened national security. The authorities' containment effort—indiscriminate round-up and detention of Japanese women—backfired, sparking massive grassroots protest. Middle-class women leaders fiercely opposed the indiscriminate round-up of "innocent" women, insisting on the respectability of middle-class wives and mothers. Women of the left-labor front joined their middle-class counterparts and insisted on their own sexual respectability. Together these women demanded that the occupiers observe a crucial distinction between "respectable" and "unrespectable" women and called for stricter surveillance and regulation of "fallen" women as part of postwar democratization. Articulated at the intersection of Japanese nationalism and Cold War containment sexuality, feminist protestation both enforced and challenged the dominant structures of power. The chapter illuminates the problematic legacies of postwar feminism that emerged out of the intense comingling of gender, class, race, and sexual politics in the controversies.

Chapter 6 concludes this volume by highlighting the complex relation among feminism, imperialism, and Cold War containment politics that shaped the U.S. occupiers' gender reform in postwar Japan.

2

Feminism, Nationalism, and Colonial Genealogies

Women's Enfranchisement and Constitutional Revision

Beate Sirota Gordon's 1997 memoir, *The Only Woman in the Room,* opens with a chapter titled "Homecoming." The time is 1945, and the setting is Japan, where Gordon is being sent as a member of the American occupation forces. The title is "Homecoming" because to her, Japan was home. Born in Vienna in 1923, Gordon spent her childhood, the late 1920s and 1930s, in Tokyo, prior to immigrating to the United States. Japan was also where her Russian Jewish parents, Leo and Augustine Sirota, had been stranded since the beginning of the Pacific War. The foremost personal goal of her return was to find her parents, from whom she had not heard in several years.

Flying in, Gordon saw enormous devastation: "Charred ruins and solitary chimneys . . . stood up from the bare red earth like nails." As she recalls, "[l]ooking down, I knew beyond a doubt that the Japanese were finished." As her plane approached Atsugi Airport, where Douglas MacArthur had triumphantly landed several months earlier, the Americans on board were ecstatic with the panorama of their victory, but Gordon's reaction was distinctly different:

> The soldiers on the plane whistled and flocked to the windows, exulting openly, but I felt numb with shock. We were all American citizens assigned to the General Headquarters of SCAP (Supreme Commander Allied Power), where General Douglas MacArthur

was directing the occupation, but at the moment I was brought up short by the differences between us. To me, Japan meant home, the country where I had been brought up and where my parents still lived.[1]

Following the account of her arrival, Gordon's memoir takes us back to the Sirota family's emigration from Europe to Japan in the 1920s, when Leo Sirota, a renowned pianist, was invited to chair the Piano Department at the Japanese Imperial Academy of Music in Tokyo. Her life story then proceeds in chronological order: her growing up in prewar Japan, moving to the United States to attend college, obtaining American citizenship, returning to postwar Japan and authoring the women's rights articles in Japan's new constitution, and finally moving back to the United States to pursue her career and family life.

Central to her narrative is her involvement in the revision of Japan's constitution, a revision intended to transform Japan's political, economic, and social systems. In her early twenties and fresh out of college, she had absolutely no constitutional or legal knowledge. She was confident, however, that she "knew" Japan, especially women's lives, because of her childhood experience in prewar Tokyo. Being "the only woman" on the all-American—and all white and almost all male—team drafting the constitution, she was driven by the conviction that she alone was responsible for emancipating Japanese women. Using the Weimar and Soviet constitutions as her model, she drafted women's rights articles. That the articles pertaining to women's rights in the new constitution were written singlehandedly by a woman member of the U.S. occupation forces has not escaped the attention of women's studies scholars. In both Japan and the United States, Gordon has been celebrated as a symbol of international feminism, a woman who brought emancipation to Japanese women.

Gordon is not the only member of the occupation forces hailed as a liberator of Japanese women. General Douglas MacArthur continues to be a central figure in the narratives of Japanese women's emancipation in the U.S. occupation of Japan. As the story goes, even before MacArthur reached Japan, he spoke of his deep concern for the low status of Japanese women, telling an aide that the liberation of women would be one of the priorities of his democratization efforts. In his autobiography, *Reminiscences*, MacArthur, who embodies American military prowess, portrays himself as a staunch advocate of women's causes. His support for women's suffrage provoked heavy criticism from those who believed that Japanese women, confined for centuries in their feudal and patriarchal tradition, would be unable to exercise political rights. However, asserting absolute confidence in Japanese women, MacArthur granted them the right to vote, thereby ensuring his renown as an advocate and liberator of Japanese women.[2]

In existing occupation narratives, MacArthur and Gordon are thus celebrated as champions of Japanese women. According to these narratives, acting on strong, personal beliefs, the two initiated remarkable reforms in the earliest days of the occupation, instituting gender equality, striking a fatal blow to indigenous male domination, and opening a new chapter in the history of Japanese women.

It is curious, to say the least, that a European Jewish woman has become the celebrated figure in the narratives of the American emancipation of Japanese women, standing as feminist emancipator alongside an unapologetic, autocratic general who embodied American imperial masculinity. Strikingly, in these narratives Japanese women's historical and political agency is erased, leaving them invisible in the story of their own emancipation. They are portrayed simply as fortunate recipients of American-initiated reform efforts, finally liberated from centuries of patriarchal oppression by their beneficent occupiers. Not only does the history of their political struggles prior to and during the occupation become invisible in this narrative; their complex and problematic involvement in pre-1945 Japanese nationalism and colonialism also gets erased.

In this chapter I examine two exemplary feminist liberation narratives in the U.S. occupation of Japan: MacArthur as initiator of women's suffrage, and Gordon as author of the women's rights articles in the new constitution. I argue that rather than unambiguous symbols of Japanese postwar rebirth and American democratic leadership, women's enfranchisement and constitutional revision were closely intertwined with the histories of American and Japanese feminism, nationalism, and imperialism prior to and during the occupation. What has been celebrated as the pure and unquestionable moment of Japanese women's "emancipation" was in fact deeply enmeshed with, and indeed enabled by, the problematic dynamics of nationalism and imperialism in the late nineteenth and early twentieth century.

More specifically, for the Japanese, the political debates surrounding women's suffrage and constitutional revision became an arena where prewar and wartime discourses about women, family, and nation would be rearticulated. Nationalist expressions were officially censured during the occupation, but gender reform ironically provided a space where Japanese politicians, including feminists, could publicly express nationalist sentiments concerning women, family, and national and racial superiority. Occupied Japan also proved significant for American gender and nationalist politics. Frequently comparing Japanese gender relations to more "emancipated," "progressive," and "democratic" American gender relations made occupied Japan a site for reiterating the superiority of American femininity, domesticity, and nationhood. Carefully tracing the historical and political dynamics that shaped gender reform in the early days of the occupation sheds light on the multiple and problematic meanings assigned to women's emancipation, Japanese women, and American women, as well as mutually enabling relationships among feminism, nationalism, and imperialism.

In the narratives of the occupation, MacArthur and Gordon stand as two iconic figures who constitute particularly concentrated sites for the production of empire. In person, performance, and even genealogy, MacArthur embodies the history of American militarism and imperialism. His grandfather, Arthur MacArthur I, was married to Aurelia Belcher whose ancestry traced back to Jonathan Belcher, a colonial governor of New England. Their son and Douglas's father, Arthur II, was a career militarist, spending many years at frontier posts in "Indian Territory," participating in the Spanish-American and Philippine-American Wars, and serving as the military governor of Manila. His wife, Douglas's mother, was Mary Hardy, daughter of a wealthy Virginia planter. A graduate of West Point, Douglas spent his life in the U.S. military. As Supreme Commander for the Allied Powers during the occupation of Japan, he played a vital role in turning the Asia-Pacific into an "American Lake," replacing the Pax Britannica and competing with the Communist bloc for Cold War hegemony.

Gordon offers an equally or even more fascinating case study of imperialism. Her personal journey from Europe through Japan to the United States mirrors the crucial geographical shift of the twentieth century. As prewar European domination shifted to postwar U.S. hegemony, her location also shifted from one imperial stronghold to another, via Japan. That she came to play a prominent role in the U.S. occupation of Japan had much to do with this transnational movement and the various privileges acquired in the process. Gordon's memoir repeats, quite explicitly, a gendered imperial narrative about white, emancipated women endowed with a mission to liberate oppressed and victimized women of color. As a result, her relationship to Japanese women has never been equal; she was, and continues to be, more liberated, more knowledgeable, and therefore superior. As an American imperial feminist liberating Japanese women, Gordon confirms and reinforces U.S. imperial hegemony in postwar Japan.

At the same time, Gordon's complicity in U.S. hegemony is never complete, as she frequently disrupts the narrative of the occupation. Recruited into the American project of nation and empire building, Gordon also resisted it. Arriving in postwar Japan, she insisted on her "difference" from other occupying Americans and expressed ambivalence toward American victory over her "home country." During the constitutional reform, her European lineage proved a source of tension, as Americans objected to her draft articles inspired by the Weimar and Soviet constitutions. Gordon's status as "other" within the American occupation forces became especially visible when her parents' tie to Russia made her suspect as a communist subversive in the emerging Cold War divisions. Despite her complicity, then, Gordon stands as an ambivalent and potentially transgressive figure in the narrative of the occupation, as she questions, challenges, and disturbs U.S. hegemony in postwar Japan from within.

Reorienting and Rehabilitating the Japanese: Imperial Governance and the Question of Agency

Japan's unconditional surrender at the end of World War II ushered in an unprecedented period of restructuring in the nation's history. Despite the overwhelming victory of the Allies, however, the occupation project was far from uniform or stable. From the very outset, two discourses of imperial governance—European and American—coexisted, resulting in different and often opposing assessments about the Japanese people's willingness and ability to initiate democratization and the nature and forms of the occupiers' interventions. Examining documents that specified the terms of surrender and occupation reveals the heavy-handed nature of U.S. domination, but also its instability and incoherence.

Historians recognize the Potsdam Declaration: Proclamation by Heads of Governments, United States, United Kingdom, and China, signed on July 26, 1945, as being of fundamental importance. This declaration demanded in no uncertain terms Japan's unconditional surrender, threatening that the alternative would be "the inevitable and complete destruction of the Japanese armed forces and just as inevitably the utter devastation of the Japanese homeland." Japan's military leaders were identified as responsible for their nation's involvement in the war: "The time has come for Japan to decide whether she will continue to be controlled by those self-willed militaristic advisers whose unintelligent calculations have brought the Empire of Japan to the threshold of annihilation, or whether she will follow the path of reason." The purpose of the postwar occupation was clearly defined as the elimination of those leaders "who have deceived and misled the people of Japan into embarking on world conquest." It affirmed that the Allied powers "do not intend that the Japanese shall be enslaved as a race or destroyed as a nation, but stern justice shall be meted out to all war criminals, including those who have visited cruelties upon our prisoners." Two elements were identified as central to Japan's postwar transformation: preexisting democratic tendencies, and the people's will toward a peaceful, democratic political system: "The Japanese Government shall remove all obstacles to the revival and strengthening of democratic tendencies among the Japanese people. Freedom of speech, of religion, and of thought, as well as respect for fundamental human rights, shall be established," along with "a peacefully inclined and responsible government

... in accordance with the freely expressed will of the Japanese people."[3] The declaration thus defines the Japanese as the chief agents of the postwar democratization of Japan, a view reiterated in the August 29, 1945, document, "United States Initial Post-Surrender Policy for Japan."[4]

The voluntary nature of Japanese democratization was similarly emphasized in another American document, SWNCC-228, "Reform of the Japanese Government System," considered, with the Potsdam Declaration, by occupation scholars as the two most important sources for constitutional revision.[5] Approved by the U.S. State War Navy Coordinating Committee (SWNCC) and transmitted to MacArthur on January 11, 1946, the document insisted on the transformation of Japan under the occupation authorities, but also cautioned MacArthur not to create the impression that reform was an imposition from above: "Only as a last resort should the Supreme Commander order the Japanese Government to effect the above listed reforms, as the knowledge that they had been imposed by the Allies would materially reduce the possibility of their acceptance and support by the Japanese people for the future."[6] Drawing on preexisting American imperial discourses, documents of the surrender and occupation projected the postwar reconstruction not as a coercive imposition, but as providing guidance for an indigenous population toward democracy and freedom in accordance with "the freely expressed will of the Japanese people."

Yet, occupied Japan constituted a dynamic discursive field where the apparatus of domination was never uniform or stable but always challenged and contradicted from within. The source book used to train occupation personnel reveals a drastically different understanding about the occupation's mission that denies any possibility of Japanese self-transformation and calls for coercive interventions by the occupiers. In a blatantly Orientalist tone reeking of colonial discourse, *Civil Affairs Handbook, Japan* defines the occupation's objective as nothing less than civilizing and modernizing a Far Eastern nation mired in premodern culture and centuries-old tradition. Any Japanese ability for self-transformation goes unmentioned; indeed the Japanese people as a whole are stripped of their own agency. In a chapter entitled "Cultural Characteristics," the *Handbook* provides a detailed discussion of the Japanese character. The arguments invoke a binary notion of the West and its others, constructing Japan in terms of its lack of Western characteristics such as rationality, individualism, scientism, egalitarianism, democracy, and modernity. The *Handbook* explains that the peculiar character of the Japanese is traced to their "illogical" and "unscientific" language, "a fanatical pride in race," and "feudalism," a catch-all term used to point to Japan's presumably premodern, uncivilized condition.[7] Because of the living legacy of feudalism, the *Handbook* argues, the Japanese willingly subordinate themselves to higher authorities, such as the Emperor, and lack the ability to adhere to more abstract principles.

The feudal legacy has bequeathed a very hierarchical and regimented social structure in which the individual has no place to express personal opinions. Combined with a fanatical pride in their nation, these characteristics induced "the extreme of chauvinism" observed during the war:

> [N]owhere else on earth is there a people with a record of such long-term, imposed restraints, dating back to the early feudal times. The Japanese are hot-blooded emotional people who have been regimented from the cradle to the grave, by their government, by strict and hidebound traditions, by parents, teachers, bosses, police, and superior officers in the army. The very strictness and severity of life produces a frustration that may explode in violent action. . . . The emotions that other peoples discharge in occasional anger, grousing, and quarreling, the Japanese store up and discharge all at once. Drink will sometimes set it off; war has done it, as evidenced in the atrocities of Nanking and Bataan.[8]

Unlike in enlightened Western societies, this oppression produced little social dissent, partly because Japanese social structures are too rigid to allow for dissension, but more importantly because the Japanese individual is "willing to be regimented . . . (and) happiest when he is told what to do." "As individuals," the *Handbook* states, "the Japanese have little opportunity for self expression since the pattern and philosophy of Japanese life circumscribe and restrict them. They exist as units of a family, as objects of the state, as parts of a group to which they are always subordinated." In the family, "(a)n individual member has very little opportunity for personal self expression" and thus "does not exist as an individual at all." Beyond the family, the state binds its subjects to "the Emperor as the father of the great family of the nation." "The paternalism" in the state and the family robs the person "of his individualism and of his initiative," and thus "he shrinks from the responsibility of making an individual decision."[9] The *Handbook* clearly moved from holding a handful of leaders accountable for Japan's wartime behaviors; the Japanese as a whole were seen as fanatical, with no sign of peaceful or democratic inclination, and a highly questionable ability to vote freely and to transform their society according to the principles of democracy. The occupiers could no longer assume preexisting democratic tendencies among the Japanese. Democratizing Japan would require firm-handed and coercive interventions.

Repeating a familiar gendered trope of colonial racism and imperialism, the *Handbook* invokes the figure of colored women to emphasize the inferiority of a non-Western nation, turning Japanese women into the repository of racially inferior, premodern, and chauvinistic culture and tradition. The

Handbook's frequent focus on the "feudal" tradition and its negative impact on women provide a static and ahistorical picture:

> In the traditions of the feudal period the Japanese woman was expected to be obedient, chaste, industrious, and quiet ... These feudal patterns have persisted to a surprising degree into modern times ... [the description of] the Japanese woman's life is almost as accurate for the period 1890–1930 as for the feudal period.[10]

Male chauvinism is thus a constitutive and unchanging part of Japanese culture and society, as are helpless women victims with no agency of their own. Such an image of Japanese women follows the well-recognized pattern of Western colonial discourses where "the agency of women, the colonized and the industrial working class are disavowed and projected onto anachronistic space: prehistoric, atavistic and irrational, inherently out of place in the historical time of modernity."[11]

The *Handbook* draws on discourses of sexuality in addition to gender and race. Its discussions of prostitutes and geisha—the foremost object of Western fascination—rely on "a fantastic conflation" of multiple vectors of power to further mark Japan's inferiority.[12] According to its argument, Japanese nation-racial inferiority is evident in the treatment of women whose sexual subjugation not only points to the existence of indigenous male domination but reveals women's inability to recognize their own oppressions, the ultimate sign of human degradation. As the *Handbook* points out, licensed prostitution, the very existence of which demonstrates the cultural inferiority of the East, dates back to the premodern, feudal era. This tradition caused Japan considerable embarrassment on the international scene when it failed to meet the 1925 League of Nations mandate to prohibit traffic in women and children. The inability of the Japanese—or at least the Japanese state—to meet universal (i.e., Western) standards of sexual respectability was considered as a sign of its cultural and racial inferiority. Even worse, women are unaware of, and indeed content with, their own enslavement: "These girls (i.e., geisha) are not unhappy, as a rule. It has been their life since girlhood and in this realm, as in all others in Japan, women are trained not to think or desire beyond their own realm."[13] Reminiscent of the exotic harem women that so captured the European colonial imagination, prostitutes and geisha stand as evidence of the cultural and racial inferiority of the Japanese in the American imagination.

As Japanese women were incapable of recognizing their own oppressions under indigenous male domination, an impetus for social change had to come from elsewhere, namely the West. As the *Handbook* tells it, Western influence already improved the lives of Japanese women. From 1915 until

1935, as Western ideas, fashion, and education came to Japan, women began to enjoy more freedom. Some gained access to higher education, wore "American clothes," "bobbed their straight stiff hair, and had 'permanents' in the approved fashion," and became doctors and lawyers, and so on. University students participated in radical social movements, including the 1918 rice riots. There was also "a real feminist movement" and "Japanese women became more than mere dolls." The *Handbook* also acknowledges some form of agency in Japanese women. Although women of the upper class are most often modest and obedient, they "exert a quiet back-of-the-screen power." Lower-class women "worked alongside their husbands in the rice paddies and home industries and, being economically indispensable, were almost equal in status with their husband." Wartime mobilization further drew women into the public arena, where they proved to be an important economic resource for the nation. Younger women "are making money of their own and are perhaps beginning to lose some of their subservience to men."[14]

The Japanese woman of the *Handbook* is more often than not portrayed as a victim without agency—neither to feel unhappiness or even to recognize her own oppression, continuing to live mired in feudal and premodern customs and tradition. Only Western influences could alter these conditions. However, the *Handbook* also invokes an image of Japanese women who are capable of exerting limited power and influence, within the home and family, and even in social movements, including feminism, which suggests that women themselves could be agents for personal and social changes. As I argue, these competing understandings of Japanese women led to different visions and strategies of American interventions, and to less than uniform reform discourses and practices. Japanese women constituted an ambivalent and even contradictory site in the occupation politics as they both justified and called into question American interventions in postwar Japan.

The *Handbook* portrayed a Japan formidably different from the West. Yet emphasizing America's will to liberate the Japanese, MacArthur was firm in his belief in American ability to transform Japan and its people. In fact, the Japanese made a "better pupil" than the occupied Germans, more willing to learn and ready to change their ways:

> The German people were a mature race. If the Anglo-Saxon was say 45 years of age in his development, in the sciences, the arts, divinity, culture, the Germans were quite as mature. The Japanese, however, in spite of their antiquity measured by time, were in a very tuitionary condition. Measured by the standards of modern civilization, they would be like a boy of 12 as compared with our development of 45 years. Like any tuitionary period, they were susceptible to following new models, new ideas. You can implant

basic concepts there. They were still close enough to origin to be elastic and acceptable to new concepts.[15]

MacArthur and his occupation forces thus launched a civilizing mission with the firm belief that they could transform—could "educate" and "train"—the racially inferior other.

Race alone, however, does not explain the zeal and commitment with which the occupiers worked to reform the Japanese women. If the Japanese as a whole were racially immature, childlike creatures who needed to be taught by "adult" Americans, the Japanese woman—the ultimate girl-child—was an even more worthy candidate for emancipation, growth, and transformation. Articulated at the intersection of race and gender discourses, liberating Japanese women from Asian patriarchal oppressions became a significant project. Success would provide powerful evidence of the humane and generous intentions of the American reformers, and solidify the notion that the United States was truly a leader of freedom and democracy in the postwar world. Yet, how to implement gender reform remained a contentious issue, as the occupation's interventions in Japanese gender relations would soon give rise to numerous tensions, contradictions, and contestations, destabilizing from within the American hegemony in postwar Japan.

Women and Empire in Japan's Modernity

Despite the occupiers' understanding of Japanese women as agentless, innocent, helpless victims of indigenous male domination, even a cursory review of Japanese modern history tells a far more complex story. The gender relations encountered by the occupiers were in fact a product of Japan's modernity, and of its own as well as Western imperial dynamics. Japanese women were never innocent bystanders or helpless victims, but rather complicitous participants in these dynamics. In particular feminist leaders were willing supporters and participants, actively pursuing material and discursive opportunities in the nation's modernization process. As Japanese women's movements were enabled by Japanese and Western racism, nationalism, and colonialism, feminism's "imbrication" with modernity constituted a salient feature. The occupiers' belief in Japanese women's victimhood that generated the extraordinary zeal for "women's emancipation" was predicated on the erasure of the problematic history of women, nation, and empire.

To make sense of the theorizing I present concerning postwar gender reform and its imbrication with nationalism and imperialism, a brief review of pre-1945 Japanese history is necessary. Japan's modern history cannot be understood apart from imperialism, its own as well as Western. Imperial expansion pried Japan open in 1853, when the arrival of American Commodore

Matthew Perry and his "black ships" ended Japan's long isolationist period. Japan's forced entry onto an international stage rife with Western imperial competition was followed by the restoration of the Emperor and efforts to build a modern nation-state. To fend off the Western colonial powers, the Japanese state launched massive modernization efforts, centralizing its political control, developing the economy, building and strengthening the military, and consolidating a national identity of racially homogenous citizens subject to the Emperor. Central to this process of modernization was Japan's own expansionist move as an emerging colonial power. As Tani Barlow succinctly summarizes, Japan's modernity was critically shaped by its "double relation" to colonialism: "Japan's state builders, threatened by U.S. and European colonialism, turned to consolidation of the nation through the colonial occupation of neighboring territory in East and Southeast Asia."[16] Japan's own development as a colonial power in Asia since the late nineteenth century was carried out in the name of liberating Asia from the rule of Western colonial domination. In reality, however, creating the Greater East Asia Co-prosperity Sphere entailed the subordination of other Asian nations under Japanese rule.

Japan's double relation to colonialism provided a crucial context for gender relations in general and feminist politics in particular, creating an intimate and problematic connection among women, nation, and empire. With modernization, the category of Japanese women emerged, heavily invested with new political significance as female national subjects. The manner in which women became incorporated into Japan's modern polity closely resembles the gendered patterns of nation-state building identified by Floya Anthias and Nira Yuval-Davis. As they argue, women become participants in nation-state building processes in such capacities as biological reproducers of offspring, reproducers and transmitters of culture, signifiers of national and racial boundaries, participants in nationalist movements, and so on.[17] In other words, women become a site of the production and reproduction of the national and racialized subject and subjectivity. In Japan, motherhood, and to an extent wifehood, came to be articulated as a core aspect of Japanese women's national identity. *Ryōsai kenbo* (good wives, wise mothers), a construct simultaneously informed by race and gender, rendered women as preservers and repositories of Japanese racial and national purity and strength. As Kathleen Uno states, "Modern Japanese nationalism produced 'good wife, wise mother' along with compulsory education, industrialization, military modernization, and constitutionalism."[18]

The Imperial Constitution of the late nineteenth century codified women's place in the emerging nation-state. Written by the ruling oligarchy in 1889 and bestowed by the Emperor as a "gift," the constitution institutionalized the notion of *kokutai*, or national polity, in which sovereignty resided in the Emperor himself, and the nation's populace were his "subjects." Articulated at the intersection of gender and race, Japanese national polity was imagined in terms of family blood relations whereby the whole nation was constructed as an extended and racially homogenous family headed by the Emperor, the nation's benign and beneficent patriarch. As reproducers of the national subjects, Japanese mothers thus became politically significant, taking on a specific, gendered role in modern nation-building.

Women's incorporation into national polity resulted in both limitations and opportunities, pointing to a complex and contradictory relation between women and nationalism. On the one hand, as female subjects of the modern nation-state, Japanese women were doubly subordinated under imperial as well as patriarchal domination. The Civil Code, promulgated in 1898, defined *ie*, a clanlike multigenerational family unit, as the basic unit of the national polity headed by the Emperor. Its household head, usually the oldest male, held various rights over his subordinates. These included decisions regarding the domicile, marriage, and divorce of family members. In the system of succession, the family name, the family inheritance, the rights of the household head, and the right to perform family rituals and ancestor worship were handed on to the oldest son. This left women legally subordinated to the power of the male household head. In addition, the family functioned as a moral institution, demanding of its members filial piety and obedience to the male head. This was part of the larger national project of preserving the imperial nation's *junpū bizoku*, or beautiful custom and tradition. Women's obedience to the family head was a significant obligation that was not simply legal but moral, not simply individual but national.

Notwithstanding legal codification of women's subordination, Japanese modernity also provided new opportunities and resources, facilitating women's willing participation in nation and empire building. As Japan ferociously pursued colonial expansion in neighboring countries, the discourses of motherhood became increasingly articulated in relation to militarism and imperialism, defining women and their bodies as the primary site of national reproduction and imperial expansion. Bearing and rearing citizen-soldiers, Japanese women were to make a specifically gendered contribution to the nation's mission to establish the Greater East Asia Co-Prosperity Sphere. Biological reproduction of male offspring became a salient focus in the state mobilization of women. Equally important were Japanese women's moral and spiritual contributions to the nation. By staying away from "dangerous" and "subversive" thoughts such as socialism, communism, and anarchism, they were to be the nation's moral backbone, properly transmitting imperial nationalism to future subjects of the nation.

Many, if not all, Japanese women actively participated in the state's mobilization efforts. *Dainihon Kokubō Fujinkai* (All Japan Women's Defense Association), established in 1932, is one example of a state-led women's mobilization where nationalism and colonialism led to more discursive and material resources for women. With the objective of mobilizing middle- and working-class housewives and mothers for the state's war efforts, this nation-wide women's organization provided numerous opportunities to participate in public activities as well as a new discursive space to imagine and articulate female national subjectivities. Through this organization, women performed various public duties and contributed to the imperial nation in a specifically gendered manner by cheering newly drafted soldiers, visiting families of the drafted and the war bereaved, visiting hospitalized soldiers, making care packages to be sent to the soldiers at the war front, and so on. As well documented by Japanese historians, this and other state-led organizations gave women a sense of excitement and purpose, even empowerment, in otherwise confining social and cultural contexts.[19]

The problematic location Japanese women occupied in the nation's colonial modernity becomes especially obvious once the experiences of "other women" are taken into account. Similar to the colonial constructions of European and American women, the category of Japanese woman was always articulated through its others, creating race- and class-based hierarchies among the women who came under Japanese colonial control. In Japan's modernization process, rural and poor women bore the brunt of Japan's hasty industrialization. They were treated as an expendable and cheap labor source in emergent industries such as textiles and in the sex industry.[20] On the periphery of Japanese nation-state building were Okinawan, Taiwanese, and Korean women, newly incorporated as racialized and colonized minorities. The economic, cultural, and social marginalization these women experienced was specifically sexualized, as they were frequently cast as sexually disrespectable and expendable, in direct and explicit contrast to sexually respectable and therefore racially and nationally superior Japanese women. The potent nature of gender-sexual-racial dynamics in Japanese colonialism manifested itself most blatantly in the system of military sexual slavery. Institutionalized in the aftermath of the Rape of Nanking in 1937, where a staggering number of Chinese were killed, raped, and tortured by the Japanese, military sexual slavery systematically exploited as sexual slaves Korean, Chinese, and other Asian and Pacific Islander women under Japanese colonial rule.[21]

The emergence of Japanese modern feminism is inseparable from these historical and political dynamics, confirming Inderpal Grewal's observation that feminism is deeply intertwined with and enabled by racism, nationalism, and imperialism. While Japan closely followed her observation, its double relation to colonialism also provided a unique context for the emergence of pre-1945 feminism. Two instances of feminist mobilization—the temperance and suffrage movements—illustrate how Japanese modern feminism was mediated simultaneously by its own nation's colonial modernity and by Western feminisms, whose discourses and practices were informed by Western imperial dynamics.

Nihon Kirisutokyō Fujin Kyōfūkai (Japan Women's Christian Temperance Union, or Japan WCTU) presents a fascinating example of complex enmeshment of feminism, racism, and imperialism, as Western imperial feminism provided the inspiration and organizational resources for Japanese women leaders who went on to challenge, but also promote, the nation's colonial modernity. Japan WCTU emerged as a national organization in 1893, sparked by Josephine Butlers's campaign for the repeal of the Contagious Disease Acts in Britain, as well as WCTU activities in the United States. Founded by progressive individuals, women's rights activists, and Japanese Christians, Japan WCTU played a central role in the prewar women's suffrage and union movements. Despite its progressive and frequently oppositional stance on many issues, the organization became an agent of Western imperial feminism on the one hand, and of the Japanese state's sexual and moral regulation on the other.

American feminists, including WCTU leader Mary Clement Leavitt and suffragist Carrie Chapman Catt, firmly believed in their missions to rescue and emancipate women in non-Western societies and vigorously tried to internationalize their organizations. This drive often followed the movement of American imperial expansion, and was informed by a feminist orientalism that circulated the discourses of superior, emancipated American women and oppressed, racially inferior sisters in need of Western guidance. In the case of the WCTU, the organization "constituted an important vehicle for the assertion of the values associated with one kind of American dream at a time of broader economic, political, and cultural expansion of Western societies." By becoming an agent of "cultural imperialism," women's temperance efforts to liberate their foreign counterparts from indigenous patriarchal subordination "became enmeshed in the extension of European values and in the domination of a larger portion of the globe by the imperial power."[22] Japan became one of the sites where the WCTU tried to expand its evangelical and imperial influences.

Japan WCTU's connection to Western imperialism went beyond the ties to its parent organization in the United States. The moral reform Japan WCTU pursued had much to do with its liberal and humanitarian principles, but it was also driven by the intention to "modernize the sexual mores of the populace along the lines of contemporary British and American societies." Following the assumption of Western moral, sexual, and cultural superiority, the Japanese crusaders were on a mission to transform existing, un-Christian sexual relations to those that fit the Christian doctrine of monogamous marriage. With their earnest pursuit of moral and sexual regulation, they were initially at loggerheads with the Japanese state, which advocated the continuation of state-licensed prostitution.[23] By the 1930s, however, Japan WCTU came to participate in the state's moral and sexual surveillance of the population, providing the state with Western expertise and technologies for maintaining moral and sexual purity. This collaboration culminated in 1935 with the formation of *Kokumin Junketsu Dōmei* (National Purification Federation), an organization that, with full support of the state, pursued the sexual and moral purity of the nation by espousing a eugenicist, nationalist notion of the "purification of blood."[24]

Japan WCTU's collaborations with the state were not limited to the domestic context; it also directly and indirectly supported Japan's expansionism abroad. For example, as Japan's colonial interest in Korea was becoming increasingly obvious at the end of the nineteenth century, Japan WCTU began to advocate sending Japanese women to help liberate Korean women from indigenous, oppressive social conditions. Just as their Western counterparts saw opportunities for women in colonial expansionism, Japan WCTU perceived Korea as a place that would provide various opportunities to Japanese women as teachers, doctors, and reformers. In the 1930s, as Japan proceeded with its brutal invasion of China, Japan WCTU openly denied the colonial nature of the actions taken by the Japanese military.[25]

Fujin Sanseiken Kakutoku Kisei Dōmei, later *Fusen Kakutoku Dōmei* (League for Women's Suffrage), which played a significant role in the prewar women's suffrage movement, similarly reveals the intertwining nature of feminism, militarism, and colonialism. Like Japan WCTU, Ichikawa Fusae, a prominent suffragist in pre-1945 Japan, had close and often direct connections to Western, especially American, suffrage movements. During her two-and-a-half-year stay in the United States, Ichikawa's direct contact with the National League of Women Voters, and especially with the National Women's Party and its leader Alice Paul, whom she met in 1922, inspired and emboldened her to initiate a suffrage movement in Japan.[26] On her return, she became the leading figure of the League for Women's Suffrage, which she helped to found in 1924.

The prewar Japanese women's suffrage movement never accomplished a massive mobilization, nor did it achieve its ultimate objective of suffrage. Nevertheless, Ichikawa and other suffragists pushed the Japanese state, inch by small inch, toward the enfranchisement of women, with major political parties, policymakers in the Diet, and state bureaucrats beginning to endorse varying and limited degrees of women's enfranchisement. Their endorsement should not be taken, however, as evidence of their support for gender equality. Some political parties saw women as a source of votes. Others saw Western women's suffrage as a model of modernization that Japan should emulate. State bureaucrats saw middle- and upper-class women voters as a conservative "stabilizing force," who would "help to check the rise of radical male candidates from the ranks of workers and tenant farmers." Yet others supported women's enfranchisement in villages, towns, and cities because of their "feminine" contribution to public issues such as "schools, sewers or public toilets."[27] In 1931, the Japanese cabinet introduced a bill in the Diet that would have allowed women to vote and hold offices at city, town, and village levels, but not at the prefectural level. Although this bill passed the Lower House, it was defeated in the House of Peers.

Both the temperance and suffragist movements suggest women's complicity in Japan's racial, national, and colonial politics. As Suzuki Yūko's study suggests, despite their critical distance from, and indeed frequent challenges to, many of the state's patriarchal and nationalist discourses and practices, well-known feminist leaders like Ichikawa Fusae; Hiratsuka Raichō, a figure synonymous with a well-known feminist literary circle, *Seitō* (Blue Stocking); and Oku Mumeo, another leading figure in the prewar feminist movement, could not envision women's empowerment outside the context of Japan's colonial modernity. Disturbing consequences of feminism's imbrication with nationalism, militarism, and colonialism are evident especially in the case of Ichikawa. Her single-minded pursuit of women's participation in national polity, without any serious critique of that polity, led her to collaborate with the imperial nation-state during World War II. Understanding women's participation in the public arena to be a step toward women's emancipation, she zealously pursued women's mobilization for the war efforts, often even critiquing the state's underutilization of women.[28]

The involvement of organizations like Japan WCTU, and of individuals like Ichikawa, in the problematic processes of Japan's modernity reveal that the state of gender relations in the prewar years was far more complex than the narrative of passive victimhood advanced by *Civil Affairs Handbook, Japan*. Despite American emphasis on the oppressive nature of the prewar Japanese state, Japan's nationalist and colonialist politics provided the crucial, enabling context for an indigenous prewar imperial feminism. This intimate yet problematic relation between feminism, nationalism, and imperialism did not cease with the surrender, but continued to shape gender reform during the occupation.

"The Noble Influence of Womanhood and the Home": MacArthur and Women's Enfranchisement

In the postwar Japanese memory, women's enfranchisement and constitutional revision signify the nation's new beginning. Women's enfranchisement finally put an end to centuries-old feudalism and chauvinism, and the promulgation of the "peace constitution" allowed Japan to leave behind its dark and violent past. Japanese women's transformation also confirmed American democratic leadership, and especially that of MacArthur, who single-handedly brought down Japan's patriarchal culture by granting women suffrage. The congratulatory narrative of the occupation's gender reform, especially women's suffrage, constitutes a common discursive site for occupiers as well as occupied to articulate their own national self-understandings and postwar hegemonic orders. Despite numerous tensions and disagreements, MacArthur and Japanese male politicians tapped into the shared discursive repertoires to define women's suffrage as a means to maintaining the stability of the postwar nation and home.

From the very beginning of the occupation, women's suffrage held an important symbolic meaning for all. Japanese women leaders who had been fighting for the cause since before the war considered women's enfranchisement their priority and resuscitated their activities immediately after the surrender. Among them was Ichikawa Fusae, the leader of prewar suffrage movement, who considered it critical that women's suffrage be obtained as a result of women's political mobilization and not imposed by the foreign occupiers. As early as August 25, 1945, Ichikawa organized more than seventy women leaders into *Sengo Taisaku Fujin Iinkai* (Women's Committee to Cope with Postwar Conditions) to deal with the defeat and reconstruction. At their first meeting on September 24, women's suffrage and the expansion of women's political roles were identified among the top priorities of postwar political activism. For Ichikawa, women's suffrage was a particularly urgent issue. Once the occupation began, American occupiers would order the Japanese government to give women the right to vote. With Japanese women's longtime involvement in the suffrage movement, Ichikawa thought it "unbearable" that women's suffrage be imposed by the foreign occupying forces and not granted by the Japanese government as a result of prewar women's mobilization.[29] Ichikawa went to work, visiting a number of Japanese politicians and urging them to support her cause.

Japanese male leaders were not adverse to the idea of women's suffrage. At a meeting of the newly formed Shidehara Cabinet on October 9, 1945, Home Minister Horiuchi Zenjirō, sympathetic to Ichikawa's cause since before the war, suggested that women be granted suffrage. Prime Minister Shidehara Kijūrō agreed, arguing that because of women's contribution to the country during the war, they deserved the right to vote. Women were indeed worthy, as he noted: Just the night before, when his car had run into a ditch, the housewives in the neighborhood had come out and pushed his car back onto the road, proving themselves useful members of the community. The cabinet members unanimously agreed to grant women suffrage.[30]

Two days after the cabinet meeting, and before the Japanese cabinet had taken any action on their decision, however, MacArthur met with Prime

Minister Shidehara and handed him the famous five-item reform demand. At the top of the list was women's suffrage, calling for "[t]he emancipation of the women of Japan through their enfranchisement."[31] Missing an opportunity to grant women suffrage was a source of frustration for Japanese male leaders. As Horiuchi later told Ichikawa, the prime minister, on seeing the first reform item, made a point to MacArthur by stating that the Japanese cabinet had already decided to grant women suffrage. To this, MacArthur simply replied approvingly, directing him to take care of the rest of the reforms in the same manner. In his conversation with Ichikawa, Horiuchi insisted that it was the Japanese government, not MacArthur, that had granted women the right to vote; it was simply the case that MacArthur's five-item reform directive was announced before the Japanese government had time to complete the procedure for changing the election law. He lamented that the Japanese public would wrongly think that women's suffrage was granted by the foreign occupiers.[32] In the earliest days of the occupation, women's reform already became a contentious political issue where indigenous and foreign male authorities competed against each other for the claim of women's emancipation.

The symbolic significance of women's enfranchisement in the occupation politics became all the more salient during the eighty-ninth session of the Imperial Diet in December 1945, where the cabinet's proposal regarding women's suffrage was discussed at length. While the passage of the proposal was guaranteed, the Diet members, all male politicians, nonetheless raised several concerns, turning the session into a politicized arena to articulate their nationalist anxiety. In the face of defeat and foreign occupation, male policymakers showed much resilience in rearticulating pre-1945 nationalist discourses concerning women and family and resisting a new gender order introduced by foreign occupiers. For instance, during the deliberations regarding the potential conflict between women's entry into the public, political sphere and the maintenance of the Japanese family system that constituted the foundation of Japan's colonial modernity, members of the Diet worried that, once granted suffrage, women would step out of their rightful place as mothers and wives in the home and family. How could women be allowed to participate in politics while keeping intact the beautiful tradition of the Japanese family system? Wouldn't women's suffrage harm the Japanese family system, which was the backbone of the nation? The vital connections among women, family, race, and national polity of pre-1945 Japanese modernity and colonialism were thus reiterated in the suffrage debates, and later surfaced again in the Diet debates over constitutional revision.

The Japanese cabinet representatives attempted to address the questions raised by the Diet members. Far from challenging the gendered nationalist argument presented by the Diet members, the cabinet representatives confirmed it, reemphasizing as an argument for women's enfranchisement the connection among women, family, and nation. Referring to women's mobilization during the war, the cabinet representatives argued that Japanese women had invaluable opportunities to participate in various social activities, and as a result, women now had at least some familiarity with social issues. Furthermore, women could be educated about how to exercise their voting rights, and taught political and social matters. The cabinet representatives also assured the members of the Diet that women's participation in politics would not undermine the nation–family system. Rather, women voters would make invaluable contributions to the postwar nation. Women, they said, were simplistic and straightforward; such qualities might be usefully applied to the discussion of certain issues. To demonstrate women's inclination to moderation, they pointed out that voting patterns abroad showed that women voters were more likely to be middle-of-the-road than extreme left or right. In postwar Japan where the existing social order was going through rapid change, they argued, the nation would benefit from women's inclination to moderation. In short, the government supported women's suffrage because of their contributions to the war effort, and because of their conservative and stabilizing influence in a nation anticipating drastic, foreign-led transformation.[33]

On December 17, 1945, the election law was revised to grant Japanese women the right to vote. SCAP initiated a massive campaign to inform Japanese women about their new right, and on April 10, 1946, the day of the first postwar election, 66.97 percent of registered female voters turned out to vote. Female political candidates were also quite popular in this election, as thirty-nine women were elected to the Diet. Japanese women thus made an official and successful entry into national politics.

What did MacArthur think about this major transformation in Japanese women's lives? Did his views concerning women's suffrage differ from those of Japanese men? MacArthur shared a stunningly similar vocabulary with the Japanese cabinet, articulating Japanese women's role in terms of their contribution to the stability of the nation and home. He expected suffrage to allow Japanese women to exert "the noble influence of womanhood and the home which has done so much to further American stability and progress."[34] At a meeting with the thirty-nine newly elected women in the Diet, he made it clear that women should contribute to postwar Japan "without sacrifice of the important position of women in the home." Far from being the impetus for political emancipation, women's enfranchisement was defined as a stabilizing social force.[35]

MacArthur's views on Japanese women's suffrage need to be understood not only in relation to the Japanese context, but also to the American discursive landscape. Indeed, the connections MacArthur made among women, family, and the stability of the nation echoed the wartime and postwar political discourses in both Japan and the United States. Despite American assumptions about the differences between Japanese and American gender relations, women's familial role constituted a significant component in American nationalist discourses during World War II. As Sonya Michel points out, in the wartime United States, "the family was regarded as a key link in the nation's defenses and women were deemed essential to the family's survival and stability." This "not only reinforced traditional views of women's role but also invested the family with major political significance, thus making it more difficult for women to challenge the social division of labor without appearing treasonous."[36] Not only was a traditional family invested with a set of new political meanings in the context of war and nationalism, but women would be held accountable for familial and social stability and the maintenance of American democracy. As feminist studies of the Cold War United States repeatedly show, such wartime discourses concerning women, family, democracy, and national security continued into the postwar years, and were rearticulated with increasing urgency as a key to the Cold War victory of American democracy over communism. As is clear in MacArthur's statement, Japanese women's enfranchisement became an occasion for articulating not only Japanese but also American discourses of women, family, and national stability.

Women's suffrage provided MacArthur an ideal opportunity to publicize and promote the United States as a new, democratic leader in the postwar world. Japanese women—exemplary pupils in the American school of democracy—were perfect poster girls for selling American democracy internationally:

> Women of Japan are responding magnificently to the challenge of democracy; their record of participation in the general election on 10 April sets an example for the world . . . Japanese women are displaying an increasing interest in political, social and economic affairs which exceeds the most hopeful anticipation of political observers. It attests to the powerful appeal of the democratic idea and to the enthusiasm with which Japanese women are discarding the age-old bonds of convention.[37]

Oppressed for centuries, Japanese women were now awakening to a new democratic spirit, thanks to American interventions. The picture of Japanese women enthusiastically casting their first vote and thus stepping out of feudalism and into modernity was exquisite proof of the appeal and desirability of (American) democracy, attesting to the generous and beneficent nature of the guidance the United States, and specifically MacArthur, could provide. Yet as postwar Japanese and American memories indicate, this narrative suppresses, if not erases, a complex range of political and historical dynamics that informed gender reform, especially women's complicity in pre-1945 racism, nationalism, and colonialism. A similar, although perhaps far more complicated erasure was performed in yet another narrative of women's emancipation: the codification of gender equality through constitutional revision.

Constitutional Revision and the Cold War Rivalry

If the first pillar of women's emancipation in occupied Japan was women's suffrage, the second was the codification of gender equality through constitutional revision. Intended to replace imperial sovereignty with popular sovereignty, to renounce war, and to guarantee civil rights, the revised constitution has been considered evidence of the progressive, liberating intent of the American occupiers and of the successful Japanese transformation they enabled. In the narratives of constitutional revision, Beate Sirota Gordon stands as the iconic figure, as women's studies scholars and Gordon herself emphasize her ingenuity and belief in gender equality as the leading causes for the inclusion of women's rights articles in the new constitution.

A closer examination, however, reveals a far more complex and turbulent picture of the U.S. hegemony in its making. As I argue, constitutional revision was a political process through which the United States struggled to establish its domination in early postwar Japan, performing multifaceted negotiations by engaging in a series of political and rhetorical manipulations. Within this context, Gordon played an extremely ambivalent role by simultaneously promoting and destabilizing the U.S. claim as a nation of democracy and gender equality.

On one level, reform efforts were visibly shaped by geopolitical rivalry between the United States and other Allied nations. An all-American team from the Government Section (GS) of SCAP, many of whom knew little about Japan, drafted a new constitution under conditions of great secrecy and in extreme haste—little more than a week—in early February 1946 precisely to circumvent the involvement of other Allied nations. Within occupied Japan, who would be in charge of authoring the new constitution was an equally contentious issue. Despite the fact that SWNCC-228 called for constitutional revision as an expression of "the free will of the Japanese," the occupiers officially excluded the Japanese from this normatively domestic affair, but also tried to keep the American origin of the constitution secret. Indeed, while the new draft constitution upheld the ideal of freedom of thought and speech, "Criticism of SCAP Writing the Constitution" constituted a formal category used by the Civil Censorship Detachment of SCAP to maintain the secret of constitutional authorship.[38] Within this context, the conservative Japanese cabinet had an extremely awkward role to perform. Adamant about preserving the prewar social order, especially imperial sovereignty, the cabinet nonetheless was forced to pretend that the American draft constitution advocating popular sovereignty was its own work, defending it against numerous, vehement objections from Diet members. By doing so, they secured the continuity of the Imperial Household and helped MacArthur maintain the myth of beneficent democratic reform. The articles on women's rights in the new constitution emerged under these convoluted political conditions.

A brief chronological description of constitutional revision from Fall 1945 to Spring 1946 helps set the context for analysis of women's rights articles.[39] Initially, MacArthur intended to let the Japanese themselves revise the Imperial Constitution. On October 4, 1945, Prince Konoe Fumimaro, a special appointee of the Office of the Privy Seal, met with MacArthur, leaving with the impression that he had been entrusted with the task of drafting a constitution. On October 11, however, MacArthur met with Prime Minister Shidehara Kijūrō, presenting him with two separate directives, one for a five-item democratization reform, the other for liberalization of the constitution. This led to a brief rivalry for authorship between Prince Konoe, who represented the Imperial Household, and *Kenpō Mondai Chōsa Iinkai* (Committee to Study Constitutional Problems), or the so-called Matsumoto Committee, appointed by Prime Minister Shidehara and led by State Minister Matsumoto Jōji. However, on November 1, 1945, as it became increasingly likely that Konoe would be prosecuted as a war criminal, SCAP withdrew its support, leaving the Matsumoto Committee as the officially appointed body in charge of constitutional revision.

Although the Matsumoto Committee intended to work in secret, away from the scrutiny of the Japanese public and SCAP, its draft constitution was leaked to the press and published in the Mainichi Shinbun on February 1, 1946. While the version that was published was not the committee's final draft, the scoop nevertheless exposed the extremely conservative intent of the committee, which would have maintained imperial sovereignty, defining Japanese citizens as *shinmin*, or subjects. At that time, the first priority of the Japanese cabinet was to preserve *kokutai*, or national polity—most importantly the Emperor and the imperial system—and the committee's draft contained language to achieve this end. This draft proved to be extremely unpopular. Editorials in the Mainichi denounced it, arguing that the draft's provision concerning the imperial system was no different from the one in the Imperial Constitution and that the use of the notion of shinmin was too anachronistic. Furthermore, the editorial argued, the draft failed to provide the equal educational rights, gender equality, and racial and ethnic equality without which democratization would be incomplete.[40] Clearly, the Japanese cabinet failed to sense not only the wishes of SCAP but also the popular senti-ment for social change, including gender equality. Prompted by this public outcry, SCAP ordered the Matsumoto Committee to officially submit its entire draft to headquarters by February 8, 1946. However, SCAP had already concluded from the published text that the Matsumoto Committee was inca-pable of revising the Imperial Constitution in a way that would satisfy the requirements of the Potsdam Declaration. As a result, SCAP decided to take over, to hold its own "constitutional convention," in absolute secrecy and with no Japanese participation. Drafting was to start on February 4 and to be completed by February 12, 1946.

SCAP's rushed and secret constitutional revision had much to do with the emerging Cold War geopolitical context. Already the Cold War rivalry between the United States and the Soviet Union over control of Japan was coming into play. Since before the end of World War II, the United States and the Soviet Union began to compete for postwar dominance in both Europe and East Asia, but the Americans had the advantage. The overwhelming U.S. military mobilization in the Far Eastern theater, culminating in the use of the atomic bombs that forced the Japanese surrender, made the United States dominant in the occupation. However, the Soviet Union and other Allied countries objected to the privileged American position and demanded fuller participation.

It was within this context that debates regarding the status of the Emperor, especially the possibility of trying him as a war criminal in an international court, took place among MacArthur, the U.S. government, and the other Allies. In November 1945, MacArthur had received instructions from the Joint Chiefs of Staff to collect information and evidence for a possible trial. However, MacArthur was strongly opposed to putting the Emperor on trial, arguing that the imperial institution and the Emperor himself could be utilized as a "stabilizing force" in occupied Japan. He made his case in his January 1946 response to the Joint Chiefs, arguing that no evidence requiring a trial had been found. If the Emperor was to be tried, MacArthur insisted, the whole of Japan would resist. Enormous chaos and disorder would follow, even escalating to "guerrilla warfare in the mountainous and outlying regions" and "all hope of introducing modern democratic methods would disappear." To cope with such chaos and disorder, "a minimum of a million troops would be required which would have to be maintained for an indefinite number of years." MacArthur's assertions effectively killed any further talk within the U.S. government of a trial of the Emperor.[41]

However, other Allied nations demanded the abolition of the imperial system and the trial of the Emperor for war crimes. In late 1945, these nations were instrumental in forming the Far Eastern Commission (FEC), a coordi-nating body of Allied nations established to curtail exclusive U.S. control of occupied Japan.[42] The FEC was a compromise between the United States and the Allies: The United States retained the right to issue interim directives on urgent matters in the process of the occupation, but it could not issue directives on matters concerning constitutional revision. With the activation of the FEC scheduled for February 26, 1946, MacArthur faced a limited window of opportunity. Once in place, the FEC would be sure to intervene in the constitutional revision, especially regarding the Emperor and the imperial institution. His exclusive control forfeited, MacArthur would be required to consult with and obtain agreement from the FEC concerning all constitutional reforms. MacArthur had to act swiftly. He needed a new constitution that would maintain the Emperor, satisfy the Potsdam Declaration, and be approved at least on the surface by the Japanese. With the Matsumoto Committee draft failing to fulfill these requirements, MacArthur convened the "American Constitutional Convention." Thus inscribed onto the origin of constitutional revision in postwar Japan were geopolitical struggles involving Western powers.

No Japanese representative was officially invited by SCAP to participate in drafting the constitution. MacArthur assigned the task to the Government Section (GS) of SCAP, instructing its chief, Courtney Whitney, in the so-called MacArthur Note, on key sections concerning the status of the Emperor, the nation's right of self-defense, and the "feudal system," among others.[43] On February 4, 1946, Whitney announced to the Public Administration Division staff in the GS that they would have a "constitutional convention." An all-American team was expected to draft an entire constitution and submit it to MacArthur by February 12. Those present at the meeting were immediately divided into Steering Committee, Legislative Committee, Executive Committee, Civil Rights Committee, Judiciary Committee, Local Government Committee, Finance Committee, Committee on the Emperor, Committee on Treaties and Enabling Provision, and Committee on the Preamble. Each subcommittee would write an individual chapter, to be approved by the Steering Committee.

The Steering and the Civil Rights Committees had the central roles in drafting articles pertaining to women's rights. Consisting of three male American lawyers—Colonel Charles Kades, Commander Alfred Hussey, and Lieutenant Colonel Milo Rowell—and a woman, Ruth Ellerman, who kept copious notes on the proceedings, the Steering Committee had strong legal background but little familiarity with Japan. In contrast, the members of the Civil Rights Committee—Lieutenant Colonel Pieter Roest, Harry Emerson Wildes, and Beate Sirota Gordon (then Beate Sirota)—had little legal training or expertise, but much familiarity with and firsthand experience in Asia. Significantly, moreover, the Civil Rights Committee's composition was more European than American. Originally a Dutch citizen, Roest had studied medicine at Leyden University, received a PhD degree in anthropology and sociology from the University of Chicago, and done postgraduate work in international relations at the University of Southern California. His academic experience included teaching at a small college in Madras, India, and conducting research on the Indian caste system and other subjects related to the Middle East and Asia. Wildes had studied economics at Harvard, and obtained an MA and PhD from the University of Pennsylvania, and a second doctorate in humanities at Temple University. From 1924 to 1925, he had taught economics at Keiō University, an elite private college in Japan. The third member of the Civil Rights Committee, Sirota, who had personal connections to prewar Europe and Japan, was assigned to define the new legal status for Japanese women.

The Only Woman in the Room:
Beate Sirota Gordon and Imperial Feminism

In the narrative of the occupation, Gordon stands as a matching icon to MacArthur. Like MacArthur, Gordon constitutes a concentrated site for the production of empire where multiple vectors of power converge. As revealed in her autobiography, *The Only Woman in the Room: A Memoir*, it is through the figure of Gordon, both as a participant and an author-narrator, that three critical imperial processes—European, Japanese, and American—come together to shape the politics of Japanese women's emancipation, inseparably linking feminism and imperialism in the U.S. occupation of Japan. Despite her complicity in the politics of empire, however, Gordon also subverts postwar U.S. hegemony by insisting on her difference from and superiority to other American occupiers and questioning the American claim as the nation of democracy. The twin themes of complicity and subversion thus animate Gordon's story, turning her into a dynamic figure who disrupts the dominant narrative of the occupation.

Gordon's life began in Europe as the child of an elite Jewish family. Her father, Leo Sirota, a Russian Jewish emigre from Kiev, was a renowned artist in turn-of-the-century Vienna, a highly cosmopolitan center of imperial Europe and capital of the Austro-Hungarian Empire. An enormously successful concert pianist, he was famous in Europe and acquainted with prominent artists and intellectuals who filled the salon reigned over by her mother, Augustine Sirota, also a Russian Jew and a well-known socialite. Born in Vienna in 1923, Gordon grew up amidst cultural sophistication, fame, and privilege, developing a strong identification with Europe.

How Gordon came to spend her childhood in Tokyo is inseparable from the history of Japan's imperial expansionism. In 1928, while on concert tour in Manchuria, where Japan was increasing its imperial control, Leo Sirota met Yamada Kōsaku, a famous Japanese musician. Impressed by Sirota's performance, Yamada invited Sirota to chair the Piano Department of the Japanese Imperial Academy of Music in Tokyo. The Sirotas moved to Japan in 1929, setting up house in Tokyo's exclusive Nogizaka neighborhood and re-creating the cosmopolitan life of artists and intellectuals that they had enjoyed in Vienna. Leo Sirota continued to enjoy fame and patronage as a concert pianist and a revered master to Japanese students. Augustine Sirota ran the household with an array of Japanese maids and servants, holding lavish parties and entertaining the guests with Viennese, Russian, and Jewish dishes. The family residence became a "Viennese salon" once again, which such Japanese elites as the Tokugawas, Mitsuis, and Konoes frequented.

The childhood Gordon depicts in the memoir is a blissful one. Under the guidance of her liberal-minded and artistic parents, she studied music, modern dancing, and several foreign languages. Her formal education, initially supervised by a governess from Estonia, occurred briefly at a German school, followed by enrollment in an American school in Tokyo. As a young child, Gordon thrived in such an environment, and a sense of innocence and joy permeates her recollection of "home." Yet, such recollections depend on erasing several important factors shaping her life in Japan. Gordon never once mentions Japanese imperialism. Equally absent are the enormous economic and cultural privileges she enjoyed as a child of European emigres in Asia. The Sirotas' privileged and yet secluded life in Japan shared striking similarities with those of Europeans in colonial outposts, despite Gordon's Jewish background. In both instances, seemingly innocent lives, and a sense of entitlement to a foreign country as their "home," were inextricably intertwined with geopolitical hierarchies that endowed the West and its imperial agents with material and cultural superiority. Their lives remained within elite European circles, occasionally including indigenous elites. Despite the severe (and often self-imposed) seclusion these Europeans experienced in foreign lands, they often claimed to "know" the indigenous culture and population. The Sirota family's life in prewar Japan, and Gordon's later claim to know Japan, especially its women, closely replicated this colonial pattern.

Western women's location in imperial politics had additional complexities as they frequently engaged in "domestic imperialism," reproducing Western domestic lives in foreign lands, lives that signified their racial and cultural superiority. To accomplish this specifically gendered and racialized imperial task, Western women were dependent on indigenous women who as maids and servants were a cheap source of labor. Gordon's mother was no exception: In a country far from her origins, she tried to re-create the lifestyle of European, more specifically Viennese, cosmopolitan artists, using indigenous labor. In her recollections, Gordon recounts one of the maids, Mio, who served the Sirota family in Nogizaka. Notwithstanding her attachment to this Japanese woman, who she calls "friend" or "reliable older sister," Gordon fails to acknowledge the material and other inequalities that defined their relationship. She never questions, for example, how her mother's relative freedom from domestic toil or her own privileged childhood in Japan had much to do with their access to material and other privileges, a status embedded in their relation to Mio. Instead, in her narratives, Mio becomes a symbol of the Sirota family's friendship with "ordinary people." Gordon's longing for "home" as an innocent and blissful place hinges on erasing gender, race, class, and imperial hierarchies that infused the very domestic space she inhabited as a child.

Following the accounts of her childhood and wartime relocation to the United States in 1939, Gordon's memoir moves to her return to Japan in 1945 as an American citizen and member of the U.S. occupation forces. Occupied Japan was to become the place where Gordon would try out the "progressive" lessons learned at Mills College in San Francisco: Middle- and upper-middle-class women should have a challenging career and also run a household. On February 4, 1946, she was rather informally assigned to the team of American occupiers in the GS who were to rewrite the Japanese constitution. With relish Gordon recalls the suggestion by Roest that was to change her life: "You are a woman; why don't you write the women's rights section?" She was thrilled with this offer. At the same time, the weight of responsibility was overwhelming. The makeup of the drafting team—almost all of whom were considerably older American men with substantial legal backgrounds—was intimidating to her. The only knowledge she had of any constitutional or legal matter was what "came straight from my high school social studies classes." Yet whatever hesitation she felt was quickly replaced by a "tremendous sense of mission."[44] She firmly believed that it was "our job to introduce the concept (of civil rights) to Japan in a detailed and concrete way."[45] An imperial feminist consciousness—that as "the only woman in the room" she was in charge of rescuing Japanese women—drove her: "As a woman, I felt that my participation in the drafting of the new Japanese Constitution would be meaningless if I could not get women's equality articulated and guaranteed."[46] Just as Japanese women presumably needed Gordon for their salvation, she depended on Japanese women for her own self-realization. As objects of rescue and civilizing efforts, Japanese women were indispensable for Gordon's own transformation as a "progressive" woman.

Gordon was confident that she shared with MacArthur the same vision of women's emancipation. She thought that his decision to grant Japanese women the right to vote was revolutionary, and she was determined to play a part in the U.S. reform efforts to liberate Japanese women. Yet, as she recalls, she received no instructions to guide or shape the women's rights section. Existing studies show that neither MacArthur, nor other GS members, nor the U.S. government gave any specific instructions. Since the American involvement in constitutional revision was kept secret, Gordon was not allowed to contact anybody on the Japanese side, either. In short, despite their emphasis on women's reform, the occupation authorities gave little consideration and allocated few resources to the revision of women's rights in the new constitution. Rather than questioning MacArthur's commitment to women's reform, Gordon uses this episode to emphasize her own significance as "the only woman in the room," indeed in the entire occupation forces, who could represent Japanese women. Left to her own devices, she hopped into a military truck and visited libraries in Tokyo to obtain copies of the constitutions of several countries. Since the U.S. involvement was top secret, she had to act carefully, picking up a few documents here and a few more there so as not to cause any suspicion among the Japanese. In the end she brought back to headquarters a dozen or so constitutions, including those of the United States, the Weimar Republic, the Soviet Union, and the Scandinavian countries, as well as the Imperial Constitution and the Meiji Civil Code of Japan.

Gordon's commentary on the constitutional documents reveals her ambivalent position in the occupation. As she studied the Imperial Constitution, the existing Civil Code, and the published version of the Matsumoto Committee draft, she became convinced that the Japanese had no understanding of civil rights. The Imperial Constitution had so little to say about people's rights that she wondered—as had the authors of the *Civil Affairs Handbook*—why the Japanese had not expressed dissent.[47] Constructing Japanese as agentless, ignorant, and undemocratic, she justifies and reinforces American hegemony in postwar Japan. Yet she also challenges the occupiers' authority by questioning their ability to truly democratize Japan. Examining the U.S. Constitution, she realized that "civil rights were not protected by the original document of 1789, but only later, in amendments." Furthermore, American women's right to vote "was not guaranteed until 1920, with the passage of the 19th amendment."[48] In contrast, she was deeply impressed by the progressive provisions concerning women's rights in the Weimar and the Soviet constitutions, especially Article 119 of the Weimar Constitution that defined gender equality in marriage.[49] In the emerging Cold War context, where MacArthur was struggling to establish hegemony against the Soviet Union and other Allies, Gordon clearly undermined his intention by questioning the American claim as the nation of democracy and freedom and inserting Soviet and European gender discourses into the constitutional revision process controlled by the American occupiers.

In drafting the women's rights articles, Gordon tapped into her childhood memory where the Orientalist imagery of oppressed and helpless Japanese women predominated: "I tried to imagine the kinds of changes that would most benefit Japanese women, who had almost always married men chosen for them by their parents, walked behind their husbands, and carried their babies on their backs. Husbands divorced wives just because they could not have children. Women had no property rights."[50] The Sirota family's residence in prewar Tokyo, the site of imperial domesticity dependent on Japanese women's subordination to European women, now provided a space where Gordon, as an American reformer, would articulate her postwar imperial feminism. She remembered patriarchal practices that Japanese women had talked about at the gatherings hosted by her mother at the family residence, such as men adopting the children of their mistresses without consulting their legal wives. From her mother and the family maid, Mio, she had also learned of the plight of farmers and their children: "Farmers had been known to give away their children in order to cut down on the number of mouths to feed," and "during famines, girls were sold off."[51] In sum, Japanese women were "little better than chattel to be bought and sold."[52] By recirculating the Orientalist notion of Japanese women as victims without agency, Gordon was complicit not only in European and American, but also Japanese imperial politics, as such understanding erases Japanese women's participation in racism, nationalism, and colonialism. In the narrative of the occupation, then, Gordon constitutes a powerfully iconic figure who draws together three strands of imperial dynamics—European, American, and Japanese—to produce postwar Japan, and especially its women.

The original draft articles written by Gordon were extensive and detailed and significantly influenced by European social welfare philosophy. They included gender equality in marriage and family (Draft Article 18); a social welfare provision for expectant and nursing women as well as married and single mothers, and legal equality between legitimate and illegitimate children (Draft Article 19); a provision about adoption and wives' participation in decision making regarding adoption (Draft Article 20); democratic and peace-oriented education at all public and private schools (Draft Article 23); universal and free health care for children (Draft Article 24); the prohibition of employment of minors and guarantee of minimum wages (Draft Article 25); women's right to work and equal wages with men (Draft Article 26); and social insurance, including mothers' assistance (Draft Article 29). These articles "embodied [her] heartfelt wish that women and underprivileged children in Japan should benefit from such important rights as free education and medical care."[53] The draft chapter on civil rights included another important article for Japanese women. Written by Roest, Draft Article 13 proclaimed equality before the law and prohibition of discrimination on account of sex, as well as race, creed, social status, caste, or national origin.

On February 8, 1946, the Civil Rights Committee met with the Steering Committee to discuss the draft chapter on civil rights. The meeting became a contentious site where two discourses of imperial governance—European and American—collided. The Steering Committee, predominantly American in its membership, made no objection to gender equality as specified in Draft Article 13 written by Roest, or to gender equality in the family in Draft Article 18 written by Gordon, but it did object to the welfare provisions for women and children written by Gordon. The Steering Committee considered the proposed articles too minute, belonging in statutory regulations, not the constitution. Gordon responded to this, arguing that the social guarantees of welfare rights were common in European countries. She was sure, furthermore, that Japanese male bureaucrats, who would be assigned to rewrite the new civil code according to the new constitution, could not be trusted to provide adequate rights to women. "The only safeguard" was to write these rights into the constitution. Roest supported Gordon's argument, emphasizing the status of Japanese women as utter victims of indigenous patriarchal oppressions; indeed they were no better than "chattels." A constitutional guarantee of women's social rights was therefore absolutely necessary. Wildes seconded this. However, Milo Rowell, a member of the Steering Committee, objected that such a provision would provoke strong objection from the Japanese government, resulting in rejection of the entire draft constitution. Wildes's response to this is revealing because it articulated the long-standing imperial assumption of the "white men's burden." He insisted that they had the "responsibility to effect a social revolution in Japan," and for this, the constitution would be the most expedient means to effect "a reversal of social patterns" in Japan. However, the Steering Committee objected to the notion that they were to "reverse a social pattern." Rowell argued that they could not "impose a new mode of social thought on a country by law."[54]

The debates between the two subcommittees not only reflected a difference in American and European legal traditions. They reflected, however unwittingly, a long-standing difference in the method of imperial governance. The European-influenced Civil Rights Committee insisted on a drastic intervention in indigenous culture, determined to initiate the reversal of social patterns in postwar Japan. On the other hand, the Steering Committee members insisted, at least rhetorically if not in reality, on an important tenet of American overseas rule: training and nurturing of natives, rather than a blatant imposition of the foreign system, however superior that might be.

Since no compromise could be reached, the two committees consulted with Whitney, the GS Chief. Whitney ruled that minute details would be taken out of the draft and that a general statement regarding social welfare would be included. Gordon was extremely upset with this: "With each cut [of her articles] I felt they were adding to the misery of Japanese women, such was my distress, in fact, I finally burst into tears."[55] Her memory of losing this battle to the Americans is indeed bitter and long-lasting: "To this day, I believe that the Americans responsible for the final version of the draft of the new constitution inflicted a great loss on Japanese women."[56] Overtly contradicting the occupation's claim as the liberator of Japanese women, Gordon charges the Americans with harming Japanese women by rejecting the European welfare philosophy she tried to introduce to postwar Japan.

The draft constitution was completed on February 12. Reflecting complex and convoluted political dynamics, it began with a preamble in which the Americans have the Japanese declare popular sovereignty:

> We, the Japanese People, acting through our duly elected representatives in the National Diet, determined that we shall secure for ourselves and our posterity the fruits of peaceful cooperation with all nations and the blessings of liberty throughout this land, and resolved that never again shall we be visited with the horrors of war through the action of government, do proclaim the sovereignty of the people's will and do ordain and establish this Constitution, founded upon the universal principle that government is a sacred trust the authority for which is derived from the people.

This was followed by Chapter I, "The Emperor." Article 1 in this chapter stated, "The Emperor shall be the symbol of the State and of the Unity of the People, deriving his position from the sovereign will of the People, and from no other source." Chapter III, "People's Rights and Duties," authored by the Civil Rights Committee, contained the following articles on gender relations:

> Article 13. All natural persons are equal before the law. No discrimination shall be authorized or tolerated in political, economic or social relations on account of race, creed, sex, social status, caste or national origin.

> Article 23. The family is the basis of human society and its traditions for good or evil permeate the nation. Marriage shall rest upon the indisputable legal and social equality of both sexes, founded upon mutual consent instead of parental coercion, and maintained through cooperation instead of male domination. Laws contrary to these principles shall be abolished, and replaced by others viewing choice of spouse, property rights, inheritance, choice of domicile, divorce, and other matters pertaining to marriage and the family from the standpoint of individual dignity and the essential equality of the sexes.

The several articles pertaining to welfare that Gordon had originally proposed were reduced to one:

Article 24. In all spheres of life, laws shall be designed for the promotion and extension of social welfare, and of freedom, justice and democracy. Free, universal and compulsory education shall be established. The exploitation of children shall be prohibited. The public health shall be promoted. Social Security shall be provided. Standards for working conditions, wage and hours shall be fixed.[57]

Gordon had tried to specify women's welfare rights, but Draft Article 24 eliminated any reference to women.

The American constitutional convention thus scripted a draft constitution with content that was drastically different from either the Imperial Constitution or the Matsumoto Committee draft. The next step was to convince the Japanese government to accept the draft and present it as the cabinet proposal to the Diet. On February 13, 1946, Whitney, Kades, Rowell, and Hussey met with representatives of the Japanese cabinet: Foreign Minister Yoshida Shigeru, State Minister Matsumoto Jōji, and two others. The Japanese representatives were only expecting to hear SCAP's responses to the Matsumoto Committee draft that had been officially submitted on February 8. Thus it came as a complete surprise to the Japanese when they were informed that SCAP rejected the Matsumoto Committee draft and were presented with the completed American draft constitution. Whitney explained the reasons for rejection as follows:

> [T]he draft of the constitutional revision, which you submitted to us the other day, is wholly unacceptable to the Supreme Commander as a document of freedom and democracy. The Supreme Commander, however, being fully conscious of the desperate need of the people of Japan for a liberal and enlightened Constitution that will defend them from the injustices of the arbitrary control of the past, has approved this document and directed that I present it to you as one embodying the principles which in his opinion the situation in Japan demands.[58]

Whitney continued, with language that was nothing if not a thinly veiled threat:

> The Supreme Commander has been unyielding in his defense of your Emperor against increasing pressure from the outside to render him subject to war criminal investigation. He has thus defended the Emperor because he considered that was the cause of right and justice, and will continue along that course to the extent of his ability. But, gentlemen, the Supreme Commander is not omnipotent. He feels,

however, that acceptance of the provisions of this new Constitution would render the Emperor practically unassailable. . . . General MacArthur feels that this is the last opportunity for the conservative groups, considered by many to be reactionary, to remain in power; that this can only be done by a sharp swing to the left; and that if you accept this Constitution you can be sure that the Supreme Commander will support your position. I cannot emphasize too strongly that the acceptance of the draft Constitution is your only hope of survival.[59]

That the postwar constitution, presumably a document expressing the Japanese will for freedom and democracy, was in fact authored by the Americans and forcefully handed to the Japanese cabinet is not the only irony here. More strikingly, the legal document that would have the most authority in postwar Japan—that codified a drastically new, democratic social order, including in particular popular sovereignty—was presented to the Japanese cabinet in exchange for the survival of the imperial throne, the protection of conservative ruling elites, and the political containment of the left.

Despite Whitney's strong language, the Japanese cabinet representatives were not ready to give up the Matsumoto Committee draft, and over the next several days they tried to negotiate its acceptance. In the end, however, the Shidehara cabinet had no choice but to accept the American draft. On February 22, they capitulated and began to prepare the Japanese-language text of the American draft constitution. On March 4, the Japanese cabinet representatives led by Matsumoto Jōji presented to the GS a draft constitution, presumably based on the American text. The two sides then sat down to go over the text. From the very start, the GS representatives, especially Charles Kades, were alarmed by what they found. To begin with, the Japanese draft constitution omitted the entire section of the preamble, in which "We, the Japanese People" proclaimed popular sovereignty. Throughout, there were many words, concepts, and phrasing in the Japanese draft that the GS could not agree to, such as the Japanese omission of social rights provisions, including those pertaining to women's rights.[60] Extremely tense discussions followed, and before long the two sides were deadlocked. Exasperated, Matsumoto left the meeting, never to return. This left Satō Tatsuo, Matsumoto's assistant, alone, with two Japanese interpreters at the table, clearly outnumbered by the members of the GS. At around 6 p.m. on that day, Satō and his interpreters were informed that the final draft constitution must be completed then and there. The GS and Japanese representatives were locked in the negotiating room and undertook the arduous process of (re)writing the entire constitution. Relying on translators and Japanese–English dictionaries, they worked for approximately thirty hours without a break. Gordon was at this meeting as a translator, and thus able to witness the Japanese responses to her draft articles. Once again, she was "the only woman in the room."

By the time the discussion of the civil rights chapter began, it was already 2 a.m. According to Gordon, the Japanese side objected to many of the articles in this chapter, including those pertaining to gender equality, "as fiercely as they had argued earlier on behalf of the emperor." This time Kades was on Gordon's side. He told the Japanese, "This article was written by Miss Sirota. . . . . She was brought up in Japan, knows the country well, and appreciates the point of view and feelings of Japanese women. There is no way in which the article can be faulted. She has her heart set on this issue. Why don't we just pass it?" The personalized appeal worked. According to Gordon, since she had been helping the Japanese translate and even elaborated their arguments to the Americans throughout the meeting, the Japanese representatives by then viewed her in favorable terms. Kades's comment and appeal were followed by "stunned silence." In the end, the Japanese accepted the inclusion of gender equality, remarking nonetheless that it was not a full acceptance of or agreement with the ideal of gender equality, but simply a concession to the occupiers' demand: "All right . . . we'll do it your way."[61]

On March 6, 1946, the content of the new draft constitution was released by the Japanese cabinet, followed by a strong endorsement by MacArthur: "It is with a sense of deep satisfaction that I am today able to announce a decision of the Emperor and Government of Japan to submit to the Japanese people a new and enlightened constitution which has my full approval." He went on to praise the new constitution:

> It provides for and guarantees to the people fundamental human liberties which satisfy the most exacting standards of enlightened thought. It severs for all time the shackles of feudalism and in its place the dignity of man under protection of the people's sovereignty. It is throughout responsive to the most advanced concept of human relations—is an eclectic instrument, realistically blending the several divergent political philosophies which intellectually honest men advocate.

The new constitution "places sovereignty squarely in the hands of the people" and renounces "war as a sovereign right of the nation." With these transformations, MacArthur proudly declared, Japan was to begin a new phase in its history, leaving its past behind: "The Japanese people thus turn their backs firmly upon the mysticism and unreality of the past and face instead a future of realism with a new faith and a new hope."[62] That the American-authored constitution had been forced onto the Japanese cabinet in exchange for the Emperor's and their own survival was mentioned nowhere in his statement.

Shortly after the promulgation of the Japanese constitution, Gordon's involvement in the occupation ended. Returning to the United States in 1947, she married a fellow occupier, James Gordon, and pursued a career and family life in New York. Yet, Gordon continued to be part of unfolding stories in occupied Japan, which was increasingly involved in Cold War divisions. One episode in particular, although not included in her memoir, sheds light on her unique and often precarious location in the occupation narratives. A memorandum, "Leftist Infiltration to SCAP," issued by the Military Intelligence Section on April 23, 1947, which contains detailed documentation of "patterns of infiltration," "leftist subversion of the occupation," "leftist case histories," and so on, dated February 27, 1947, characterized Gordon and a list of other occupiers as "pro-leftist and pro-Communist," and warned of their intention to subvert the occupation policies.[63] The documents reported communists' "infiltration" of SCAP, especially in the GS, and their participation in international espionage activities. As Japan was becoming "an Asiatic barrier to Communism" at the time, these internal "subversives" were deemed to pose a serious threat to the U.S. occupation of Japan: "[l]eftist personnel holding responsible positions in SCAP have given every indication of a relentless effort to subvert the Occupation," and thus their presence "constitutes a direct menace to the security of the United States and the progress of the occupational program in Japan."[64]

More specifically, the Military Intelligence Section identified a number of characteristics of the subversives: Russian background, matriculation in U.S. colleges and universities, recent acquisition of U.S. citizenship, employment in government positions under the guise of experts, interests in research activities as a means of accessing classified materials, and critical stance toward the occupation policies. It was suggested that those who fit this profile were frequently found among intellectuals, artists, musicians, and writers. According to the Military Intelligence Section, every action taken by Gordon and her parents was a sign of subversiveness. Not only were Leo and Augustine Sirota originally from Russia and currently stateless, they were also musicians. The reason for their move to Japan and the special status they seemed to have enjoyed there were unclear and therefore suspicious. Gordon's employment in the GS of SCAP, as well as her recent acquisition of U.S. citizenship, also fit the profile of a subversive. Referring to Gordon's brief involvement in the task of purging Japanese officials accused of war responsibilities, the memorandum had this to say:

> Miss Sirota has unquestionably inherited from her father an overwhelming dislike for the Japanese police and bureaucracy. Now passing as an "expert" on Japanese affairs, this young girl finds herself in a position of unusual responsibility in this headquarters. In this

position she takes a virtually childish glee in venting her fury and suppressed hatred as an "expert" on the purging of Japanese officials. There is something inconsistent, if not dangerous, in a young, immature person of this kind of obscure background with belatedly acquired United States citizenship . . . wielding the power of the United States and the prestige of the Supreme Commander on matters which vitally affect the success of the Occupation and the ultimate security of the United States.[65]

No action was taken based on this accusation. Yet, the document sheds light on Gordon's precarious position within the occupation forces. Despite her complicity in the U.S. occupation of Japan, as a young, European-born woman, often critical of SCAP policies, Gordon was also an alien, and thus potentially subversive element, in a postwar military project that was overwhelmingly American and masculine. In the emerging Cold War context where differences were often a cause for suspicion, Gordon was perceived as an ambiguous, even potentially dangerous figure.

Praised as an American feminist foremother in the current revisionist historiography, Gordon in fact provides a far more complex and dynamic story of feminism, the U.S. occupation of Japan, and the politics of Cold War empire building. At first glance, she is a feminist version of MacArthur, a female icon of colonial missionary enthusiasm who undertook Japanese women's liberation as part of the "white women's burden." Closer examination reveals, however, that her complicity in postwar American hegemony was never complete, as she not only questioned the American claim as the country of democracy but also injected European and Soviet discourses of gender and family into an American constitutional convention. Her lack of allegiance to the United States did not go unpunished. A new immigrant with a significant tie to Russia, she was suspected as a communist subversive and alien other who would jeopardize the U.S. Cold War national security. Gordon's narrative thus marks women's reform as an ambiguous site, foreshadowing the contradictory and transgressive dynamics of gender reform that followed constitutional revision.

Defining Gender and Family in the Postwar Nation: Feminism and Nationalism in the Japanese Constitutional Convention

The Japanese discussions of the draft constitution took place at the Ninetieth Imperial Diet Sessions, convened in June 1946 and including thirty-nine newly elected women members of the House of Representatives. From June through October, the members of both the House of Representatives and the House of Peers discussed the meanings and consequences of a new constitution for postwar Japan. While the American draft became the postwar Japanese constitution with remarkably few revisions, the Diet sessions nonetheless became a contentious arena where Japanese policymakers engaged in rhetorical maneuvers to preserve preexisting national and gender orders. Particularly important to observe is Japanese women's complicity in postwar nationalism. Katō Shizue, a leading feminist politician, played a visible role, articulating postwar nationalist understandings of women, family, and tradition and reestablishing the vital connection between feminism and nationalism in the emerging Cold War context.

The newly formed and conservative Yoshida cabinet faced an extremely awkward and difficult job. Besides presenting as its own the draft constitution authored by the foreign occupiers, Prime Minister Yoshida Shigeru—an autocratic politician and staunch supporter of the Emperor system—and his cabinet had to defend popular sovereignty and other progressive provisions, including gender equality, against any opposition from Diet members. Yoshida considered the capitulation to American reformers, including constitutional revision, only a temporary compromise, indeed a tactic to hasten the end of the occupation. Once independence was regained, Yoshida thought, various reforms imposed by the Americans would be revised.[66]

One tactic the cabinet used was obfuscation. Cabinet representatives responded to many of the sharp questions from Diet members with unclear and ambiguous answers. In particular, Kanamori Tokujirō, Minister of State and spokesperson for the government, excelled at this strategy. Knowledgeable about legal matters, he had worked in the Legislation Bureau prior to the war and had written a book on constitutional issues, but unlike many other bureaucrats, he was also well versed in literature and eloquent in speech, and often used literary expressions, rather than legal language, to obscure the issues at hand and to avoid answering questions that would put the cabinet in a difficult position. Pressed with a question of whether the new constitution would change the nature of *kokutai*, or Japanese national polity, for example, Kanamori answered, "Even if the water flows, the river does not."[67] To respond to the same question, he also drew from Copernican theory to make a point about the unchanging nature of national polity: "Whether the argument has been that the sun rotates around the earth, or that the earth rotates around the sun, the movement itself has not changed from ancient times to today."[68] The Japanese performance in the drama of postwar constitutional revision matched, if not surpassed, that of the American occupiers.

Predictably the debates in the Diet focused on national polity, sovereignty, and the Emperor. Both conservative and progressive members pushed the government to clarify the exact nature of the changes that would take place in national polity. The cabinet's argument went as follows: Although the Emperor, defined as the symbolic head of the nation, was to lose his political power, this would not cause the slightest change in national polity, the essence of which was fundamentally spiritual, not political. The Emperor had been and would continue to be the center of *akogare*, popular yearning and admiration, regardless of his political status. The Emperor and the Japanese population would spiritually and psychologically be united as one for eternity. Thus, the argument ran, while proclaiming popular sovereignty, the new constitution would not change the nature of national polity nor the relationship between the Emperor and his people. Kanamori frequently relied on the notion of *akogare*, thus frustrating the Diet and earning mockery from the press and public. The media ridiculed Kanamori, calling him "*akogare* minister," and the draft constitution was labeled the "*akogare* constitution."[69]

The discussions in the Diet on postwar gender relations were inseparable from this major question about national polity. The meanings of Draft Article 22 (Gordon's Article 23), which called for equality of sex in the institution of marriage, were fiercely debated. Would the article result in fundamental change in the existing family system, especially the elimination of *katoku sōzoku*, the patriarchal system of succession, and *koshuken*, the rights of the household head? The conservative politicians saw the article as a major threat to the physical as well as the moral and spiritual survival of national polity. Without the family system, they demanded to know, how would one ensure the continuation of the nation and its *junpū bizoku* (beautiful customs and traditions)?[70]

Especially notable in the debate were the thirty-nine newly elected women in the Diet. In particular, Katō Shizue—a member of the Socialist Party, leading "feminist," birth control activist, and favorite of the American occupiers—strongly supported Draft Article 22.[71] Despite her feminist oppositional stance toward male politicians, Katō's arguments were informed by discourses of gender, race, and nation, defining Japanese family as the core of postwar national polity and women as the preservers and promoters of racial strength. In the special session on July 6, 1946, she challenged the government's tactics of obfuscation, and pressed its representatives to clarify the many ambiguities and contradictions:

> I recall the Prime Minister stated that we must preserve the beautiful virtues and customs of the traditional Japanese family system. My understanding of his statement is that we need to retain the traditional strength, virtues and honor of families that the Japanese have constructed over a long period of time, the spirit of harmony and mutual cooperation among family members, the custom of being polite and diligent, or in sum, the moral and virtuous aspects intrinsic

in the Japanese family institution. Or, did the Prime Minister rather intend to say that statutes on succession and family rights in the existing Civil Code should be considered as virtuous aspects of our family system and thus be retained?

She would have had no problem if Yoshida had only meant preserving the moral aspects of the family, but would obviously have objected had he meant preserving the existing Civil Code:

> Needless to say, our family life is the basic unit that most fundamentally defines the character of our society and nation-state. Whether we lead a solid family life or not has a grave impact on the development of our nation and race. Even if laws and statutes provided sweet-sounding phrases such as a guarantee of basic human rights, we could not expect to have national strength nor cultural development, were our citizens to be isolated individuals. The superior national life would be based on solid families as the core units.[72]

Katō clearly advocated the notion that family as a moral institution was vital for the nation and its tradition. Her point of contention was that existing statutes would not foster such a family institution or traditional virtues and morality. As she argued, many of the Meiji Civil Code statutes, including the rights of the household head and the system of successions, would conflict with the idea of family proclaimed in Draft Article 22. Specifically she pointed out that the Meiji Civil Code defined wives as legally incompetent, and thus nullified their abilities to take legal actions or hold property. She emphasized that Draft Article 22 would unmistakably necessitate elimination of these statutes. In advocating for the improved status of women, she not only rearticulated the preexisting nationalist connection among women, family, and national and racial strength that supported Japanese colonialism, but echoed MacArthur's sentiment concerning enfranchised women as the source of postwar social stability.

The discussions in the Diet focused on the meanings of gender equality, a notion extremely difficult to define and open to interpretation. Katō presented her own understandings of gender equality, arguing that although women were essentially equal with men, they should still be treated differently from men. Given their reproductive role, women must be given special protection as mothers. Presenting her own definitions of equality and difference, she argued that these two concepts were not in conflict:

> I understand that the phrase "essential equality of the sexes" means that men and women are essentially equal in terms of their basic

humanity. I would like to know if my understanding is correct. I agree with such a notion of equality, but I also want to point out that women have a special and important mission to bear and rear children. Therefore I see the need to legally state both a principle of gender equality and also a principle of protection of motherhood. . . . If the constitution mechanically states that men and women are equal before the law, in their real lives men and women would experience inequalities. We need to specifically state in the constitution that we protect the interests of mothers and children and that the state will take responsibility for the lives of widowed mothers.[73]

She then proposed welfare provisions for mothers, especially widowed mothers, arguing that Draft Article 25, which specified the right to employment, should include some state protection for working mothers. In postwar Japan, with a large number of women having lost their husbands in the war, widows and the economic hardships they faced presented serious problems. Katō was particularly concerned with this segment of the population. Thus a proposal for protection of mothers that had been raised by Gordon but eliminated was once again brought up by Katō.[74]

How did the government respond? Minister of Health Kawai Yoshinari agreed with Katō on the notions of equality and difference:

"Essential equality of the sexes" that is stated in Draft Article 22 points to equality between men and women in terms of their basic humanity. Thus we need to acknowledge the fact that mothers with children have distinct economic and other types of social burdens. In addition, we should also acknowledge a natural division of labor whereby men are expected to participate in the labor market, if not because of their physical propensity, at least because of our custom and convention.[75]

However, Kawai went on to argue that it was not necessary to specify protection of mothers with children in the constitution. Since differences between men and women were so obvious, he said, future welfare statutes would naturally treat men and women differently without any specification in the constitution. Unconvinced, Katō continued to insist on constitutional protection of war widows with children, who in her eyes were the victims of the war. In doing so, Katō, like Gordon, argued that Japanese women, cast primarily as mothers and wives, were victims, whether of war or the patriarchal family institution.

As the leading feminist politician in occupied Japan, Katō's complicity in nationalism is extremely problematic. In her deliberations concerning postwar education and gender, Katō was particularly explicit in defending the nationalist construct of good wives and wise mothers, and emphasizing women's contribution to postwar Japanese society through their familial roles:

> For a long period of time, school education for girls and adult education for women have been defined in terms of nurturing "good wives and wise mothers" (ryōsai kenbo). Generally speaking I agree with the principle of "good wife and wise mother." And I think being a good wife and wise mother should be understood in terms of its broader implications of being a mother for our society as a whole. But we cannot overlook the fact that in the past the education based on this principle has been dictated by feudalistic moral codes.... Therefore I need to hear some clarification about how education of future children and especially girls would be conducted.[76]

Tanaka Kōtaro, Minister of Education, responded by noting that the principles of good wife and wise mother and an emphasis on traditional national virtue were not inherently negative. As he pointed out, the idea of good wives and wise mothers existed even in Western culture as well. Thus it was not the idea itself, but the implementation during the war years, that was wrong. The new educational principle for women, according to Tanaka, would be to "set down the exemplary feminine path for women so that women would be educated as wives who would take on the entire responsibilities of family education and everyday sustenance of family lives, as citizens, and as members of the human race."[77]

Far from criticizing the nationalist discourse of good wife and wise mother, Katō fully agreed with Tanaka's argument. In her closing statement, she emphatically stated that in the past Japanese women had been endowed with excellent qualities and characters, as was even acknowledged in Western literature. Yet, because of a temporary surge of an excessive "feudal" ideology of good wives and wise mothers, they had been prevented from fully realizing these inherent qualities. Once provided with education based on a broader perspective, the excellence of Japanese women would once again be acknowledged all over the world. Her statement was nothing less than a nationalistic exaltation of Japanese womanhood. As the preservers of national and racial strength, Japanese women were once again assigned to a specifically gendered task of reproducing the postwar nation. Not surprisingly, her male colleagues received the statement with applause.[78]

In the House of Peers, the debates continued to focus on Draft Article 22 and its impact on society. The arguments presented by the Peers were in many ways similar to those presented in the House of Representatives, although often more pointed and detailed. The House of Peers included a number of scholars more knowledgeable about constitutional and legal matters than their counterparts in the House of Representatives. As a result, the tone and content of the debates often became quite academic. The discussions here often were like "lectures at the university."[79] The Peers grilled Kanamori and other cabinet representatives about the consequences of Draft Article 22 on the existing family system, especially the rights of the household head and the system of inheritance. They pressed the cabinet representatives over and over again to admit that Draft Article 22 would result in an overhaul of the existing family system. The government representatives tried hard to evade the issue. Finally, however, they acknowledged that the rights of the household head and succession would be abolished.

In the end, the new constitution proclaimed popular sovereignty and gender equality. Article 24 (Draft Article 22), which advocated gender equality in the marital union, necessitated revision of the Meiji Civil Code, and the New Civil Code eliminated the rights of the household head to decide its members' domicile, marriage and divorce, and rights of succession. It eliminated wives' incompetency in terms of property, provided the same grounds for divorce to wives and husbands, and granted both fathers and mothers the same parental rights over children. In terms of inheritance, surviving female spouses were to get an equitable share. Thus Article 24 significantly improved the postwar legal status of women.

Yet, what kind of political and discursive significance these debates assigned to postwar Japanese women is a different matter. The Ninetieth Imperial Diet served as the contentious discursive arena in which Japanese politicians negotiated postwar national and gender orders, resisting and subverting the radical potential of constitutional revision. Even though popular sovereignty and gender equality were written into the new constitution under the pressure of American occupiers, it was the cabinet and the Diet that assigned specific meanings to such terms, reinscribing prewar discourses of women, family, and nation. The conservative politicians and the cabinet representatives insisted on a spiritual and moral understanding of national polity, especially concerning the Emperor as its core. Similarly, while the proclamation of gender equality and the subsequent civil code revision marked a significant break from the prewar gender and national orders, the deliberations in the Diet constructed understandings of family and femininity that, to a remarkable degree, maintained the presurrender nationalist orders.

Katō Shizue played a complex role in this process. A champion of women's causes, who insisted on eliminating the legal subordination of women in the new Japan, she also insisted on the continuing significance of *ryōsai kenbo*, good wives and wise mothers, and their role in maintaining *junpū bizoku*, beautiful customs and virtues of the nation, thereby leaving a clear imprint of the problematic legacies of modernity in the postwar articulations of female citizenry. By deploying such familial and nationalist terms in defining postwar gender orders, she collaborated not only with Japanese male politicians, but with MacArthur, who defined the role of enfranchised women—Japanese and American alike—as contributing to the order and stability of their respective nations. The complex and problematic connection between feminism and nationalism forged in the course of Japan's colonial modernity was thus allowed to persist in postwar Japan despite, or because of, the U.S. occupation. As I demonstrate, the convergence of feminism, nationalism, and imperialism observed in the course of Japanese constitutional debates continued to shape the gender reform process in occupied Japan, which was increasingly articulated through Cold War political and cultural imperatives.

3

Feminism, Domestic Containment, and Cold War Citizenry

On August 9, 1946, the *Sea Star*, a converted cargo ship full of Americans, was nearing Tokyo Bay after a two-week journey from Seattle. On board was Carmen Johnson, an American woman in her mid-thirties on her way to join the U.S. occupation forces in Japan. Born into a Swedish-American lower-middle-class family in Elkhorn, Wisconsin, and raised in the Midwest, Johnson had no knowledge of the history or language of Japan. To her, the country was an exotic and faraway place, yet she felt no fear. On the contrary, she was eager for the experience. Johnson had joined the Women's Army Auxiliary Corps (WAAC), which later became the Women's Army Corps (WAC), and had been sent to Florida for basic training, and then later to Officer Candidate School in Iowa. Stationed in California, she had worked with Air Force combat intelligence during World War II. Throughout her military experience, she had come to appreciate the challenges of new places, meeting people, and tackling demanding jobs. Japan would be her next adventure, albeit on a different scale. As Mt. Fuji rose before her, she stood on the deck of the ship, excited about what lay ahead: a new job in a country she had only dreamed of.

What motivated Johnson to apply for a position with the U.S. occupation forces in Japan? The immediate postwar years were a time of economic retrenchment for many American women. Just as wartime mobilization had required the mass entry of women into the public domain, the end of the war and postwar demobilization required that women go home. Like many other WACs, Johnson was being demobilized. However, the taste for adventure and the economic independence she had acquired during the war were hard to give up. With no intention of settling down, she sought an alternative; the U.S. government's recruiting of personnel for the occupation of Japan thus came as welcome news. Not only would she have a job, but also a chance to go abroad. Johnson immediately made up her mind to join the occupation forces.

Johnson's autobiography, *Wave-Rings in the Water: My Years with the Women of Postwar Japan*, documents her experience in occupied Japan.[1] Her admitted ignorance of Japanese history, culture, and language was matched by a keen desire to learn. She constantly sought opportunities to meet with Japanese, especially women, outside of her job, offering English conversation classes, giving lectures, and meeting and talking to ordinary Japanese people wherever she went. When her first appointment as a clerk and typist in Nagoya ended in the summer of 1947, she looked for a more challenging position, and in an interview at Eighth Army Headquarters in Yokohama, she requested—rather daringly—a post away from the major urban centers. The interviewers warned her that an assignment in an isolated rural area meant difficulties in getting supplies, the presence of few other American women, a lack of facilities for women occupiers, and other inconveniences. None of these conditions discouraged her. She was delighted when she was given the position of Women's Affairs Officer on the island of Shikoku. Her responsibility was to "democratize" Japanese organizations, especially women's, in four prefectures: Ehime, Kagawa, Kōchi, and Tokushima. Johnson was to experience the occupation from a vantage point distinctly different from Beate Sirota Gordon's—far away from the center and at the grassroots level.

As its subtitle suggests, Johnson's autobiography is a tribute to Japanese women who she came to know during the occupation. Page after page, she describes her encounters with maids and waitresses, housewives and mothers, interpreters and assistants, as well as with leaders of women's organizations. Although consumed with curiosity about the unfamiliar country and its people, she was also aware of the Japanese gaze back at the occupiers: "Whether we were more curious about the Japanese or they about us was an unanswered question."[2] In stark contrast to Gordon, whose narratives focus on herself as "the only woman in the room" in charge of emancipating Japanese women, Johnson understands the occupation in far more inclusive, and on occasions even seemingly egalitarian, terms. To her, Japanese women were collaborators and coparticipants in democratization. She saw herself as there to aide these women's struggles. Reading Johnson's autobiography next to Gordon's, we begin to sense the diverse backgrounds, motives, and perspectives of the women occupiers.

Notwithstanding MacArthur's enthusiastic proclamation of women's liberation, it was American women like Carmen Johnson, and not the Supreme Commander or other high-ranking male officers, who carried out the arduous and demanding tasks of reaching out to and educating Japanese women about the democracy and gender equality codified in the new constitution. Without language skills or knowledge of Japanese society, the Americans nonetheless believed that they were ideally equipped to teach Japanese women. After all, they had grown up in the model democracy—the United States—and while not all the American women involved in the reform identified themselves as feminists, their visions and objectives clearly focused on the emancipation of Japanese women from indigenous male domination.

Some of the American women reformers served as Women's Information Officers or Women's Affairs Officers in the Civil Information and Education Section (CI&E) of SCAP. Others were invited to Japan as "visiting experts." Still others—the wives of the male occupiers—acted as self-appointed teachers of democracy to their Japanese maids and servants.[3] Unlike Gordon, these American women often worked side-by-side with Japanese women to transform Japan from a feudal, traditional society to a modern, democratic one.

Enthusiasm for gender reform was not confined to those stationed in Japan. American women's organizations eagerly wrote letters to Tokyo headquarters, checking on the progress of reform and offering resources and assistance. Many volunteered to go to Japan to disseminate the American way of life. Japanese women enthusiastically welcomed these Americans, asking for advice and suggestions and developing close working relationships. Thus, a network of American women reformers and Japanese middle- and upper-class women emerged, working together on a feminist agenda to emancipate Japanese women.

This chapter questions the well-accepted notion of the CI&E gender reform as a successful instance of women's emancipation and explores the intimate although hitherto underexamined connections between feminist mobilization and Cold War containment politics in occupied Japan. I analyze how Cold War cultural dynamics not only enabled feminist mobilization that was complicit in postwar American hegemony, but also produced numerous contradictions and ironic consequences that challenged the dominant apparatus of power. During the occupation, gender reform was clearly informed by the Cold War. To start, the democracy disseminated in occupied Japan was undoubtedly American, always already imagined in opposition not only to Oriental feudalism, but increasingly to communist totalitarianism. In their attempts to reform Japanese women, American women occupiers' reform disseminated—often by skits and role playing—their own American, white, middle-class notions of femininity, domesticity, and heterosexuality as the path to democracy. At workshops, conferences, and training programs, Japanese women were required to enact, often repeatedly, American notions of democracy, domesticity, and femininity. Faultless performance was taken as an indication of successful democratization. Importantly, SCAP's strategic reliance on skits and role playing for gender reform was strikingly similar to the Cold War U.S. civil defense program that repeatedly used drills to prepare for possible nuclear attacks by the Soviet Union. The mastery of civil defense skills was considered a moral and ethical obligation, ensuring the survival of the American way of life against the Communist menace. In the world of civil defense, "survival was reduced to the performance of routines."[4] Given Japan's significance in U.S. Cold War foreign policies, it is no surprise that the occupation's gender reform similarly focused on the performance of routines. Despite its geographical distance from the United States, occupied Japan became an important site for articulating Cold War practice, even prior to its full flourishing in the United States.[5]

By playing out their roles in the Cold War project, American women—both those stationed in Japan and those in the United States—were participating in a mission of national and international significance. Japanese middle-class and elite women never disappointed the Americans, enthusiastically studying, advocating, and performing the "American dreams" of democracy and gender equality. What is indeed striking about gender reform during the occupation is the strong sense of excitement and empowerment shared by both groups. American and Japanese women tapped into the same discursive repertoire of democracy, jointly participating in the feminist project of transforming women's lives, shaped and driven by emerging Cold War political and cultural dynamics.

The Cold War era has been considered a time of loss for women, spawning a postwar cult of domesticity, confining women within the sphere of home and family, and eroding whatever gains had been made during World War II. As the conventional argument goes, during the Cold War, the containment of communism went hand-in-hand with the containment of women.[6] However, recent feminist studies have begun to question this "conservatism-and-constraints approach," calling for more nuanced and complex understandings of the Cold War and its diverse implications for women. For instance, Laura McEnaney's study of the U.S. civil defense program argues that the Cold War tenets of femininity, domesticity, and anticommunism produced "more, rather than less, opportunity for women's activism." Because it "was a malleable and widely applicable construction in the Cold War years," McEnaney notes, American women often appropriated "the post-war cult of domesticity" in pursuit of feminist political objectives.[7] Building on McEnaney's insight, in this chapter I argue that in occupied Japan the Cold War also facilitated, rather than suppressed, feminist mobilization of American and Japanese women, providing them with opportunities and resources and turning them into complicit participants in Cold War cultural and political dynamics.

At the same time, the relation between the Cold War and feminism was far from simple, as feminist mobilization also produced numerous instances of disruption, resistance, and contradiction, challenging American hegemony from within. Although ardent promoters of the U.S. Cold War missions, American women reformers sometimes doubted MacArthur's—and their own—ability to democratize Japan. Japanese middle-class women leaders, "poster girls" for U.S. democratic leadership, were aware of U.S. discrimination against women and minorities and willing to point out the fallacy of holding up the United States as the model democracy. Furthermore, Japanese and American women developed close working relationships and sometimes strong personal bonds, causing much suspicion and anxiety among American male occupiers and subverting the Cold War heterosexual normativity. Thus, neither Japanese nor American women's complicity in the Cold War was ever simple. Feminist mobilization in occupied Japan was a frequently contradictory and unpredictable process, resulting in unexpected and even subversive outcomes that exceeded all expectations. Hegemony's inability to sustain itself—its frequent "leakage" in the midst of Cold War containment culture—constitutes a dominant theme in this chapter.

Civil Information and Education and Cold War Indoctrination

The U.S. occupation of Japan set for itself an extremely ambitious and thoroughly ambiguous goal. Not only would it restructure social institutions, it would transform the minds of the Japanese. The task of instilling the spirit of democracy into "feudal" and "premodern" Japanese minds was assigned to the CI&E Section of SCAP. "One of the explicit purposes of the Occupation," the CI&E document "Mission and Accomplishment of the Civil Information and Education Section" states, "has been to give the Japanese an opportunity to discard those of their past ways which made them a menace to the rest of the world and to establish democratic principles in all spheres of political, economic and cultural life." For this purpose, the CI&E would "deal largely with intangibles, with matters closely related to the thought and culture patterns of the Japanese people."[8] Repeated use of the terms "reorientation" and "rehabilitation" emphasized the CI&E focus on reforming the minds of the Japanese. Indeed, the United States believed that the war and subsequent occupation were not simply a military confrontation, but an "intellectual war" as well. "Total victory" meant not only subjugating the

Japanese military force, but changing "the basic thinking of the Japanese masses."[9] This "intellectual warfare" continued after the surrender, with the CI&E a central agent in waging the war.

CI&E activities were wide-ranging, following patterns well observed in other U.S. Cold War interventions abroad.[10] So-called information centers were established in major cities. Also offered were library services, which included showing motion pictures and playing music. Radio programs, workshops, and lectures were other means of information dissemination, as was translating English materials into Japanese. By 1949, the CI&E had translated more than sixty books, including *Abe Lincoln Grows Up* by Carl Sandburg, *The Republic* by Charles Beard, and *Babe Ruth* by Bob Considine.[11] The occupation forces labeled the function of the CI&E "educational," but its activities clearly positioned it as a propaganda machine transmitting American values, norms, and ideals to the occupied territory and transforming the minds of the Japanese.

Despite the heavy-handed nature of American Cold War domination, its operation in Japan was far from coherent or stable, with gender reform becoming a major site of its articulation as well as unraveling. A significant portion of gender reform was assigned to low-ranking CI&E Women's Information Officers or Women's Affairs Officers. As with Beate Sirota Gordon and the constitutional revision process, American women in the CI&E were not given a blueprint for gender reform. The symbolic importance assigned by MacArthur to Japanese women's liberation was belied by the lack of planning and resources assigned to gender reform, leaving the American women occupiers to implement from scratch the enormous project of transforming Japanese gender relations. At the center of this ambitious, although virtually unplanned reform project was Ethel Weed, the head of Women's Information Officers, both those stationed in Tokyo and those in local areas. She was in charge of devising, implementing, and monitoring numerous reform activities. Other sections within SCAP, such as the GS, the Economic and Scientific Section (ESS), and the Public Health and Welfare Section (PHW), often consulted with her on women's issues. In the existing historiography, Weed, like Gordon, is granted a pivotal role in implementing the ideals of gender equality and democracy in postwar Japan. However, resituated within the context of Cold War containment politics, the nature and consequences of Weed's and other American women's involvement in the occupation take on drastically different and far more ironic and ambiguous meanings. On the one hand, these American women were agents of U.S. imperial expansionism, soliciting Japanese women's participation in containment politics and thereby re-creating a problematic tie between women and imperialism. On the other hand, however, women occupiers also played a subversive role as their participation in the foreign occupation not only contradicted the

Cold War ideal of domestic femininity but also resulted in the formation of a female homosocial sphere of American and Japanese women, generating much anxiety among male occupiers.

Ethel Weed was born in Syracuse, New York, in 1906, and raised in Cleveland, Ohio, by her father, Grover Weed, an engineer, and her mother, Berenice Weed, a homemaker. The first in the family to obtain a college degree, she majored in English. After graduation, she worked as a journalist for the *Cleveland Plain Dealer*, and then as a public relations specialist for various civil organizations, including the Women's City Club in Cleveland. With these credentials, she enlisted in the WAC in 1943, and helped recruit women to the military. While at Officer Candidate School, she learned about the military's plan to send a group of American women to Japan as part of the occupation forces. The prospect intrigued her and she got herself appointed to a place in the occupation.[12] In contrast to Gordon, but like Carmen Johnson and many other occupiers, Weed had no prior exposure to Japan, no knowledge of things Japanese, and no language skills. A crash course given to occupation personnel at Northwestern University was her only preparation. Single and in her forties, with experience primarily in public relations, Weed was to play a crucial, and extremely problematic, role during the U.S. occupation of Japan.

As Lisa Meyer points out in her study of women in the U.S. military, as the first cohort of women enlistees, WACs like Weed and Johnson were pioneers, breaking conventional gender expectations, and entering a previously all-male domain. Those who advocated the formation of the WACs often thought of women's entry into the military as a way of improving women's status and gaining for them full citizenship in the United States. On the other hand, women enlisting in the U.S. military during World War II were under constant scrutiny and regulation, with their sexuality a focal issue. Those who opposed the enlistment of women perceived "women soldiers" as "mannish women" or "lesbians," and therefore a threat to the existing gender and sexual order. To cope with the opposition and anxieties surrounding women in the military, both male and female leaders demanded that the WACs present an image of impeccable respectability, with white, middle-class femininity and sexual restraint fully in place. Ironically, for the WACs themselves, the result was a work environment closer to the prewar labor market, rigidly segregated by gender, race, and class, than it was to the wartime civilian labor force, which provided certain openings for women.[13]

Wartime and postwar sexual politics within the U.S. military were full of contradictions and ironies. As John D'Emilio documents, World War II military mobilization, and especially the sex-segregated nature of the military, "created a substantially new 'erotic situation' conducive both to the articulation of a homosexual identity and to the more rapid evolution of a gay subculture."[14] However, this newly emerging sexual community immediately came under strict surveillance once the war was over. Gays and lesbians were not only labeled and stigmatized as "sexual perverts," but in the emerging Cold War context, they were perceived as contaminating "normal" individuals and as breaching national security through their alleged communist connections. Discourses of sexual containment were inseparable from discourses of national security and the containment of communism.

Occupied Japan was no exception. As one former WAC recalls, a major "witch hunt" took place in Tokyo in the early days of the occupation, during which some five hundred women, suspected because of their alleged lesbian sexual orientation, were court-martialed, tried, and dishonorably discharged.[15] Postwar sexual anxiety was expressed in other far more subtle ways as well. In addressing the newly elected thirty-nine women of the Diet, MacArthur defined their mission as a "stabilizing force" in postwar Japan, and strongly advised them against forming a "woman's block" vis-à-vis Japanese men in the Diet. MacArthur's warning against a "woman's block," which was repeatedly expressed by other male occupiers, was more than a conservative male sentiment against "women's rights movements." Within the context of Cold War gender-sexual politics, such statements reflected a strong suspicion, even fear, of a female homosocial sphere.[16] In occupied Japan, then, Cold War containment strategies often "leaked," with gender reform turning into a major site of disturbance. Assigned to play a central role in disseminating Cold War notions of femininity and sexuality, the reform network of American and Japanese women ironically became a space contaminated by possibilities of gender-sexual subversion.

The Strongest Democratizing Force in the World of Women: American Women Leaders and Cold War Feminist Mobilization

In occupied Japan, Ethel Weed proved to be an effective organizer of a vast network of women, which included individuals like Mary Beard, well-known woman historian, and organizations like the General Federation of Women's Clubs. Some organizations contacted headquarters in Tokyo, some wrote directly to MacArthur, and others wrote to Weed. The extensive correspondence records between the United States and Tokyo headquarters indicate that talk of Japanese women's emancipation—and U.S. leadership in that project—was a circulating discourse, traveling back and forth between the Americans at home and those stationed in Japan. The organizations that corresponded with Tokyo headquarters including the American Association of University Women, the General Federation of Women's Clubs, and the National Federation of Business and Professional Women's Clubs, had deep connections to Cold War politics back home, often criticizing the government's underutilization of "women power" and promoting women's participation in the public sphere.[17] By 1951, these middle-class women's organizations, together with the National Association of Negro Business and Professional Women's Clubs, National Federation of Republican Women, the Women's Division of the Democratic National Committee, and others, formed umbrella organizations such as the Advisory Committee for Women's Participation and the Assembly of Women's Organizations for National Security.[18] Far from content with the postwar ideals of femininity and domesticity, American women leaders actively sought opportunities to participate in the Cold War. Within this context, the U.S. occupation of Japan offered a welcome chance to make a womanly contribution to the postwar nation as well as to expand their organizational activities abroad.

As Laura McEnaney documents, American women's eagerness to participate in the Cold War often baffled male policymakers who lacked a well-defined plan of how to utilize women. In U.S.-occupied Japan, American women leaders' enthusiasm about gender reform also resulted in bewilderment among the occupation authorities who had only expected their limited involvement. The correspondence records between the General Federation of Women's Clubs and Tokyo headquarters shed light on the makeshift nature of American hegemony that was simultaneously bolstered and challenged by American women leaders' demand to participate in the occupation. Early in the occupation, Hazel Moore, a member of the federation, requested information about the occupation. In response, Weed sent an article entitled "Progress of Japanese Women," with a photograph of newly elected women in the Diet. In the article, Weed drew a dramatic picture of the changing lives of Japanese women. In comparison to pre-1945 Japan, Weed wrote, when women had suffered from absolute subjugation, it was remarkable to witness the many achievements Japanese women had accomplished since the beginning of the occupation. "Without sacrificing their important position in the home," women from all walks of life were now "rebelling against ancient custom, thinking for themselves and comparing their lives with those of other women in democratic countries" who would be sympathetic to their struggles, "since the social, political and economic rights for which they are striving are the universal hopes of women everywhere."

As Japanese women strove for these universally desired rights, Weed reported in the article, American women were providing an important model. Japanese women were eager to learn democracy, and "insatiable in their desires for bulletins, pamphlets, news releases and all information pertinent to activities of women in democratic countries, particularly American women." While a multitude of CI&E activities were helping Japanese women, Weed considered the help from organizations in the United States to be a vital part of the reform process. American organizations had been sending material to Tokyo headquarters, which the CI&E distributed to libraries and information centers all over Japan. Japanese women were so eager to learn democracy that they were often "seen copying the printed material for the use of their friends, and often the material soon becomes thumbmarked and worn." Weed ended her article by quoting MacArthur, who had congratulated Japanese women for their "vital influence upon all public affairs" and "courage and will to work with the exemplary devotion for the common welfare of the Japanese people." This article was reviewed by the Public Relations Office of SCAP before being sent out to the General Federation of Women's Clubs. Not only were there no objections to publishing the article in the United States, but the office gave the article high marks, as it provided "an excellent opportunity to subtly 'sell' the occupation."[19]

The federation's response exceeded SCAP's expectations, however. Not at all content with simply sending materials to Japan, the federation demanded that its members directly participate in the occupation, subverting SCAP's intention to use women only for the occupation's propaganda purpose. Sara Whitehurst, Extension Secretary of the Foreign and Territorial Clubs of the General Federation of Women's Clubs, started intense negotiations with Tokyo headquarters. A veteran of women's club movements, Whitehurst was to become a leading figure in the Cold War mobilization of American women. Appointed chief organizer of the Advisory Committee for Women's Participation in 1951, she worked as a liaison between women's organizations and the federal government. Yet, even prior to her work with the committee, Whitehurst had become deeply involved in the Cold War, drawing on the dominant discourses of democracy and anticommunism to promote her organization's expansion in Japan against the male authorities' intent.

On January 14, 1948, Whitehurst wrote Senator Alben Barkley, asking for his support in sending representatives of the federation to Japan: "[W]omen leaders from the General Federation, if sent to Japan or invited by General MacArthur, could make a definite contribution to the advancement of his program for the democratization of the women of that country." She insisted on performing a "womanly duty" for the nation in the emerging Cold War context: "The woman's club, as exemplified in this country, is, we feel, the strongest democratizing force in the world for women. We are even having inquiries from Japanese women, asking how to go about organizing women into clubs—asking for help in planning constructive educational programs which will help them become 'like United States women.'"[20] Tapping into the dominant discourses of nation and democracy, Whitehurst nonetheless challenged the Cold War gender order by identifying women, not men, as "the strongest democratizing force in the world for women" and claiming the central place for American women in the male-dominant occupation project.

In support of the federation's request, Senator Barkley wrote a letter of inquiry to Tokyo headquarters. In reply, MacArthur acknowledged the invaluable contribution American women could make to the occupation by guiding "inexperienced" Japanese women, but also expressed ambivalence about their direct involvement in the occupation. Gender reform, wrote MacArthur,

> is a work to which we here attach the utmost importance because of belief, encouraged by what they have done since the war, that on the future of Japan her women will exert an influence comparable to that of American women on our own national life. They are eager to overcome their social inexperience of past years and to organize for democratic purposes. And not unnaturally they look to the women of the United States for inspiration and assistance.[21]

Yet, MacArthur was reluctant to invite the federation's representatives to Japan, ostensibly because of inadequate facilities for such visitors. However, an internal memo reveals a different concern. At the time, the CI&E was trying to dismantle the Japanese women's national federation, which had been formed to assist the state during World War II. It was feared that the American women from the federation would advocate for a federation-based women's organization in Japan, undermining the occupiers' efforts to "democratize" Japan.[22] At a more fundamental level, however, MacArthur's ambivalence might have to do with an equally or more serious challenge Whitehurst posed to the Cold War ideals of femininity and domesticity. Rejecting the idea that women as a "stabilizing force" would contribute to the postwar social order by exerting feminine influence from home, she insisted on women's direct involvement in the Cold War, even in a foreign occupation.

The federation continued its negotiations with Tokyo headquarters. In a letter to MacArthur on March 22, 1948, Whitehurst explicitly challenged MacArthur's authority by pointing out that the occupation's gender reform had been ineffective and that Japanese and American women were requesting service from the federation. To prove her point, she quoted from a Japanese woman's letter sent to the federation: "Please help us to organize. General MacArthur gave us the vote, which is wonderful; formerly we were slaves; now we are maid-servants. We hope we may become companions with our husbands in the home. Please help us to become free women." She also quoted from an American occupier's letter, which pointed out the ineffectiveness of gender reform in Japan and solicited the federation's help: "I shall appreciate information relative to instructions on procedures, etc. If we can find simple, dynamic means of promoting the information and activities which we suggest be utilized by the women of Japan, we will have at last made a beginning of arousing their interest." "Leaders for such work must be briefed by leaders who have had years of experience in such a field," Whitehurst argued, and the federation was ready to offer the necessary resources and expertise. In promoting her organization's participation in the occupation, Whitehurst once again couched her argument in the language of the Cold War:

> We are most anxious to help preserve our democratic form of government and to help the women of other countries to follow in our footsteps rather than succumb to a totalitarian form of rule. We believe that contact between non-governmental groups will be beneficial and that we can be of immense help to you if you will give us the opportunity.[23]

The federation's campaign to send its representatives to Japan was aggressive and insistent, indicating both SCAP's continuing resistance and women's persistent tenacity. On July 8, 1948, J. J. Blaire Buck, president of the federation, wrote directly to MacArthur, reiterating the significant role American women's organizations were ready to play in the Cold War: "We believe that the General Federation has in existence more extensive machinery than any non-governmental women's organization to interpret and promote throughout the world the American Way of Life." However, aside from its contribution to the project of national significance, the federation had its own reasons for wanting to send its members to Japan. Its proposed contribution to the occupation was inseparable from the organization's drive to recruit membership in the Far East. Reminiscent of the early-twentieth-century international suffrage movements, the federations' expansion abroad went hand in hand with American imperial expansion.[24] As Buck explained, she, together with Whitehurst, had already received an invitation to visit their member organization in the Philippines. They had also been hoping to visit Korea, where they would "study ways and means of reaching the 4,800,000 members in the Federation of Korean Women's Clubs, recently affiliated with us through the help of Mrs. Helen Nixon, Advisor to the Women's Bureau of the United States Army Military Government in Korea." Japan would be, they were confident, another site where they could resuscitate and expand club membership.[25] Her appeal worked. In a July 26, 1948 letter, MacArthur finally consented to their visit.[26]

American women's complicity in the Cold War U.S. imperialism was not limited to the federation. Many of the American women who wrote to Tokyo headquarters frequently thanked and congratulated MacArthur, showing their support for his operations in occupied Japan. While the occupation authorities used such support to boost their own images, American women also took advantage of the occupation to promote their own political and organizational agenda. Sally Butler, President of the National Federation of Business and Professional Women's Clubs, wrote in her letter of January 23, 1948: "Through you, general, we are addressing our formal appreciation to the Military Government of Japan on the enfranchisement of Japanese women. We wish to congratulate the government on its awareness that a progressive movement to give women the vote is sweeping the world."[27] Later in the same year, Butler wrote another letter to MacArthur, thanking him for appointing Doris Cochrane as a consultant to the CI&E. Cochrane had served as Director of Legislation and Public Affairs for the National Federation of Business and Professional Women's Clubs. In addition, she had worked as Information and Liaison Officer in the Department of State, Division of Public Liaison. With her experience in the United States, where she had displayed "a deep understanding [of] the problems inherent in informing less oriented women of governmental activities," Cochrane would be ideal, Butler said, for the work needed to improve Japanese women, obviously another group of "less-oriented" women. Butler suggested that MacArthur grant Cochrane a personal interview when she arrived in Japan,[28] a suggestion that was well received. Following the by now familiar pattern, an internal memo went from the CI&E to the office of the Commander in Chief; given Cochrane's "wide contacts with women's groups in the United States," her interview "would react to the benefit of the command."[29] Once in Japan, Cochrane's close working relationship with Weed was widely publicized.

There were many other letters by American women addressed to MacArthur. These letters reveal that American women's understandings about the occupation were often informed by the interanimating terms of religion, nation, and purity, forming a typical Cold War discursive trope.[30] Mrs. M. W. Aleta Jessup of the Women's Auxiliary to the National Council of the Protestant Episcopal Church in Little Rock, Arkansas, wrote to MacArthur on November 21, 1949, that she and fellow Episcopal women would study Japan during the Lenten season. She asked him to send a "message of directive" to this group of women.[31] Augusta Kent Hobbs, educational secretary of the Diocese of Maryland, asked MacArthur to send a personal message to the forthcoming meeting of the Church and the Triennial Convention of the Women's Auxiliary of the Church. The topic at the meeting, as well as in "every parish and mission of the Episcopal Family," would be Japan. For Hobbs, the U.S. occupation of Japan entailed a specifically gendered vocation Christian women should pursue. Invoking the Cold War discursive connection among women, religion, and nation, she asked him to suggest the kind of contribution that "Christian womanhood might make to the womanhood of Japan."[32] Not all the letters MacArthur received were positive or congratulatory, however, as the triangulated discourses of gender, religion, and nation also provided a space to articulate criticism to MacArthur's operations in Japan. On January 20, 1951, Mrs. Cora Brunemeir of the Women's Christian Temperance Union of Southern California wrote criticizing the alcohol consumption by occupation personnel: "We are facing a terrible enemy in Communism; but the enemy of our own making is far more ruinous. Liquor is doing its deadly work in our armed forces. WHY do we permit it?" Indeed, "the present mess we are in in Korea, may well be the result of boozy planning." She called on MacArthur to "stand pure and clean so that God may perform His will through you."[33] The letter's anticommunist sentiment was increasingly salient at this time, and notably here was linked to the discourses of Christianity, national might, temperance, and purity.

Japanese Woman as a Force in History: Mary Beard and Critique of Gender Reform

Among the many exchanges between the United States and Tokyo headquarters, correspondence between Weed and the well-known historian Mary Beard is particularly noteworthy. In her pioneering study of Beard's influence on Weed, Uemura Chikako, drawing from Susan Pharr's study, argues that their relationship was part of "an alliance of liberation," and that their correspondence contributed immeasurably to the successful outcome of gender reform. As a mentor and friend, Beard shared her perspectives, suggestions, and beliefs, especially about the centrality of women in history and the importance of a woman's standpoint; Weed used them in her project to emancipate women in occupied Japan.[34] A careful examination offers a drastically different picture, however. The correspondence between Beard and Weed constituted a space where Cold War American hegemony was simultaneously bolstered and challenged. While advocating the postwar ideals of gender, family, and sexuality, Beard and Weed developed a strong personal bond with each other, disturbing Cold War heterosexual normativity in a subtle yet significant way. The relationship between the two was subversive in another way, as they came to question the occupation's basic premise, especially the occupiers' ability to transform Japanese gender relations. Considering herself the authority on Japan, Beard perceived American women leaders to be unqualified as reformers and even chastised Weed for her lack of understanding of Japanese women. The exchange between Beard and Weed thus reveals a dynamic interweaving of hegemony and subversion, recasting the occupation's gender reform as an incoherent, often internally divided and unpredictable project.

Beard's involvement in the occupation, especially her arguments concerning women, needs to be analyzed in relation to the history of feminist movements. She had been part of the American women's suffrage movement, associating with feminist leaders such as Carry Chapman Catt, Alice Paul, and Jane Adams. Following women's enfranchisement in 1920, however, Beard began to distance herself from the movement. As the Women's Party, led by its charismatic leader Alice Paul, began to mobilize for the passage of an Equal Rights Amendment (ERA), the feminist community became divided, with many, including Beard, taking a strong anti-ERA stance. Over the following decades, Beard not only continued to express her opposition to the ERA, because of the negative impacts she believed it would have on working women, but became critical of a feminist understanding of women as subjugated victims under male domination. All over the world, she argued, women had been a significant "force in history," actively participating in society and making numerous contributions to "civilization." Women's power, and especially their civilizing presence, must be recognized

Despite her harsh criticism, Beard never gave up on the idea of women's empowerment. She pursued her own vision of feminism, calling it on one occasion "The New Feminism." Through lectures, radio addresses, and such publications as *America through Women's Eyes* (1933), *Woman as Force in History* (1946), and *The Force of Women in Japanese History* (1953), she continued to argue for the powerful presence of women in history. She was also active in educating the public about women's contributions to history, advocating women-centered curricula. She initiated, although never completed, a project to establish the World Center for Women's Archives, to collect and preserve historical source materials that would shed light on women's contribution to history worldwide.

Existing studies often characterize Beard's thesis as contradictory, even flawed. As Nancy Cott points out, to prove her theory about the centrality and powerfulness of women in history, Beard frequently relied in her writings on "overly facile judgment that one woman's, or a few women's, attainment of a certain status or privilege signified that women in general had the same opportunity."[35] Dismissing feminist arguments about women's oppression as the "subjection theory," Beard also failed to address the marginalization of women in society and overlooked the structural sources of gender inequality.[36] American women's mass entry into industry and the military during World War II confirmed her thesis about women's centrality in history, but also undercut her conviction about women's civilizing influence that should have made them opponents to war.[37] Beard's position was appreciated neither by feminists nor antifeminists.[38] Having no academic affiliation and overshadowed by the success of her husband and well-known historian Charles Beard, she often suffered from isolation. With many of her projects less than successful, she felt at times a "gnawing sense of failure."[39] Approaching her seventies by the end of the war, she saw in the U.S. occupation of Japan an affirmation and vindication of her long-held belief about women's centrality in history.

Correspondence between Beard and Weed began in the early days of the occupation. Like many other American women, Beard admired MacArthur's leadership, not least because of his attention to Japanese women's rights. "The whole procedure in Japan relative to enlisting the force of women on the side of democracy is so superior as intelligence to the military occupation in Germany that General MacArthur's leadership in this respect shines with brilliant illumination," she wrote in one of her earliest letters. She also praised Weed and her role in the occupation: "I rejoice also that you are his brilliant associate. There should be someone among the officers in Germany alive enough to realize the gravity of neglecting liberal-minded German women."[40] Despite her training as a historian, she was extraordinarily uncritical, even blind, toward MacArthur's place in the genealogy of American imperialism, or his appropriation of feminist discourses for the purpose of establishing American hegemony in postwar Japan. Impressed by MacArthur's foresight in mobilizing women, in a letter of August 15, 1946, Beard asked if he had thought of this alone:

> You may hesitate to tell me how General MacArthur arrived at his decision to enlist women so fundamentally in his crusade for the democratic way in Japan. But this I long to know: whether it sprang wholly from his mind and spirit or whether one or more of his counsellors [sic] likewise thought it was the right course to take. The failure of the AMG in Germany and Austria to rally women to its side has surely been a serious mistake.[41]

Weed did not reply immediately. In an internal memo sent to the Chief of the CI&E on August 29, 1946, she explained that she had been in correspondence with Mary Beard, "foremost American historian" who had been "the source of much inspiration and encouragement regarding the work here." She then asked for a conference with "someone close to the Supreme Commander" to respond to Beard's inquiry.[42] Weed's inquiry was sent from the CI&E to Colonel H. B. Wheeler. Once again, a note attached to this memo reveals SCAP's intention to use the topic of gender reform in Japan for Cold War propaganda purposes. It was suggested that granting an interview to Weed would be beneficial from the perspective of pubic relations, and would "enhance the prestige of the Command in Japan and abroad." Subsequently, the Chief of the CI&E, Colonel Nugent, received a memo repeating a grand narrative about MacArthur, women, and the march of progress, and once again defining American and Japanese women as the source of stability for their respective nations:

Mrs. Beard should be informed that General MacArthur for many years has considered the intervention of American women into American politics as one of the greatest stabilizing events in our political history. Because of this view, his initial planning of policy to govern in the occupation of Japan laid particular emphasis upon the early emancipation of the women and their encouragement toward independent political thought and action. While on board his plane "Bataan" en route to Japan on 30 August 1945, the depth of this purpose was made clear to the members of his staff then accompanying him when he prescribed that such action would be within the foremost of early directions designed to establish the overall pattern in the reorientation of Japan.

The memo went on to state that MacArthur was "particularly gratified at their response to the challenge of the first general election following their enfranchisement." He was confident that Japanese women were "bringing the shaping of future Japanese national policy under the direct influence of the wisdom of the home."[43]

A few months later, Beard received Weed's response. Beard could barely contain her excitement; she was ecstatic to learn that it was MacArthur's decision to enlist Japanese women to the project of occupation: "I've got something in this document indicative of General MacArthur's conception of the family as the core or heart of society and of women as its prime guardian. . . . That General MacArthur should associate the care and nurture of the family with political democracy—and do this in his own mind, not just by pressure from another mind—gives him a standing in my mind which is at the top of my judgment of a statecraft." Clearly she saw in MacArthur a person who understood and acted on a notion of history very much like her own. She would "not only treasure this reply," but "use it as a precious historic document— with good effect." She told Weed that she planned to include the information in an article she was going to write. She "needed this very kind of statement to help me in my effort to do something to socialize our ultra-feminists who so tragically overlook the role of the family even in a democracy." Perhaps with a hint of irony, Beard noted that had MacArthur not emphasized the importance of family and women, she would have been forced to "go back to Confucius" to find such a statement, which would have been "unfortunate," since Confucius was a "feudalist" who supported "totalitarianism."[44]

In her letters, Beard defined women and family as the backbone of the nation. Such gendered understanding had been prevalent in American wartime discourses, but was quickly becoming the central part of Cold War containment narratives. The triangulated themes of gender, nation, and the Cold War were more explicitly articulated in another letter written on the same day. Comparing the U.S. occupations of Japan and Germany, Beard deemed gender reform in Germany too slow and too worrisome. Enlisting "anti-Nazi and anti-Communist women" in Germany was crucial, or the occupation would not only "fall short of its goal" but "be more seriously a failure." In Beard's mind, the success of the occupation hinged not simply on enlisting women, but on doing so as an anticommunist measure.[45] As she told Weed several years later, communism was a threat to "democratic liberties," and as far as she was concerned, there was "no true communism in the Society [sic] system."[46]

While often complicit in Cold War containment discourses, the correspondence also became a critical space to question the very premise of the occupation. For instance, Weed's letter of February 12, 1947, reveals a rarely expressed sense of unease about her work:

> It is very difficult to extol women and constantly work for their equal representation in government, etc., and at the same time to avoid "exalting women to excess." Personally, I hate even the thought of a real matriarchy. I believe that men and women have their separate contributions to make to the world, and that the contributions of both are needed for a peaceful and well-integrated civilization. They must work together.

Weed even contradicted the popular understandings of MacArthur as the liberator and of gender reform as emancipating helpless and agentless Japanese women. Contrary to SCAP's publicity efforts, and despite her own article sent to the General Federation of Women's Clubs, Weed expressed a firm

> conviction that women in Japan have given a great deal more to their country than they have ever been given credit for. One point that I continually have to emphasize here is the fact that whatever has been done by General MacArthur, has come as result of achievements of Japanese women in the past, of their desire for equal opportunities, and strong feeling that women and men must together build a new world.

Written just a few days after the failed February 1 nationwide worker-initiated general strike, Weed's letter is revealing in another way. In the preceding weeks, occupied Japan had witnessed an enormous surge in labor mobilization, with a strong showing by women of the left-labor front under Communist leadership. "Democratization" was going too far—exceeding the level the occupiers were willing to permit. MacArthur intervened, prohibiting the strike and dealing a severe blow to the Japanese left. Reflecting on this turmoil, Weed pondered the political future of the country, and especially the influence of the "right" and the "left." Japan was at a "crossroads," and Weed felt uncertain about prospects for successful democratization, wishing for "some magic way" to accomplish it: "People have, in the vote, a very powerful weapon but at their present stage of development the masses are at the mercies of either the extreme left or the extreme right, whichever group speaks the loudest."[47]

Weed's letter drew an emotional response from Beard: "Your fine letter of February 12 makes me want to write you with a torrent of words because it goes to the core of society and ranges outward to all its periphery. The convictions you declare to be your own are mine too." Like Weed, Beard believed that women everywhere had made specific womanly contributions to "civilization," and that contrary to a feminist notion of subjugated womanhood, Japanese women had clearly been a "force in history." Such understanding explicitly challenged the dominant, Orientalist image of Japanese women as helpless victims under indigenous male domination. However, Beard's celebration of Japanese women's contributions to civilization was no less problematic, as it concealed the complicit roles Japanese women had played in pre-1945 racism, nationalism, and colonialism.

In the same letter, Beard responded to Weed's uncertainty about U.S. operations in Japan and offered advice as well as comfort:

Dear young woman, you are not too impatient in your situation, with your responsibility, for without impatience, you might dawdle. But cultivate as much of it as you can by trying to hold the long view. I speak like a granny but, being very old now, maybe I have some warrant for counseling you, since you have asked me whether you are too impatient while you also say that you know things take time. Certainly they do. No revolution could change a people overnight.

Japan's postwar situation was not unique, Beard noted: "Japan at the crossroads? Yes she is. So is every other nation and people." Keeping a system of democracy in Japan—or anywhere else—requires "eternal vigilance with immense knowledge of this system and strong appreciation of its value." Thus, "we are all in the same boat as far as having to rule out magic is concerned and stick to the faith that we have taken the right road ourselves."[48]

Despite her strong admiration for MacArthur and Weed, Beard also explicitly challenged the occupation's basic premises as well as its personnel, defining Japanese women, not the American occupiers, as the central force in postwar democratization. To begin with, she considered U.S. democracy less than perfect, citing the nation's "backward" attitude toward the history of women.[49] She was no less critical of American women and their understanding of their own history, which she believed few truly did. Women leaders in the

United States were "mental children," unqualified to guide Japanese women, and poor models for independence.[50] Beard, who considered herself an expert on Japan, was appalled at the "naivete" and "colossal" ignorance of the American occupiers. "What burns me up is the ignorance of our women and men who assume to know what other people must do to be saved and at once," she wrote. "I am positively stunned at the light-mindedness with which some of our people think they can rush into such a strange-to-them situation and even set up the right system of education for the Japanese." Instead of relying on missions sent from the United States, such as the education mission, she thought it "so infinitely preferable for the women of Japan to be encouraged, as you encourage them, to think and act from their own intelligence and understanding of what it means to emerge from feudalism to self-government."[51] In yet another letter, Beard faulted the occupation's "acculturation policy" of imposing American values on the Japanese and advocated for "adaptation to firmer native values."[52]

Critical of gendered imperialist assumptions among the occupiers, Beard did not always approve of Weed's actions in Japan, either. Indeed it is questionable how much of Beard's insights, including her critique of the U.S. occupation, Weed thoroughly understood and shared. A rare moment of disagreement appeared in a 1949 letter from Beard to Weed. Beard objected to the title Weed had given an article, which Beard hadn't read: "The Emergence of Women." Japanese women were not simply "emerging," Beard wrote, as women had always been a force in the history of Japan.[53] Indeed, Weed's article presented a picture of women who had just emerged from shackles of male domination:

> Legally, socially, politically, and economically, the role of the Japanese woman up to the time of the Occupation was practically a non-existent one. In the home her role was one of obedience and service. In society she was scarcely recognized. Traditionally she was to go no place without her husband's permission. Legally, she was an incompetent. Economically, she had practically no independence.

Such a situation was "abhorred" by a small number of women who "had come in contact with the western world" or had "thought of people as individuals." However, they had been unable to reach the masses with their political message. In contrast to prewar conditions, the article continued, women's lives since the end of the war had witnessed remarkable changes: "an ever-increasing improvement in the status of women," and "their emergence from the feudalistic atmosphere in which they have lived and worked for generations." Making these postwar changes permanent features of Japanese society, Weed pointed out, would require "a vast amount of re-education," and eradicating "(p)ast traditional indoctrination." However, women had clearly taken the first major step toward a democratic future.[54]

The tone and content of the article differ significantly not only from Beard's position, but also from views expressed in Weed's own correspondence. How are we to understand the discrepancy? Part of the answer lies in the specific location of Weed within the occupation as a whole. Despite her often sensitive observations about the occupation's mission, and especially her awareness of women's contribution to society prior to the war, she was not always free to express her views. She was, after all, part of the CI&E, an agency engaged in numerous propaganda and indoctrination programs. She was also, of course, part of SCAP, whose overriding purpose was to establish U.S. cultural hegemony in postwar Japan. The narrative of the American rescue of Japanese women was a powerful tool in the American propaganda effort, indeed critical for establishing U.S. leadership not only in Japan, but also internationally. Constructing Japanese women as victims without agency—until the arrival of American occupiers—was a critical part of this narrative, which Weed could not openly contradict. The gap between her public pronouncement about the occupation's gender reform and the sentiments expressed in her correspondence indicates the difficult and often contradictory position the women occupiers were forced to take. Of course it is indeed questionable if Weed herself was free of the gendered American imperial discourses that informed the understandings and actions of so many of the occupiers. Reform efforts were driven by notions of Americans as rescuing and liberating Japanese women, and more often than not, Weed actively participated in this endeavor.

The U.S. occupation of Japan and its gender reform created a common discursive space in which, for various reasons, and with varying agendas, American women who went to Japan and who stayed behind imagined and talked about Japanese women. Occupied Japan became a major site for American women to articulate postwar feminism that was deeply informed by Cold War nationalism and anticommunism. The network of American women was far from uniform and coherent, but was all the more dynamic for its numerous contradictions, challenges, and subversive possibilities. Seeking to expand their organizational influence abroad, women leaders drew on Cold War discourses of women, nation, and democracy to challenge and subvert the narrative of women and domestic containment. Despite her harsh criticism of "feminists" and "naive occupiers," Beard, too, articulated her own vision of Cold War feminism, imagining herself playing a part in the emancipation of Japanese women and the struggle against communism. The occupation let Beard validate her vision of women as a central force in history—a vision, Beard believed, she shared with MacArthur. At the center of the women's network, Weed played an extremely ambiguous role, sometimes promoting and at other times questioning the American claim as the liberator of Japanese women. Correspondence between American women and Tokyo headquarters thus sheds light on the precarious nature of American hegemony in its making that was simultaneously bolstered and challenged by American women.

Impossible for Japan to Copy America: Japanese Women Leaders and Resistance to Cold War Indoctrination

Both at Tokyo headquarters and in local areas, American women occupiers actively recruited Japanese women to serve as vital sources of information, coparticipants in the project of women's emancipation, and indigenous advocates for a gendered Americanization of postwar Japan. Japanese women turned out to be more than willing participants in Cold War feminist mobilization. Collaborations resulted in a mutually beneficial, although clearly unequal, relationship: It provided the Japanese women with otherwise unavailable opportunities and resources, and the American occupiers with indispensable interpreters, aides, and informants for carrying out gender reform.

In recruiting Japanese women, SCAP relied on a familiar imperial strategy—enlisting indigenous elite women as informants and advocates for American rule. The gendered and classed nature of this strategy was best exemplified in SCAP's selection of Katō Shizue, previously Baroness Ishimoto, as the spokesperson for Japanese women. Fluent in English and elegantly dressed in a kimono, Katō exemplified the newly emancipated woman whose aristocratic bearing often awed the occupiers. Under the aegis of the American forces, her political career as the preeminent Japanese feminist flourished. She was the leading figure among the thirty-nine women members of the Diet who made their formal entry into the hitherto exclusively male Japanese political system, and played a prominent role at the Japanese constitutional convention as the spokeswoman for Japanese women.

Katō's extremely privileged background and especially her ability to travel abroad and pursue her ambition to become a "new woman" in prewar Japan resemble that of Beate Sirota Gordon.[55] The daughter of a wealthy family and the wife of a baron, Baroness Ishimoto was one of the most visible women's rights activists. Her family's fortune and stature, and the support of her idealistic husband who advocated socialism and Christian humanism gave her rare opportunities to venture out of traditional feminine roles. When it was extremely rare for Japanese women to travel abroad, she accompanied her husband to the United States and Europe, becoming acquainted with notable Americans including Margaret Sanger and Mary Beard. After a one-year stay in the United States, she went back to Japan and participated in the women's suffrage movement in the 1920s, introducing and promoting the notion of birth control and becoming known as "Japan's Margaret Sanger."

In the 1920s and 1930s her activities often involved bridge-building between Japanese and American women. She brought Margaret Sanger to Japan, and made it her mission to disseminate information about Japan and its women to an American audience. Launching successful lecture tours in 1931 and 1937, she spoke on such topics as the Japanese birth control movement, Japanese aesthetics, and the Japanese women's movements. She published an English-language autobiography, *Facing Two Ways: The Story of My Life*, in 1935 as another way of informing Americans about Japanese culture. With help from her friend and mentor Mary Beard, who edited the entire manuscript, her book chronicles her struggles against feudalism and tradition and her self-transformation into a modern, feminist subject. Published not only in the United States, but also in England and Sweden, the book was a success.

The Baroness's overseas success was in striking contrast to her increasingly difficult life in Japan. Her marriage was dissolving. As Japan entered its ultranationalistic era in the 1930s, many political movements and organizations were suppressed. Her advocacy for birth control came into conflict with the state's policy of population and territorial expansion. Her personal association with Katō Kanjū, a socialist, leading labor activist, and chair of the Proletarian Party, made her guilty by association. Her involvement in the popular front movement and her opposition to Japanese militarism were perceived as "anti-national" and "dangerous." In 1937, she was arrested and imprisoned for two weeks, and her birth control clinic was closed by authorities. Following this, she withdrew from political activity. However, the war years were not entirely bleak. After much difficulty, she was finally able to divorce her aristocratic husband, who had become increasingly involved in Japan's colonial expansionism, and in 1944, she married Katō Kanjū.

As soon as the war was over, her fortunes changed. In October 1945, the Katōs received a surprise visitor, Lieutenant Tsukamoto, a Japanese American soldier, who delivered a message from SCAP, requesting interviews with Katō Shizue for her assistance in gender reform and with her husband on labor issues. They were subsequently taken to the CI&E for interviews and discussions. Katō Shizue was an ideal person for SCAP. She had been listed as a "friendly person" by the U.S. Office of Strategic Services as early as 1941; the U.S. government had obtained intelligence from former American missionaries in Japan that Katō Shizue was "anti-militaristic, and pro-American";[56] and her autobiography documented her prewar connection to the United States.

Just as the occupation catapulted Gordon to prominence, it was a catalyst in Katō's rise as the leading women's rights activist, highlighting an enabling aspect of U.S. Cold War imperialism in postwar Japanese feminism. Similar to Weed's central position in the American women's network, Katō played the pivotal role in creating a network among Japanese women and functioned as a liaison to American women occupiers, especially Weed. Katō suggested to the CI&E six women who would be useful in the occupation's gender reform: Kubushiro Ochimi, a suffragist and leading member of Japan WCTU; Ichikawa Fusae, a leading activist in the prewar suffrage movement; Kawasaki Natsu, another suffragist; Kaneko Shigeri and Yamataka Shigeri, activists in the prewar birth control movement; and Gauntlett (nee Yamada) Tsuneko, an active member of the Japan WCTU and the suffrage movement.[57] The core group of Japanese women thus formed to assist Weed was from a middle- and upper-class background, and most had close associations with prewar feminist movements that had been deeply complicit in Japan's racism, nationalism, and colonialism. In addition, Katō recommended Japanese women with English-language skills and education who could work as aides and translators for Weed, who relied on the information these Japanese women brought to her, their translation skills, and their service as aides and assistants.

Outside of the core group identified by Katō, many other women participated in gender reform, recruited at meetings and interviews organized by Weed. A wide range of information was collected from the interviews and copiously documented: women and welfare policies, political parties and their women's platforms, labor movements, prostitution and sexual regulation, grassroots democratization efforts, and much more.[58] Takahashi (nee Tomita) Nobuko, who was recruited at the suggestion of Katō, worked as a translator and assistant for Weed, remembering her as a superb organizer and coordinator, skillful in soliciting the involvement of Japanese women in various programs. Weed expected Takahashi and other women to be more than simply translators and interpreters; she asked them for suggestions and ideas concerning gender reform.[59] Even though the information that Japanese women provided might not always have led to immediate action, these interviews provided an occasion to air their concerns to the occupation authorities. Thus CI&E gender reform gave Japanese women leaders not only a sense of empowerment and excitement, but also access to numerous otherwise unavailable opportunities and resources. By providing a new political space for Japanese women, Weed played a critical role in eliciting their willing participation in Cold War feminist mobilization.

Yet, such gendered Cold War containment strategies often "leaked," as the occupiers' intention to create loyal allies among Japanese women sometimes resulted in unintended consequences. The case of the *Fujin Minshu Kurabu*, or Women's Democratic Club, a women's organization inaugurated with Weed's endorsement on March 16, 1946, sheds light on a double theme of Cold War hegemony and subversion. Prominent Japanese women leaders, such as Katō Shizue, Matsuoka Yōko, Miyamoto Yuriko, and Akamatsu Tsuneko, belonged to this organization, which played an important role in occupied Japan, publishing its own newspapers, creating branches in local areas, and addressing such women's issues as food shortages, women workers' rights, women's suffrage, and political education. Celebrated as a symbol of Japanese women's democratization, the club was nevertheless plagued by Cold War ideological controversy even before its inauguration. At the very first preparatory meeting, the meaning of "democracy" became a source of contention and bitter debate among its members. For Katō, democracy was the system practiced in the West; that is, by the United States and some European nations. For Miyamoto, closely affiliated with the Communist Party, Katō's notion of democracy was outdated, as the United States and Europe exemplified "bourgeois democracy," while "real" democracy was the system emerging in China.[60] This gulf was unbridgeable, and before long, Katō and her supporters resigned from the organization, leaving the Women's Democratic Club, and especially its official newspaper, as a critical space for women of the left-labor front to resist occupation policies by advocating Soviet and Chinese women's lives as the ideal.

As the most prominent feminist leader chosen by SCAP, Katō's strong anticommunism should be noted as it sheds light on the important connection between the occupiers' gender reform and Cold War containment politics. She was indeed a passionate anticommunist activist. By 1951, she became involved in the Moral Re-Armament (MRA) movement, an international evangelical movement established by Frank Buchman before the war that continued to play a salient role in the postwar decades. Advocating peace and Christian morality, the MRA was explicitly anticommunist.[61] After attending the MRA's international meeting in Michigan in 1951, Katō and her husband established an MRA branch in Japan. By the following year's meeting, Katō had become a vocal advocate of MRA principles, even urging Americans "to be alert to the menace of communism and to work to overcome poverty and overpopulation, society's twin devastations."[62]

A double theme of hegemony and subversion is salient in other instances of gender reform, especially in a Cold War feminist project called the Women's Reorientation Program. At a time when overseas travel was almost impossible for most Japanese, the CI&E sent a group of Japanese women leaders to the United States so that they could learn "democracy" firsthand.

Sending leaders to the United States was an important part of Cold War indoctrination efforts in Japan and at many other sites.[63] As Yukiko Koshiro documents, the leadership program in occupied Japan often took an overtly anticommunist tone. American policymakers perceived the program as a crucial way of "gaining Japan's help in resisting Communist Pressures,"[64] as the January 1950 trip clearly demonstrates. A group of fourteen Japanese leaders, mostly Diet members and presumably all male, visited the United States. While their tour in South Carolina and California went smoothly, their visit to Boston met with anti-Japanese hostility originating from wartime animosity. The City Council banned the delegates from entering City Hall, alarming SCAP who became concerned that Japanese communists would use the incident to create anti-American sentiment. A corrective measure was immediately taken. In a subsequent trip to the Capitol, the U.S. Senate went out of its way to welcome the Japanese delegates. Senator Joseph McCarthy was among them, extending an individual welcome to the delegates during a recess.[65]

While the anti-Communist sentiment was evident in the case documented by Koshiro, Cold War indoctrination efforts were also informed by gendered and gendering dynamics. As Elaine Tyler May points out, Cold War culture was "more than the internal reverberations of foreign policy, and went beyond the explicit manifestations of anticommunist hysteria such as McCarthyism and the 'Red Scare.'"[66] Indeed in the case of the Japanese women's leadership program, various strategies adopted by the authorities were not simply reducible to an overt anticommunist sentiment. Informed by Cold War understandings of women, family, and containment, the leadership program focused on inculcating a historically specific notion of female citizenry among Japanese women leaders.

In 1950, Ethel Weed escorted eleven Japanese women leaders to the United States: Akamatsu Tsuneko, a Socialist member of the House of Representatives; Egami Fuji, Chief of the Women's Division of the Broadcasting Corporation of Japan (later NHK); Gotō Shun, Vice Chief of Women's Sections of the Democratic Liberal Party; Kume Ai, attorney and advisor to the Domestic Relations Court; Marusawa Michiyo, Chief of the Women's Section of the National Railway Workers Union; Nomura Katsuko, a member of the Central Committee of the Japan Consumers' Union League; Ōmori Matsuyo, Chief of the Home Demonstration Section of the Ministry of Agriculture and Forestry; Tanino Setsuko, Chief of the Women in Industry Section of the newly created Women's and Minors' Bureau (WMB); Togano Satoko, a Socialist member of the House of Representatives; Tokahashi Nobuko, a member of the Women's Section of WMB and previously a translator and assistant for Weed; and Itō Kazuko, an interpreter for the CI&E. The group was promoted as a "cross section of the feminine leadership which emerged in Japan's postwar era."[67] Prior to their departure, MacArthur granted an audience to the delegation, congratulating them for having exhibited a "magnificent response to the challenge to womanhood under a democracy," and for having "fully justified my faith in the part Japanese women were destined to play in the transformation of a completely regimented society into one composed of individuals each of whom . . . is free, by demonstrating their capacity to assume the co-equal responsibilities of citizenship in a democratic state." He assured the delegates that they would be well received in the United States, and encouraged them to "observe and to study the practical application of American democracy in every phase of American life." "The distinctions between American and Japanese traditions," he told them, "are basically distinctions between the concepts of freedom and regimentation, and that all people who cherish individual freedom may draw heavily upon American experience and example without the slightest impairment of native culture." He encouraged the delegates not only to study American democracy carefully, but also to tell the Americans that Japanese women were "a vital and beneficial force in the evolution of Japanese democracy, and writing an inspiring record to encourage the enlightened progress of less unfortunate women of other races."[68]

Once in the United States, the women traveled across the continent, witnessing "(American) democracy" in action. Weed carefully documented the experience. From her report to the CI&E chief, one can see how intense and deeply gendered this indoctrination effort was, with American and international women's organizations playing a salient role in creating pro-American and anticommunist agents among Japanese women leaders. The delegation visited many organizations, including the YWCA, the League of Women Voters, the Women's Bureau, the Department of the Army, and labor unions. From coast to coast, local civic organizations, women's groups, and churches extended enthusiastic welcomes. Tokahashi and Togano attended the national convention of the League of Women Voters in Atlantic City, their expenses partially paid by the Carrie Chapman Catt Fund. Not only did they have a chance to observe a meeting "run according to strict parliamentary procedure from beginning to end," they addressed the convention, speaking of the progress Japanese women had been making. Their presentation was received with much enthusiasm on the floor of the convention.[69]

A visit to the United Nations (UN) provided an important opportunity for Japanese women to speak with UN delegates from around the world and to expand their contacts beyond American men and women. There Kume and Tomita had a chance to meet representatives of international women's organizations such as the International Federation of University Women, the International Alliance of Women, the International Council of Women, and the International Federation of Business and Professional Women's Clubs, all of which expressed interest in forging an affiliation with Japanese women. In addition, Japanese delegates met with representatives from countries such as Greece, India, Turkey, and France. As Weed reported, the visit held much significance in the Cold War context as it "provided opportunities for learning first-hand of the undemocratic practices of the Communist-backed Women's International Democratic Federation which organization has tried to make inroads into Japan."[70]

The delegates' experiences in the United States went beyond meetings and contacts with women's organizations and involved learning of American domesticity as the path to democracy. To stretch their funding, the delegates often prepared food for themselves; for this, they were taken to supermarkets where "individuals prided themselves on shopping like American house-wives."[71] Each delegate also had a chance to experience an "American home" firsthand, spending "a total of at least two weeks in private homes and despite difficulties managed to visit average workers and farm homes." Everyone "had at least one opportunity to cook in an up-to-date American kitchen."[72] Weed even sent some delegates to the Connecticut home of Mary Beard, who was delighted by the visit.[73]

Playing "American housewife"—going to a supermarket and cooking in an American kitchen—seems innocent enough. However, placed in a preexisting imperial cultural pattern that constructed Western domesticity as a marker of Western racial and cultural superiority, such teaching of Western domesticity to native women becomes part of a "civilizing effort." During the occupation, the pattern was repeated with additional complexities originating from a new historical context, the Cold War.

In discussing Cold War gender politics, it is by now almost customary to cite the 1959 "kitchen debate" between Richard Nixon, then the vice president of the United States, and Nikita Khrushchev, the premier of the Soviet Union, as a primary instance of gendered Cold War articulation.[74] It was indeed an unforgettable performance. At the site of the American National Exhibition in Moscow, Nixon emphatically argued that the American suburban home, equipped with modern household appliances, such as a "built-in panel-controlled washing machine," allowed women to perform household labor more efficiently and thus to enjoy "freedom" and a good life. American women owed this to capitalism, free market enterprise, and the abundance of consumer goods. All of this, Nixon insisted, demonstrated the clear superiority of American capitalism to communism. Khrushchev flatly disagreed. He pointed to Soviet women workers as evidence of the superiority of communism. Under the communist system, he argued, women were free of "capitalist" assumptions about gender roles, and participated in productive activities. The debate gave new meaning and status to the "American kitchen," endowing it with political significance specific to the Cold War era.

The importance of the American kitchen—and of American fashions, supermarkets, hairstyles, and cosmetics—in U.S. Cold War diplomacy was not limited to this instance. As Robert Haddow carefully documents, "exhibiting American culture abroad" constituted a salient Cold War strategy, and things associated with American femininity, such as kitchen gadgets, played critical roles in selling the desirability of American democracy in other parts of the world.[75] To Japanese women, the American kitchen came to symbolize not only the superiority, but also the desirability, of American womanhood. It was an effective gendered means of "selling" American democracy. The American occupiers frequently emphasized the importance of "modernizing" the Japanese kitchen as a necessary part of women's emancipation. In his study of postwar Japanese culture, Yoshikuni Igarashi documents the CI&E emphasis on disseminating information about the material wealth available in the United States, including household appliances. Radio programs, films, and even exhibits at department stores introduced the American way of life as superior and desirable. American families stationed in Japan also provided "training" in American domesticity to maids and servants, and wives of male occupiers often considered it their mission to teach their servants American cooking and cleaning as a means to modernization and democratization,[76] thus mirroring the women delegates' experiences in American homes and kitchens.

While in the United States, the women delegates were besieged with invitations to press conferences, radio broadcasts, and formal and informal receptions. Representatives of various hosting agencies and organizations warmly welcomed them, and were extremely eager to help out. American sponsoring agencies, Weed noted, often inquired how to go about "maintaining constructive contact with the Japanese women leaders." She recommended that the sponsors' "very natural desire" to maintain ties with Japanese women should be encouraged, and that the Japanese delegates should be encouraged to create "an organization to fit the needs of continued study and contact with the United States."[77]

Publicity about the women's trip to the United States was no less intense in Japan. While in the United States, the Japanese women became involved in filming two documentary newsreels describing the lives of American women, which were to be released in Japan. In addition, they recorded, usually with leading American women, eight radio programs for broadcast in Japan, including "Women's Responsibilities in the World Today" with Eleanor Roosevelt, Egami Fuji, and Itō Kazuko; "Greetings to Japanese Women on the Fourth Anniversary of Woman Suffrage in Japan" with Senator Margaret Chase Smith, Akamatsu Tsuneko, and Itō Kazuko; and "The Contribution of the Women's Bureau to the Status of Women in the United States" with Frieda Miller, Chief of the Women's Bureau, Department of Labor, Tanino Setsuko, and Tokahashi Nobuko.[78] Cold War indoctrination efforts clearly involved top-level mobilization of Japanese as well as American women leaders. The women's leadership program makes it impossible to think of the 1950s as "quiet" with regard to women. A most remarkable cultural imperialism was enacted, mobilizing women not only into the public domain but also cross-nationally and producing new understandings about gender, democracy, and domesticity.

Yet, Cold War feminist mobilization also resulted in unintended and ironic consequences, as Japanese women who were recruited by Weed came to witness firsthand various shortcomings and contradictions in American democracy and began to question the occupation's basic assumptions. A roundtable discussion of the delegates published in the magazine *Kangyō Rōdō* sheds light on how American hegemony was challenged by the very women who had been selected by the occupiers for Cold War indoctrination purposes. The participants in the roundtable discussion (Egami Fuji, Gotō Shun, Tanino Setsu, Tokahashi Nobuko, Nomura Katsuko, and Itō Kazuko) were at first full of praise and admiration for the United States. More than anything else, American material wealth and the expanse of land impressed them deeply. Some even joked that they would like to be reborn as a "cow" in the United States so that they could enjoy the material abundance found there.[79]

What provoked the greatest interest, and also envy, among the women delegates was the "democratic" and "egalitarian" family life in the United States, especially the ideal of companionate marriage based on mutual love, care, and understanding. Yet, in idealizing American marriage and family, the women did not focus on motherhood and domesticity, as was frequently emphasized in Cold War containment culture.[80] Clearly deviating from the dominant narrative that emphasized motherhood and domesticity, they turned instead to American housewives, especially their freedom to participate in the public sphere, as the model for Japanese women. Because of efficient and rational cooking, sewing, and laundry, Itō pointed out, American wives were able to participate in the public sphere, through a job or volunteer work. Married women's continuing participation in the public domain contributed to a sound marital relationship based on love, Nomura observed. While staying with an American family, Gotō saw a husband volunteer to take care of domestic chores. More surprisingly, to Tomita, some wives were more educated than their husbands, yet men expressed praise and pride in their wives' achievements. How some Japanese women delegates wished to bring back such "democratic husbands" to Japan![81]

Many of the Japanese women delegates believed that in the United States "complete gender equality" was established not only in the family sphere, but also in the public spheres of work and politics. Tokahashi and Kawada pointed out that women's social status was no longer an issue, and that the women's rights movement was a thing of the past in the United States. Egami agreed completely, emphasizing that true gender equality was indeed established in the United States. Some delegates were especially impressed with the bright, happy work environment. Egami recalled that at a department store, sales clerks had looked satisfied and content and that men washing dishes at a cafeteria had been dressed like "gentlemen." Tanino confirmed Egami's observation: Every worker, whether elevator boys or cab drivers, looked extremely happy and proud of his or her work.[82] Thus women rearticulated gendered and classed discourse of American democracy as not only ideal but also successful.

Yet, women's complicity in the Cold War indoctrination efforts was once again only partial. Nomura observed that American democracy was built on the enormous economic power and wealth that the country possessed. How could one possibly transplant American-type democracy to Japan, whose economic infrastructure was so far behind that in the United States? Tokahashi pointed out that American women's high status was a by-product of the extraordinarily high level of the development of capitalism.[83] By pointing out the specific historical and economic conditions that contributed to the formation of "democracy" and "gender equality" in the United States, the delegates contradicted, however indirectly, the occupiers' discourse regarding the universality of American democracy. Other delegates made observations about the existence of gender and racial inequalities in the United States. Tanino, an expert on labor issues, mentioned difficulties faced by union women, especially their exclusion from decision-making positions. The same issues existed in Japan, she pointed out. She also recalled her conversations with African American union activists, who pointed out the problems of racial discrimination. Egami talked about a textile factory she visited in Cleveland, where the official claim of gender equality was contradicted by the reality of women's low wages. The image of gender equality in the United States could not always be taken at face value, she pointed out.[84]

A report submitted to SCAP by Marusawa Michiyo, Chief of the Women's Section of the National Railway Workers Union, further indicates that the leadership program was less than successful as a Cold War indoctrination project, failing to contain Japanese women within middle-class domesticity. Like other delegates, Marusawa admired many aspects of American society. However, she also observed that it was not completely egalitarian, pointing out the many gender-based discriminations she observed during her trip. She learned from a union worker that there were wage inequalities between men and women and that women were excluded from the higher paying positions. Labor unions also discriminated against women, excluding them from leadership positions. Observing various disadvantages faced by American working women, Marusawa commented that "the trouble (for working women) is common all over the world."[85] Even in her admiration of American women's lives, Marusawa did not buy into the dominant notions of femininity and domestic containment. Challenging the boundary between public and private, a notion crucial in the Cold War containment narrative, she instead praised the housewives who could single-handedly manage multiple domestic chores and still find time to engage in various activities outside the home:

When we stayed in a private home, the housewife took care of us in addition to tak(ing) care of all domestic works and her children. According to our schedule, she took us to the designated place by her car, made a tour together, or had an interview together, asked questions one after another, then took us back home by car, prepare supper for us and took us to many small meetings after supper. This went for a week, and still she was alright.[86]

Marusawa concluded by stating that Japan could not emulate the type of democracy found in the United States, thereby contradicting the fundamental premise of the occupation: "It is impossible for Japan to copy America which has incomparably enormous land, wealth and natural sources, and was established by people who came to this land to seek for their independence and freedom, and has now such great influence to divide this world into two parts establishing everything on its strong economic system." Rejecting the United States as the model democracy, Marusawa argued that Japan should follow its own path of postwar reconstruction and democratization, with the labor movement playing the leading role. The leadership program strengthened her resolve to work for labor organizing as well as women's emancipation: "I made up my mind again deeply that I will try my best for Japanese labor movement and emancipation of women after I came home."[87]

For the Japanese women leaders recruited by Weed, gender reform proved to be an enticing and exciting project. Their sense of empowerment, combined with intense indoctrination efforts, resulted in their strong advocacy of the American way of life as a key to the emancipation of Japanese women. They were clearly willing participants and collaborators in Cold War imperial feminism. To a remarkable degree, the gendered and classed strategy of recruiting Japanese middle- and upper-class women leaders as the indigenous agents of dissemination was effective.

At the same time, it is crucial to note disagreements and dissents. The women delegates engaged in a series of discursive practices that subverted the program's objectives of instilling faith in American democracy and producing effective propagandists. The leadership program not only allowed the delegates to go beyond the boundaries of home and nation, thereby contradicting the Cold War emphasis on domestic containment of women, but also helped them see the shortcomings and contradictions in American democracy. They recognized not only the gender- and race-based inequalities in the United States, but the impossibility of transplanting the American way of life to postwar Japan, thus rejecting the occupation's basic premise of American democracy as the universal ideal. With their newly gained ability to travel abroad, the delegates also focused on American housewives' ability to participate in the public arena, advocating it as the model for Japanese women. By publicly sharing their critical observations, they contradicted the very objective of the leadership program, their dissents creating a counterpoint to the more dominant enthusiasm surrounding the occupation's gender reform that aimed at women's containment. Doubled themes of complicity and subversion, consonance and dissonance, thus animated the occupation's gender reform, turning Japanese women into unpredictable and often transgressive agents in the Cold War.

Disseminating Techniques of Democracy: Grassroots Reform, Cold War Performance, and the Politics of Subversion

In emancipating and democratizing Japanese women, the scope of gender reform was not limited to women in leadership positions, nor to the Tokyo area. The Cold War feminist mobilization necessitated that Weed and other women occupiers reach out to the "masses" as well. They created films, radio programs, skits, exhibits, posters, pamphlets, leaflets, handbooks, and so on to disseminate the dominant notion of Cold War female citizenry. With the help of interpreters, they offered "leadership training programs" for women at the local level, as well as numerous other workshops and lectures throughout the country. Many "field trips" were made to local, often remote areas to inspect local conditions and monitor progress. Often these programs involved "visiting experts"—American women with expertise on specific issues who were invited to Japan to assist Weed and the other women occupiers. Local Japanese women flocked to these workshops and lectures, and actively participated in the occupation reform programs.

The CI&E grassroots reform was symptomatic of the Cold War. The containment ideas of femininity, domesticity, and citizenry articulated by American and Japanese women leaders were widely disseminated at the local level. Similar to U.S. civil defense exercise, American women reformers focused on performance, breaking down the complex ideas of gender equality and democracy into a series of simple skills and techniques and having Japanese women repeatedly enact them as a way of reorientation and rehabilitation. Despite the occupiers' painstaking efforts, however, the grassroots mobilization of Japanese women was once again less than successful, as local encounters between women occupiers and Japanese women resulted in even more ambiguity and ambivalence than the mobilization of women leaders, revealing the unpredictable and uncontainable nature of Cold War cultural dynamics.

In grassroots reform, Japanese women were encouraged to imitate—to physically embody—American femininity and domesticity. As in the case of the leadership program, however, the type of femininity portrayed as American, and thus ideal, simultaneously affirmed and challenged the dominant Cold War narratives of gender, domesticity, and democracy. This is reflected in one of the skits used in a training course:

> On a certain Saturday afternoon. Miyoko is making her toilet as she is going to attend a meeting of her organization. A foreign style room with a table in the middle. Three chairs around the table. The husband is coming home singing "My Blue Heaven."
>
> HUSBAND: Tadaima.
>
> WIFE: Okaeri nasai.
>
> HUSBAND: Oh, you are making your toilet. Hum, have you been eagerly waiting for my return?
>
> WIFE: I wish I could say so, but today I am going out.
>
> HUSBAND: Where?
>
> WIFE: Our organization is going to have a meeting at Mrs. Yokohama's.
>
> HUSBAND: Ah, a meeting, again? Don't go. It's all right if you don't go, isn't it?
>
> WIFE: (silent)
>
> HUSBAND: To tell the truth, I have a very nice plan. You see, I went down to Kumamoto on official business and was reimbursed more than I expected. Therefore, let's go out to see a movie tonight, ok? We have been too busy to go out together for one year, six months, 22 days, and 5 hours since we married.
>
> WIFE: Well . . . but . . . I suppose everybody is waiting for me.
>
> HUSBAND: Do you think so much of your club? It must be a mere gathering of leisure women. Give it up. Give it up.
>
> WIFE: (silent)
>
> HUSBAND: Now, come on, let's eat as soon as possible and go out.
>
> WIFE: Well I have finished eating. I put yours in the shelf. So please eat it alone. And, if you don't mind, please wash the dishes.
>
> HUSBAND: Aren't you crazy, my dear? Darling, go out with me, please.
>
> WIFE: No, I could not. I am the president and I've got to go.
>
> HUSBAND: You are determined to go, aren't you? All right. Now I order you not to go.
>
> (The players had to improvise the rest.)[88]

Needless to say, the ideal gender relationship presented here—a white, middle-class companionate heterosexual marriage—is articulated at the intersection of race, class, and sexuality. The space in which democracy and gender equality are enacted is imagined first and foremost as Western, and more specifically American: a foreign-style room, chairs, and table, and the tune of "My Blue Heaven." Japanese women were to enact and embody the femininity portrayed here as part of U.S. democratization efforts. As in the case of the "kitchen debates," we see once again the importance of American material objects as signifiers of freedom and the American home as a reservoir of democracy. In that sense, the skit is clearly a gendered artifact of Cold War imperial politics. At the same time, the skit also subverts itself by showing how the boundary between public and private could be transgressed by democratic women themselves. Rejecting the notion of domestic contentment, the female character in the skit is ready to leave home and participate in a women's organization. Rather than "a source of social stability," the femininity portrayed here is uncontainable, and thus potentially dangerous to the security of home and nation.

In the CI&E's gender reform, not only individual women but women's organizations became an important target of Cold War containment. Existing women's organizations were perceived as doubly dangerous because of their potential subversiveness in the Cold War as well as their involvement in Japan's nationalism and colonialism prior to the surrender. During the war, Japanese women had been mobilized in the state's war efforts through local and neighborhood-based women's organizations. The CI&E, and especially Weed, saw that it was imperative to reform the organizations that had mobilized women for antidemocratic and ultranationalistic purposes. Freeing these organizations from national and local government control over both finance and personnel became an important goal of the reform efforts. However, more was required. Japanese women needed skills to run an organization in a "democratic manner." To accomplish this purpose, Weed wrote a pamphlet, "Procedures for Democratic Organizations." Intended to transmit the "techniques of democracy" to Japanese women, the pamphlet discussed in an extremely mundane, detailed, and technical manner the how-to of democratic procedures. It provided instructions about voting and constitutions; the roles of chair, secretary, treasurer, and general members; the rights and duties of members; and effective discussion techniques, including how to bring motions to the floor and deal with dissenting opinions.[89] The techniques were widely disseminated and repeatedly practiced by Japanese women during the occupation. Such dissemination of the "techniques of democracy" was never innocent nor innocuous; it was symptomatic of the Cold War practice. In the CI&E's reform efforts, the complex idea of democracy was broken down into a series of simple techniques and skills, which Japanese women were required to enact repeatedly as part of their "training." Mastery of the skills was considered a sign of "successful democratization."

The emphasis on skills and drills finds an important parallel in such Cold War U.S. civil defense programs as Operation Alert and Home

Figure 3.1

Illustrations from "Techniques of Democracy: A Guide to Procedure for Japanese Organizations" created by the team of Shikoku Military Government Region to teach Japanese the basic ideas of "democratic" procedures in running an organization. These illustrations convey the ideas and aspects of democracy American occupiers tried to disseminate in postwar Japan: the significance of vote and discussions (Figure 3.1); of constitution in organizations (Figure 3.2); of women speaking up at meetings (Figure 3. 3); and of acquiring various "techniques" to achieve democracy (Figure 3.4). From the author's collection.

Figure 3.2

Protection Exercises, which trained civilians to cope with a potential nuclear crisis by acquiring a set of techniques through repeated practice. As Laura McEnaney and Guy Oakes document, the U.S. Federal Civil Defense Administration (FCDA) considered civil defense exercise a way to forge the national will and to defend the American way of life against possible communist attacks. In the Cold War United States, such exercises became moral obligations for citizens.[90]

Civil defense aimed at training the body as well as the mind. Through repeated exercise, participants were expected to master skills and techniques

Figure 3.3

until they could execute them "with an unstudied and effortless ease, even under conditions of ultimate stress." The acquisition of these skills "was regarded as habituation, a matter of changing old habits and acquiring new dispositions," which would produce "a permanent change in behavior."[91] Importantly, civil defense techniques originated from the military's training tactics, which "depended upon repeated drilling to instill in soldiers particular habits and relations to authority." Following psychological warfare theory, it

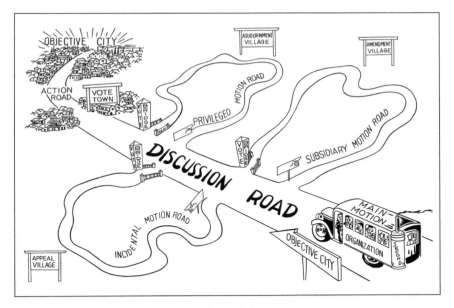

Figure 3.4

was believed that "well-trained habits resist disruption by emotion."[92] In the world of civil defense, then, emotional management went hand in hand with physical regulation; together they ensured national security.

In U.S.-occupied Japan, the CI&E resorted to similar tactics of physical and emotional regulation. The women occupiers used military-like drill exercises in their "intellectual war" to "reorient" and "rehabilitate" Japanese women, to disseminate the American way of life, and to circumvent communist infiltration into women's organizations. Weed's pamphlet, "Procedures for Democratic Organizations," was widely disseminated. In Shikoku, Carmen Johnson focused on the transmission of "techniques of democracy" as a path toward women's emancipation. Initially, she was extremely concerned about "how to present concepts (i.e., 'democracy' and 'gender equality') so strange to Japanese culture and practice": "How could women visualize the steps taken to make a motion and vote?"[93] She was skeptical about the occupation's objective, and about America's abilities to pursue, let alone achieve, women's emancipation in Japan: "The constitution gave women equality on paper, but could the customs and traditions so deeply rooted in the past be changed to comply with legal requirement?"[94] What finally assured Johnson was the incorporation of skits and role playing in the training. She wrote a skit for women to enact the procedures of making motions and voting. At a meeting in Kagawa prefecture, she picked women out of an audience of two hundred, and had them read her skit aloud. In her autobiography, she quotes from her diary's record of the event:

> I picked fifteen women at random and gave them copies of the skit to read . . . The first time was not so good but the second good enough. A few ladies were slowly catching on—just like Americans would be. After the second time, the woman who was supposedly elected president made a little speech about trying to do her best. We all had lots of fun over it. And I think they learned something from it.[95]

She found role playing so effective that she used it again at a meeting in Kōchi prefecture:

> Again, we had lots of fun with the skit. Highly successful. At the end of the meeting, I suggested we close by a motion for adjournment. We got the motion made but not seconded. So I stopped the chairman there. Then came discussion. One woman stood up and said, "I think we should do it again." Everyone just howled. So we did it again.[96]

At yet another meeting, in Ehime prefecture:

> [A]gain the play went off very well. There were a few ladies who had memorized their parts. The closing was by adjournment after a motion was made. We had to do that three times before it was done anywhere near correctly. The chairman was really very good and self-possessed.[97]

Johnson observed that Japanese women were extremely keen to play roles in the skits, which she attributed to their "earnest desire" to learn democracy.[98]

The importance of "techniques of democracy" was so paramount for Johnson that she sometimes ignored other concerns and interests expressed by the Japanese women themselves. At one meeting, a woman's club president invited Johnson to give a talk. The president was not interested in hearing about democratic procedures, however. She wanted to hear Johnson talk about "happiness." Johnson proposed an alternative topic, "How to make motions at meetings," arguing that it would be more helpful to the members of the club. To this suggestion, the president gave a blank look, confirming Johnson's belief that the president lacked an understanding of parliamentary procedure, and strengthening her determination to educate Japanese women about this important democratic practice.[99] She could not imagine that Japanese club women might be more interested in what an American woman—single, in her thirties, and stationed in a place far away from her country—had to say about happiness than they were in the mechanisms of making motions. In this instance, Johnson seems rather naive, even blind. Yet, her insistence on disseminating techniques of democracy needs to be understood in relation to the moral and ethical significance assigned to mastery of skills and procedures in the Cold War as anticommunist strategies.

That transmitting techniques of democracy was perceived as a crucial defense against communism is repeatedly observed in other women's reform efforts as well. Helen Hosp Seamans, Advisor for Women's Higher Education to the SCAP from 1948 to 1950, considered women's mastery of parliamentary procedures a key to blocking communist infiltration into civic organizations. While in Japan she attended various training programs and numerous women's meetings, including those held by the Japanese Association of University Women, the National Conference of Women Students, and the National Association of Deans of Women. She witnessed firsthand how pervasively the knowledge of parliamentary procedure was disseminated, and how frequently and "effectively" skits and role plays were used to train Japanese women in the meanings and practices of democracy. The significance of parliamentary procedure could not have been more evident at the 1949 meeting of the National Conference of Women Students. There Seamans witnessed the conference proceedings disrupted by "Communists" and their "stooges," including the student chair of the conference. The potentially chaotic situation was avoided, however, due to an intervention made by an American woman occupier who talked about "Techniques of Democracy." As Seamans recalled, this woman occupier gave "a stirring exposition of the theory of democracy," which was quickly absorbed by the students attending the conference. Danger was averted, and "the survival of democratic principles" was ensured. Clearly, parliamentary procedures was "the safeguard" against the communist menace.[100]

The women occupiers frequently portrayed their democratization efforts as successful, and transmitting the "techniques of democracy" was often a central part of their success stories. Weed's report on her field trips in southern Japan not only indicates the importance of transmitting the techniques, it documents the enormous enthusiasm with which Japanese women welcomed the American reformers and their message of "democracy."[101] Given the pervasive Orientalist understanding about Japanese women as helpless and passive victims, any action taken by Japanese women impressed American women as a sign of "progress" brought about by the occupation. Seamans, for example, thought it "a joy to see the women's faces revealing an absorption in the subject of class study,"[102] and when, one morning, she found the women rearranging the tables and chairs so that they could hear better, she concluded this was a sign that Japanese women were discarding the old ways and learning the meanings of democracy.[103]

In reality, however, the women occupiers' reform activities were not without tensions, contradictions, and ambivalence. A report filed by an occupier stationed in the central region of Japan—the Tōkai and Hokuriku areas—sheds light on the less than successful nature of grassroots reform. She pointed out that many of the training programs were not successfully followed or utilized and identified several reasons for this problem. For one, the size of the audience at the meetings, which ranged from several dozens to hundreds, was too large, limiting opportunities for discussion and demonstration. For another, the training courses relied on the assumption that the Japanese participants would transmit the information to their organizations or groups. The occupiers did not take into account the possibilities that the participants might be indifferent to the information, or that the organizations or groups might be indifferent and would not follow the instructions. Finally, the training put too much emphasis on generating leaders, and too little on developing good organizational members. Despite these criticisms, however, she never questioned the basic premise of the occupation's democratization efforts. Instead, she suggested as a corrective measure the better use of "check lists" and "report forms" to ensure the dissemination of parliamentary procedures.[104]

The ambivalent nature of CI&E reform activities is perhaps most clearly observed in the operation of a radio program called "Women's Hours," an important Cold War propaganda machinery that was deployed to disseminate the new ideals of democracy and gender equality among Japanese women. Weed's pamphlet, "Procedures for Democratic Organization," was dramatized as a skit and aired on "Women's Hours." Other topics covered included women's participation in politics, information concerning civil rights, the legal status of women, coeducation, current political and social issues, "scientific" home making, women's labor issues, and rural women's issues, among others. Many Japanese women leaders, intellectuals, and writers were invited to speak. However, on-air propaganda efforts, including the transmission of techniques of democracy, were often fraught with tensions, disrupting from within the American pursuit of hegemony. Indeed, "Women's Hours" constituted one of the rare sites where tensions between occupier and occupied broke into the open—over, ironically enough, the techniques of democracy.[105]

Nominally under the control of the Broadcasting Corporation of Japan (BCJ, later NHK), radio broadcasting was reorganized and strictly censored by the CI&E during the occupation. Out of the reorganization effort a number of new programs emerged, including "Women's Hours," which was run by a team of Japanese women, with extensive intervention from the CI&E.[106] Some of these interventions clearly resulted in new resources. By allowing the program to be produced by a staff of Japanese women, headed by a female producer, Egami Fuji,[107] the CI&E institutionalized a "women's space" within the male-dominated broadcasting corporation, literally giving women a voice. On the other hand, the CI&E imposed "American-style" radio broadcasting, which the Japanese staff found inappropriate, given the taste of Japanese listeners, and the CI&E's extensive censorship led to major disagreements and conflicts between Japanese and American women.

Despite the fact that Egami was producer, three CI&E women—Dixie Linsey, Luella Hoskins, and Jane Grills—tried to take control of "Women's Hours." The Japanese staff felt that the American women occupiers often exhibited an "excessive missionary zeal."[108] Assigned to "Women's Hours" in 1949, Hoskins was particularly difficult to work with. Although she knew nothing about radio production, immediately upon her assignment to the program, she presumed to dictate content to Egami. Hoskins had previously been stationed in the Nagoya area, where she had been in charge of "democratizing" women's organizations. Her idea was to create a program that would explain procedures for democratic organization: how to run a meeting, how to vote, how to choose the chair, and so on. Egami thought that the suggested program would be boring, and told Hoskins that she needed time to think about it. Hoskins, however, expected her ideas to be accepted without question. In a high-handed manner, she demanded that the program be made immediately. She was convinced that it would be successful, in the same way as her work in Nagoya where she had lectured to thousands of people and captured their interest. Egami did not back off, however. She cited her own credentials, which made her no less qualified than Hoskins to make decisions about programming. After all, she had spent more than thirty years living in Japan and observing Japanese women, and ten years doing radio programs. Egami also questioned Hoskins's observations about women in Nagoya. She pointed out that Japanese women were socialized to obey authority figures, and they would never contradict Hoskins, a "smartly-dressed American woman" from the occupation forces. It was doubtful, she continued, that Japanese women truly understood everything Hoskins had said about democratization. Egami's direct challenge to Hoskins's authority left the latter completely speechless.[109]

Most ironic of all, unlike the CI&E staff, Japanese women on "Women's Hours" had little time to think about the program's mission for "women's liberation" due to incessant interventions by the American occupiers. They were faced with the overwhelming task of creating a new program from scratch, which would be broadcast in the American style. They had to meet censorship requirements and deal with the CI&E staff, who were often ignorant of radio broadcasting, Japanese women's situations, or both. As a Japanese woman staff member recalled, "Since the program was live broadcast, it was like being in a war zone everyday. We barely managed to survive from one day to another. Never had time to think about liberation of women. We may have been rather unaware about what was really going on. We just worked really, really hard."[110]

The ironic consequences of grassroots gender reform were not limited to this instance. In the course of the CI&E gender reform, Japanese and American women sometimes developed strong personal bonds. SCAP's decision to relegate the task of gender reform to women ironically resulted in the emergence of a female homosocial sphere, challenging the heterosexual colonial tropes that defined the occupation as an encounter between a masculine United States and a feminine Japan and the relationship between American and Japanese women as that of adults and children, or mothers and daughters. Moreover, within the Cold War context where sexual deviation was equated with political and ideological subversion, the female-to-female bond that emerged in the course of gender reform constituted a subtle yet significant "leakage" in the Cold War containment project.

One example of such bonding is found in the relationship among Ethel Weed, Mary Beard, and Katō Shizue. The correspondence between Beard and Weed reveals the strong personal ties that developed between them. Weed, for example, expressed warm regards to Beard. Her letters were "very heartening," and provided a needed perspective. Beard was "often in my thoughts, and someday I'll fill in the gaps in my letters with the details that make life a constant surprise."[111] Beard's response to her was equally warm and full of praise: "You endear yourself to me by the qualities of mind and characters which you steadily reveal."[112] Having not yet met at the beginning of their correspondence, Weed visited Beard at her Connecticut home in 1948; this visit delighted Beard. Her follow-up letter notes: "You made an indelible impression on all of us Beards and our son-in-law Alfred Vagts as a rare human being." Beard was indeed deeply impressed by Weed: "You are so beautiful in every way—so handsome to behold and so sincerely humane—that none of us could ever forget you or remember you in any other way."[113] The bond between the two extended to include their common friend, Katō Shizue. Both were entranced by the beautiful former baroness, who was often the topic of their conversations.

In local areas, the female-to-female bond also constituted a salient theme in gender reform. Carmen Johnson found the Japanese and Japanese American women with whom she worked indispensable during her stay in Shikoku. Not only did their Japanese language skills and familiarity with Japanese culture help her reform activities; perhaps more important, they provided much needed friendship for Johnson, who was alone in an utterly unfamiliar environment. Annie Midori Bandō, a second-generation Japanese American, became one of her closest friends. Johnson "felt very secure about how my words were expressed in Japanese" when Bandō interpreted for her on numerous trips.[114] Stella Hoshimiya, another Japanese American and secretary in her office, was her roommate and frequent companion on bicycle trips. Johnson fondly recalls that Hoshimiya jovially named their single-women's quarters the "BWQ" or bachelor women's quarters.[115]

Johnson's friendships with her Japanese women assistants were similarly meaningful and rewarding. She developed a close working relationship with one assistant, Yoriko Matsumura, fondly recalling in her autobiography "taking a bath together" with her. On one trip, Johnson and Matsumura found themselves at an inn, too cold to fall asleep. Johnson asked Matsumura if she could fetch from the kitchen some hot water so that they could warm their feet. This could not be done. Johnson asked again if she could get some hot tea. Another inquiry was made. Hot tea was available. Johnson suggested to Matsumura, "Then why don't you ask for tea and warm your feet in it?" After overcoming the first shock over "this unconventional idea," Matsumura went back to the kitchen and came back with hot tea. The two women were able to warm themselves in "the hot-tea footbaths." The relationship between Matsumura and Johnson was not without moments of ambivalence. On yet another trip, Johnson and Matsumura were in a room, waiting for a vehicle to come by. Quoting from her diary, Johnson re-creates the scene: "I asked if she would like to lie down. She did but kept on her dress. When I suggested she take it off rather than wrinkle it, she said she had been taught never to undress in front of anyone else—not even her parents. I replied that was silly in my opinion and that she had seen me in my slip the day before."[116] Looking back on this trip a half-century later, Johnson wonders "if such intimate relations between a young woman and her older American supervisor were more distressing to her than I ever suspected."[117]

Helen Hosp Seamans's interactions with Japanese women who participated in the 1949 training course for prospective women deans also resulted in extremely strong, often intimate, bonds. As Donald Roden documents, Seamans's training course often emphasized the importance of "unisexual friendship among students and teachers," over and above marriage and family.[118] The training course provided a space where prospective women deans, whose ages ranged from twenty-nine to fifty-nine and many of whom were self-proclaimed "old misses," could express personal and intimate thoughts and feelings. Asked to write an autobiographical essay, one of the participants, Hayashi Akiko, confessed her infatuation with a female student she had taught. Another participant, Maeda Yoshiko, also turned the assignment into an opportunity to talk about her feelings toward women. She wrote about her "first love," a fellow female teacher, with whom she had developed a strong bond. Her decision to marry had broken Maeda's heart. Maeda was attending the training course to forget this sad episode and heal her broken heart. However, she was to experience yet another heartbreak during the training course. The rumor that Seamans was soon to marry crushed Maeda, leaving her in tears. Seamans was indeed an object of adoration among the Japanese women. Facing her impending departure, Yamada Hisae wrote as follows: "During nineteen years of extended student life, I have never received from a woman teacher the deeply moving and personal education that has come from you, Miss Hosp. Since we cannot express ourselves freely together, how could our special relationship come about?"[119]

Such feelings and sentiments were often extremely subtle, and barely artic- ulated as lesbian desires. None of the female-to-female bonds just described led to overt or covert protestation to the Cold War sexual order. Nevertheless, the strong and intimate female friendships that emerged during the occupa- tion are important for their intervention in the Cold War tenet of familial heterosexuality, and for their introduction of a narrative of homosocial desires into the occupation story. In some cases, the bonds between women were doubly subversive as they provided a space to challenge and criticize the occupation, as seen in the exchange between Beard and Weed. Ironically, it was the CI&E, the agency in charge of disseminating containment narratives in Japan, that played an instrumental role in creating such a space.

In the end, then, Cold War feminist mobilization in occupied Japan pres- ents a story that continuously subverts itself. Demanding direct participa- tion in SCAP's gender reforms, American women's organizations challenged MacArthur's male imperium. Passionate promoters of Cold War culture in postwar Japan, the American women occupiers were themselves "deviants," subverting the containment ideals of domesticated femininity and hetero- sexual normativity. Thwarting Cold War cultural emphases on mother- hood and domestic containment, Japanese women leaders returned from the United States admiring American housewives' freedom to participate in the public sphere. It is these dynamic instances of disruption, contradiction, and irony, not the "successful" emancipation of Japanese women, that makes the occupation's gender reform truly exceptional and potentially radical.

4

Women, the Cold War, and the Question of Resistance

On February 6, 1947, *Fujin Minshu Shinbun* (Women's Democratic Newspaper), the official newspaper of *Fujin Minshu Kurabu* (Women's Democratic Club), published a piece, "*Nosaka fujin ni kiku, soren no jitsujō* (Interview with Mrs. Nosaka: Social Conditions in the Soviet Union)." Nosaka Ryō—once a teacher at a women's high school, a veteran communist activist from before the war, and wife of Nosaka Sanzō—had just returned to Japan. Along with several other women, she had been invited to discuss women's lives in the Soviet Union, where she had lived for seventeen years. Conducted by the newspaper's chief editor, Matsuoka Yōko, the interview was premised on a gendered Cold War rivalry that assumed that the "rationalization of domestic labor" and "conditions at the work place" were as advanced in the Soviet Union as in the United States. Soviet women's lives could provide examples for Japanese working women, who struggled daily to build a new, democratic society in postwar Japan.

Nosaka and the other participants covered a wide range of topics that reflected postwar social conditions in Japan: high unemployment, enormous inflation, spiraling commodity prices, severe housing and food shortages, and women's economic displacement. Factories were bombed out, and even at those that were still operational, production was halted because of the shortage of raw materials. Far from sufficient to begin with, over the course of the first nine months following the surrender, government rations deteriorated both in quantity and quality. Malnutrition became widespread, and some people starved to death. Illegal economic activities, such as black-marketeering and prostitution, began to proliferate. The situation for women was especially grim. Many working women were subject to governmental and industrial demobilization. Like their American counterparts, those who had been recruited to replace male workers during the war were now being pushed out to accommodate men returning from the war front and the former colonies. As early as December 1945, the cabinet was already directing female workers to return home as a way of solving the unemployment problem; this was just the beginning of the dismissal of female workers, which continued throughout the occupation period.

In the interview, Nosaka painted an ideal picture of Soviet women's lives, in stark contrast to the difficult conditions Japanese women confronted under the U.S. occupation. In the Soviet Union, there was no discrimination against women in the workplace. Gender equality in wages and job opportunities was guaranteed, and if they possessed superior skills, women workers could even earn more than their male counterparts. Since all women worked outside the home, there were no "pure housewives" in the Soviet Union. Workers—both men and women—enjoyed their lives, combining their work life with cultural and educational activities. Food was plentiful, and distributed to all through an efficient ration system. A "free market" was also available, providing additional food items at reasonable prices. Day care was easily accessible, allowing mothers to enjoy life outside the confines of home and family. The livelihoods of women widowed during the war were protected by the state, and since unemployment was nonexistent, there was no prostitution, legal or illegal.

The explanation for the ideal state of women's lives in the Soviet Union, Nosaka pointed out, could be found in the marvelous statesmanship of its leader, Joseph Stalin, whose commitment to the people of the nation was firm and unwavering. People's welfare, rather than profit making, came first, as shown by the first major postwar state initiative: the construction of factories and housing. What a great contrast the Soviet system provided to capitalism, where people's lives were merely a secondary concern! It was no wonder that people in the Soviet Union had an abiding faith, respect, and admiration for their leader. In the Soviet Union, "Minna Stārin ga daisuki desu (Everybody loves Stalin)," Nosaka emphasized. In occupied Japan, where Douglas MacArthur and his initiative in women's liberation were widely celebrated, Nosaka made a point of praising Stalin's statesmanship and the benefits it bestowed on women. Years before the Nixon–Krushchev kitchen debate, occupied Japan became a site of gendered Cold War rivalry where American and Soviet visions of women's emancipation competed against each other.[1]

The contestatory nature of this interview becomes all the more obvious considering its timing. The interview took place in January 1947, when

Japan's left-labor front, under the leadership of the newly legalized Japan Communist Party, was gaining momentum for a nationwide general strike scheduled for February 1, 1947. A symbol of grassroots democratic mobilization, the general strike was aborted by order of MacArthur. This blatant suppression signaled the beginning of an explicitly conservative turn, or "reverse course," in SCAP's operations. Within a week, the Women's Democratic Club published Nosaka's interview, clearly a statement of opposition. It is ironic, to say the least, that the club came to take such an explicitly oppositional stance to the American occupiers, as it had come into existence under the guidance of Ethel Weed as a symbol of the democratization of Japanese women under American leadership. Contrary to SCAP's intention to nurture Japanese women's allegiance to the United States, the club and its newspaper soon became a politicized space where Japanese women could publicly protest U.S. domination.

In U.S.-occupied Japan, despite the reformers' intense efforts to disseminate American middle-class white femininity and domesticity in postwar Japan, competing articulations of democracy, gender equality, and emancipation emerged during the occupation. In this alternative discourse exemplified by Nosaka's interview, women in the Soviet Union and China embodied gender equality, freedom, and liberation. Japanese women of the left-labor front used newspapers, labor education, and other means to disseminate this alternative notion of femininity. In a radical left-labor mobilization spearheaded by the Japan Communist Party, women enacted a kind of femininity distinctly opposed to the middle-class woman surrounded by modern kitchen gadgets and content with casting votes and making motions at meetings. In the early days of the occupation, the left-labor front was extremely active, even militant, and women constituted a vital force. At work, women confronted their managers and employers, demanding better wages and improved working conditions. At union meetings, women challenged male unionists' sexism, and often pushed the leadership to take far more radical actions than initially planned. Women were on the front lines at union marches and rallies, carrying placards and waving flags. Women's sections within unions were particularly active in organizing mass women's rallies and coalitions. These efforts culminated in a women's united front, a working-class version of the "women's block" criticized by MacArthur. The women's united front developed a relationship with the Women's International Democratic Federation (WIDF), a strongly procommunist international women's organization that was critical of Western, and especially American, imperial domination in the post–World War II world. Not only did the women's actions explicitly contradict the Orientalist notion of passive and victimized Japanese women, which had legitimated SCAP's interventions in Japanese gender relations to begin with, but quite explicitly, women of the left-labor front were defying, physically as well as discursively, Cold War notions of femininity, democracy, and domestic containment.[2]

This chapter focuses on Japanese women of the left-labor front, analyzing the meanings and consequences of their resistance in the Cold War context. Just as the CI&E's gender reform continuously subverted its original intent and caused "leakage" in containment politics, leftist women's resistance frequently led to consequences that exceeded all expectations. Clearly, women of the left-labor front intended to challenge SCAP policies in Japan, pursuing varied and often extremely difficult attempts to articulate and disseminate alternative visions of postwar democratic womanhood. At the same time, however, these women's discourses and practices were never completely outside the existing parameters of power; they often inadvertently participated in and reinforced the containment narratives of gender and democracy. Calling into question the notion of "pure" resistance, in this chapter I examine various ways in which women's resistance was compromised by and recuperated back into the hegemonic orders of gender, race, sexuality, and nation.

More specifically, in U.S.-occupied Japan, women of the left-labor front occupied an iconic space where a number of discourses concerning gender and labor competed with each other. To start, they had to negotiate with the male dominant leadership and structure of the left-labor front. Like MacArthur, the left-labor front was eager to present itself as a champion of women's emancipation and granted women a prominent—if only symbolic—place in its mobilization process. In reality, the male-dominant leadership defined women as "working-class subjects," utilizing their presence for the purpose of working-class mobilization but marginalizing their gender-specific interests and concerns.

Women of the left-labor front also negotiated with the CI&E, whose American middle-class vision of women's emancipation excluded working-class women's class-specific concerns. Moreover, the CI&E's reform efforts were increasingly informed by a blatant anticommunism, seen, for example, in Ethel Weed's opposition to the Women's International Democratic Federation (WIDF). Yet, the relationship between women of the left-labor front and the CI&E was not always oppositional, as the CI&E provided important political resources. With Weed, the women were able to discuss gender-specific concerns, and the Women's Democratic Club, which became a crucial space for leftist women's mobilization, had initially emerged from Weed's gender reform efforts.

Besides the CI&E, the women of the left-labor front had to deal with the Economic and Scientific Section (ESS) of SCAP in charge of labor reform. While advocating the "emancipation of women," the ESS also pursued explicitly anti-labor and anticommunist policies. Richard Deverall, an ESS anticommunist labor educator, was particularly alarmed by the radicalization of women on the left-labor front. Exemplifying the "fantastic conflation" of gender, race, class, and sexuality, he attempted to contain these unruly, transgressive women by calling a women's section within union a "communist enclave," criticizing its existence as an antidemocratic instance of "Jim Crowism," and blaming Weed for the formation of a dangerous, "women-only" sphere.

A triangulation of the CI&E, the ESS, and the left-labor front led to political opportunities as well as constraints, creating a new discursive space in which women of the left-labor front struggled to articulate their own visions of democratic womanhood. Adopting strategies that were strongly international in scope, they turned to Soviet and Chinese women as their ideals, and tried to forge connections with procommunist women's organizations abroad. Despite their explicitly contestatory stance, however, their resistance discourses never completely transcended the dominant discursive order of the time, confirming Dorinne Kondo's critical observation that "nothing can be pristinely separated from the dominant."[3] Challenging CI&E gender reform that upheld American middle-class femininity as the ideal, leftist women leaders nevertheless insisted on their sexual respectability, thereby participating in and reinforcing the Cold War narrative of heterosexual normativity. Emphasizing political solidarity among Asian women under imperial domination, they skirted the question of Japanese women's complicity in prewar racism, nationalism, and colonialism and turned blind eyes to a complex and hierarchical relation between Japanese and other Asian women. This chapter reveals how the dynamic interweaving of resistance and recuperation animated leftist women's oppositional politics in U.S.-occupied Japan.

"Women's Action Teams Blooming in the Midst of Struggles": Gender and Class in the Left-Labor Mobilization

To contextualize the analysis of leftist women's political activism, a brief overview of SCAP's labor policies and Japanese left-labor mobilization in the early days of the occupation is necessary.[4] From the very beginning, Japanese women were an especially visible force in union mobilization, contradicting the occupiers' assumption of their docility and lack of agency. As early as October 1945, women students at a private high school in Tokyo, *Ueno Kōtō Jogakkō*, walked out to protest corruption in the administration. Their demands included the just and fair distribution of rations, the reinstatement of "good teachers," and the firing of the school principal and vice principal who were accused not only of appropriating food that students had produced on school farms but of using the produce for bribery. The students stayed out for twenty-one days. In the same month, women hospital nurses from the *Tokyo Keisatsu Byōin* went on strike, demanding an improved dormitory, wage increases, and the firing of administrators who were accused of mishandling the distribution of rations. Initiated on October 25, the strike led to the formation of a union on November 16, and ended on November 19, with most of the demands met.[5]

These and other instances of women's political activism were sparked by the democratization initiated by the American occupiers. On October 4, 1945, SCAP issued a directive, lifting prewar and wartime restrictions on civil rights. It disbanded the Japanese Special Police and abolished repressive laws, including the infamous Peace Preservation Law that had been used by the state to suppress labor and other political movements. This reform led to a release of political prisoners, including Communist Party members, who went on to play important roles in the postwar labor movements. Then on October 11, MacArthur issued his famous five-item reform, granting women suffrage and explicitly encouraging unionization. As a result, a Trade Union Law was passed on December 22, 1945, granting the rights to unionize, to collectively bargain, and to strike. Initiated by the American occupiers for economic and political democratization, these reforms opened up new space for working-class political activism.

Democratic claims notwithstanding, SCAP never intended to give full and unqualified support to the politicization of the Japanese. Only certain organizing activities were acceptable. As Joe Moore concisely argues, SCAP intended to establish in postwar Japan a "business union," or "a moderate union which did not trouble itself too deeply about politics or the internal affairs of management." Such unions were to confine themselves to "the pursuit of economic, job-oriented goals: higher wages, job security, better working conditions, and the like." These unions would avoid "representing workers as a class," and rather pursue "a 'businesslike' operation that recognized no basic conflict of interest between itself and the business enterprise."[6] Furthermore, as the ultimate authority in the occupied nation, SCAP had absolute power over the actions of labor unions and political parties. Before the occupation even began, the U.S. government was clear in its intention to ban union activities that could be considered "inimical to the objectives of military occupation," or could jeopardize "production activities and services considered to be essential to the occupation objective."[7] The phrase "actions inimical to the occupation objective" was sufficiently broad to give SCAP a great deal of discretion in negotiating with, or more often restraining and suppressing, left-labor mobilization. Thus, SCAP could encourage "business unions," while trying to

> prevent the effective political use of the workers' weapons against the liberal, capitalist regime the US was trying to construct in Japan.

SCAP was trying in effect to draw a fine line, separating the "normal" political concerns of labor within a capitalist economy from "revolutionary" actions of workers combining in a movement to wrest economic and political control from capitalist hands entirely.[8]

Within the context of the occupation and especially of the Cold War containment imperatives, the close connection that quickly developed between the Communist Party and the left faction of labor unions first surprised and then alarmed SCAP.

Despite the inherent limitations in SCAP policies, the American presence and the directives concerning economic and political democratization sent a positive signal to the Japanese. Given SCAP's intentions, it is ironic, to say the least, that the Japanese left-labor front saw the occupiers as "liberators" and that workers all over the country began to organize, with the Japan Communist Party exerting significant influence on this process. The unionization rate and membership shot up dramatically. In August 1945, unions were virtually nonexistent. By November of the same year, there were seventy-five unions and 68,530 union members, and by December there were 509 unions and 385,677 union members. One year later the numbers had increased to 17,265 unions and 4,849,329 union members, and by 1949, more than half the workers in Japan were unionized.[9] The unionization rate for women was equally or more impressive. Before the war, the women's unionization rate was less than 1 percent; by 1948, it was 45.7 percent.[10] Many unions designated sections for women members, such as *fujin kōdōtai* (women's action teams), which often developed into *fujinbu* (women's sections). Women also joined *seinen kōdōtai*, youth action teams, where young male and female workers were organized to lead radical, often militant, labor protests.

By the summer of 1946, national federations began to emerge that would coordinate these individual unions. Labor leaders initially attempted to establish one united labor front, but their efforts were unsuccessful because of a deep political schism dating to before the war. On the one hand, the right-wing labor faction, *Nihon rōdō kumiai sōdōmei*, or *Sōdōmei* (All Japan Federation of Labor), was established in August 1946, with 855,399 members, or about 22 percent of all organized workers. It drew its membership mainly from the textile and shipping industries. A few days later, the left wing of the labor movement formed *Zen nihon sangyōbetsu rōdō kumiai kaigi* or *Sanbetsu* (All Japan Congress of Industrial Unions). It had 1,631,540 members, or about 43 percent of all organized workers, and drew its primary membership from government workers, transportation, electric power, mining, and other heavy industries.[11]

Spring 1946 to February 1947 witnessed the increasing radicalization of the left-labor movement, the demands of which clearly exceeded the occupiers' expectations not only in class but also gender terms. The first postwar May Day, the so-called Food May Day of May 19, 1946 and the September Offensive and October Offensive mobilized large numbers of people, with Sanbetsu, Communist Party members, government workers, and public employees at the forefront of the labor struggles. Reminiscent of women protestors in the prewar rice riots, working-class mothers and wives also participated in these postwar rallies and marches, challenging the containment notion of domesticated femininity by waving red flags, demanding food, and criticizing the government's inability to provide the basic necessities for people.[12] Popular protests of any kind during this period were frequently associated with criticism of the government, which the population perceived as inept and hostile to popular demands. Worsening economic conditions, combined with the formation of the blatantly antilabor and conservative Yoshida cabinet on May 22, 1946, led the left-labor front to demand the dissolution of the government. Since that government was supported by SCAP, these popular antigovernment protests were also an indirect criticism of SCAP. The left-labor front clearly challenged and resisted the occupiers' efforts to contain Japanese workers' economic and political demands.

It was within these turbulent contexts that women's sections of the unions came to represent and promote female workers' needs and interests. Although issues varied from one union to another, common concerns included opposition to layoffs of women workers, the elimination of gender-based discrimination in wages and promotion, the enforcement of the Labor Standards Law, especially as it related to maternal protection provisions, the abolition of feudalistic and sexist practices at workplaces and dormitories, the improvement of welfare facilities for women at workplaces, and the provision of educational and informational activities. These demands were first raised by individual local unions and later by the national federations. The women's sections played a particularly important role in providing representatives to the unions' central committees.

Just as women's suffrage constituted a discursive site where MacArthur and Japanese male politicians competed for the claim of democracy, working-class women became an iconic figure in male union leaders' struggles against SCAP; they used a narrative of female struggles and empowerment to mark the left-labor front as an authentic space of democracy and liberation. *Rōdō Sensen*, the official newspaper of Sanbetsu, often documented women's enthusiastic participation in the left-labor front's struggles for democratization. Articles—often accompanied by photos of women unionists waving flags, holding placards, forming a scrum, or standing at the forefront of workers' marches or rallies—cast women as revolutionary figures spearheading labor mobilizations, in a marked contrast to Cold War idealization of middle-class femininity and domesticity. For example, the November 5, 1946 issue of *Rōdō*

Sensen contains an article titled "Sōgi ni hana saku fujin kōdōtai (Women's Action Teams Blooming in the Midst of Struggles)." With a photo of women protestors waving large flags and marching at the forefront of picket lines, the article reported women's participation in numerous labor struggles. In particular, *fujin kōdōtai*, or Women's Action Teams, were presented as the driving force behind left-labor mobilization. However, class, not gender, was presented as the focal point of the women's struggles. Through their participation in left-labor activities, the article observed, women unionists came to understand that women's emancipation could become possible only after the liberation of the working-class population as a whole. Such consciousness and experiences in labor struggles, the article claimed, empowered the women unionists.[13]

In a 1946 series titled "Kumiaiki o mamoru hitobito (People Who Defend Union Flags)," *Rōdō Sensen* focused on male and female union members whose work was considered exemplary. The December 3, 1946 issue introduced a young female teacher, Sueyoshi Nobuko, and her fight against anticommunism. Although only twenty-one, she was an active unionist, instrumental in organizing teachers, especially women and younger teachers, at her school. Confronted with the possible expulsion of an *akai dōryō* (red colleague) who was perceived as a troublemaker by a *handō kōchō* (reactionary principal), she mobilized teachers and started three-day marathon meetings to protest the situation. In the end, she successfully defended her colleague against expulsion and gained a promise from the principal that in the future he would never obstruct union members or their activities.[14]

That women unionists were poster girls for the left-labor mobilization is clearly indicated in another series, "Yonjūnananen no hōpu (Hopes—1947)," that exclusively focused on women unionists and their activism in the first two months of 1947, a crucial period for the left-labor activism heading toward a nationwide general strike at the time. The January 21 issue introduced Okada Toshiko, an active member of the Tokyo local of the National Railway Union. Okada is described as a young and beautiful "maiden" whose fierce fighting spirit and commitment to labor struggles often even surpassed those of male unionists. In the protest mobilization the previous year against the proposed mass layoffs of railway workers, she was instrumental in mobilizing women workers, and successfully opposed male leaders who were ready to compromise with management. Thanks to her effort, the Tokyo local became an active union, gearing up for the upcoming February 1 general strike. The rest of the series continued to describe and praise the varied and often leading roles women unionists played in left-labor struggles.[15]

Notwithstanding such public endorsement and praise, male-dominant unions were far from willing to include women as equal partners. Women unionists repeatedly pointed out the male resistance, and even open hostility.

At the preparatory meeting for the formation of a national federation of teachers' unions, for example, women unionists demanded a special provision that would guarantee a seat for a woman representative on the central executive committee. They also demanded that the federation platform include "liberation of women" on the union's agenda. Both of these demands met fierce male resistance. "Women should go back to the kitchen," male delegates shouted, or "If you women want to be equal with men, why don't you climb up to the roof and prove you can do the same job as men do," or even "You women just shut up."[16] Male unionists' hostility toward women's issues and the marginalization of women within union structures were consistently observed in other unions as well.[17]

The progressive political parties were not free of sexist dynamics either. In an interview with Ethel Weed, Nosaka Ryō acknowledged that within the Japan Communist Party she experienced "many of the problems that face women in other political parties," although the party's rule "not to criticize the party policies outside the communist circle" led to "such close supervision that this fact is not generally known."[18] In another meeting with Weed, several women members of the party discussed problematic gender dynamics within the Communist Party. The reason wives of Communist Party members were absent from political activities, they told Weed, had much to do with gender dynamics at home. Given their husbands' attitudes, women could not devote themselves fully to political activities: "Communist men resent their homes being deserted or the party contacting their wives directly." The Party was trying to address this issue "indirectly by a program of male education."[19] These women were clearly aware of and willing to challenge the image that the male-dominant left-labor front was trying to project as a democratic and liberationist movement.

Even though the male-dominant left-labor front granted women nominal significance, their gender-specific concerns were often marginalized, and even made invisible. As the *Rōdō Sensen* articles indicate, in the minds of male union leaders, class struggle took precedence over any other issue; the liberation of women could be assumed to somehow naturally follow once the working-class population was emancipated. In the left-labor mobilization, then, women were predominantly constructed as classed, but not gendered, subjects. That women's actual bodily presence was more often considered as inconvenience in the left-labor mobilization is vividly captured in the January 1, 1947 issue of *Rōdō Sensen*, which contained a workers' version of *sugoroku*, the Japanese New Year's game, depicting the progress of postwar democratization. The main characters are a male worker named Mr. Danketsu Tsuyoshi (Mr. Strong Unity) and a female worker named Miss Kōdō Taiko (Miss Action Team). Looking almost indistinguishable, both are wearing trousers and shirts and waving flags with words like "Establish

Populist Government!" and "Absolute Opposition!" Arm in arm, Mr. Strong Unity and Miss Action Team fight various obstacles, including a reactionary Japanese government, SCAP, demagoguery, and so on, to reach the goal: the establishment of a populist government for farmers and workers.[20] While this game offers an illusion of coparticipation, a closer examination shows it also erases the gendered specificity of women, constructing them as physically and politically indistinct from their male counterparts. Markedly absent in this pictorial narrative of postwar revolutionary struggles were those based on gender, including struggles against male domination within the left-labor front.

Working-Class Women and Political Agency: Helen Mears and Her Discursive Interventions

The active participation of women in the left-labor mobilization did not escape the occupiers' attentions.[21] Among them was Helen Mears, an expert on labor legislation and women's issues, and a member of the Labor Advisory Committee sent to occupied Japan in February 1946. She was rather an exception among the occupiers who frequently had no knowledge or experience of Japan. She had visited Japan twice in prewar years, and during the war, had worked as a lecturer for the Civil Affairs Training Schools that trained Americans for the postwar occupation. Her book, *Mirrors for Americans: Japan* (1948), was highly critical of American operations, exposing the limitations of many of the assumptions of the occupation and providing a refreshingly critical view of the fallacy of U.S. "democratization" of Japan.[22]

Mears's report, "Women's Labor and Political Movements," submitted to Paul Staunchfield, Chairman of the Labor Advisory Committee on June 28, 1946, is a rare and fascinating instance of discursive interventions performed by a woman occupier. Articulated at the intersection of gender and class, its portrayal of women unionists explicitly contradicted Japanese as well as American understandings of women and labor, causing a subtle yet significant rupture in the emerging Cold War orders. In the report, Mears provided information about women's activities at the two major labor federations, Sōdōmei and Sanbetsu, their affiliates, and the Japan Communist Party. She had interviewed women unionists, political leaders, journalists, and so on, and also attended women's labor and political meetings. The report identifies two new trends: (a) "the rapid increase of women in unions and the growing importance of women's sections," and (b) "the trend toward close interrelations between organized labor and the political parties." Together these trends "produced a situation of the greatest possible importance to the future of Japanese women in their society."[23]

The report highlights Japanese women's political agency in the left-labor mobilization. Mears had high praise for the woman leader of Sōdōmei, Akamatsu Tsuneko, and for its rank-and-file women members. A veteran in the labor movement and a friend of Mears since prewar years, Takamatsu exerted strong leadership, training a group of young women at Sōdōmei headquarters. These trainees' "poise and competency" was indeed impressive, but Mears was similarly affected by the rank-and-file women in the local unions affiliated with Sōdōmei. She highlighted the role of women's sections in mobilizing women, and reported that many "who head these sections seem to be astonishingly alert and responsible." A meeting at Sōdōmei headquarters provided an example of the excellent quality of the women unionists, and Mears was careful to document working-class women's resistance to male authorities. Fifty women, all heads of women's sections, met to discuss the publication of a women's labor magazine. With no prior experience in union activities or public speeches, each woman, Mears observed, "arose in turn and with poise and fluency gave an account of the development of her union and a summary of the major problems that they were concerned about, and an account of gains gotten by unionization." The women picked *Hataraku Dōshi* (*Working Comrades*) for the new magazine's name, despite "the spirited opposition of the only man present, the prospective publisher, who insisted that the name was not sufficiently feminine."[24] In another example, Mears refers to ten women section heads meeting with men from the prefectural labor offices and the employing companies. While outnumbered, the women "seemed composed and self-confident and most of them discussed their union and their job difficulties and preferences with considerable poise and vivacity."[25]

Also documented in the report is a grassroots educational effort Sōdōmei initiated for its women members to counter "a certain tendency observable in the union movement today for a small group to make a connection with a federation and bring about a unionization of a whole factory without the individuals necessarily understanding much of what it is all about." At one meeting Mears attended, Akamatsu Tsuneko, Nirazawa Keiko, and young women trained to be leaders at Sōdōmei headquarters led a discussion with a group of a dozen workers, the majority of whom were women from different factories. Akamatsu and Nirazawa began the meeting by briefly discussing the meanings of the labor movement, especially the need to "understand the problems of workers in factories other than their own and work together to improve conditions generally." Following this, the factory workers introduced themselves and described the problems found at their individual factories. Such exchanges of information among factory workers became an important educational as well as organizational tool. In a few months, some of the workers who attended the meeting began to reach out to and organize workers at other factories.[26]

The women unionists of Sanbetsu were equally impressive. The women's section of the federation and the women's sections of its affiliated unions, were successfully mobilizing and organizing women. Although Mears was less than pleased by the fact that the women's section of Sanbetsu was led by a man, she also got a definite sense that women were nonetheless extremely active, mobilizing communication workers, railway workers, teachers, and medical workers, among others. Women's sections, she noted, had a particularly important function, as they provided women with the means to bring gender-specific issues into decision-making processes at the predominantly male executive committee level.[27] While still lacking power at the leadership level, Mears observed, women unionists were extremely active at the grass-roots level "in making posters, in making and sending out leaflets, and in all of the routine work of union activities." They also "organized their share of demonstrations, rallies and strikes." Even the male head of the Sanbetsu women's section acknowledged the strength of the women union members. As he told Mears, women unionists' major contribution was "their practical brass-tacks attitude toward problems." "While men are debating some abstraction," he told her, "the women will cut through directly to the concrete problem that must be solved at once."[28]

Mears's meeting with women members of the Communist Party once again revealed the importance of women's activism in the political party with a significant influence in Sanbetsu. The party's approach to women's issues, she learned from a woman official of the government, was "more informed, conscientious, and active than in any other group." The party was providing important opportunities for these women and nurturing them to become leaders of "considerable importance." While the party leadership had a weakness of "doctrinal radicalism," Mears observed that this was "controlled in relation to grass-roots operational procedures," thanks to young women members. Acknowledging the Communist Party's connection with Sanbetsu, and the Socialist Party's with Sōdōmei, Mears considered the connections between labor unions and political parties as "probably inevitable," and "not necessarily an unfortunate development," even stating that "insofar as the political education of women is concerned, it was inevitable that labor leaders should play an important role."[29] She concluded with a strong appraisal of women in labor and political movements: "The sincerity of the women leaders is unquestionable. They believe that they are being given a wonderful chance to develop a functioning democracy on both the labor and political levels. Their faith put a great responsibility on GHQ/SCAP not to let them down."[30]

Within the context of the occupation, Mears's report is particularly noteworthy as it simultaneously challenges several competing narratives of women, labor, and politics that existed at the time. It explicitly contradicts the

Orientalist discourse of Japanese women as helpless victims by emphasizing working-class women's active political agency. Its emphasis on the intersectionality of gender and class explicitly challenges the left-labor leaders' discourses of working-class women as classed, but not gendered, subjects. Endorsing the connection between women unionists and political parties, moreover, the report counters SCAP's official policy to establish moderate unions, and especially the ESS's attempt to depoliticize and contain women's labor activism. Finally, by suggesting that leftist and working-class women play a leading role in women's political education in occupied Japan, it contradicts the CI&E's gender reform that gave Japanese middle- and upper-class women prominent roles. In sum, the report constitutes a site of oppositions by an American woman in the early days of the occupation. As discussed later, however, such oppositional discourses would soon be recuperated back into the Cold War containment narratives.

"Mannish Soviet Women," "Black Face," and Narratives of Emancipation: Nosaka Ryō and Labor Education

In Summer 1947, *Fujin Bunka Kōza* (Lectures on Culture for Women), organized by the women's section of Sanbetsu and *Nihon Minshushugi Bunka Renmei* (The Association of Japanese Democracy and Culture) took place in Tokyo, one instance of the "labor schools" that the left-labor front frequently sponsored during the occupation. The specific focus of this event was on political education for women workers. The lectures covered a wide range of topics, such as "Women's History," "Constitution and Women," "Love," "Birth Control," "Ideal Domestic Space," "Music," "Films," and "Fashion." Later, the lectures were published, including Katō Shizue's "Women and Politics," and Nosaka Ryō's "Women's Issues Today."[31] The lectures proved to be politically contentious. Katō, an SCAP favorite, and Nosaka, the head of the women's section of the Japan Communist Party, presented competing visions of postwar femininity—namely, American versus Soviet women—and turned the lecture series into a politicized space where a gendered Cold War rivalry was articulated with a focus on working-class women.

In "Women and Politics," Katō focused on the notion of "emancipated womanhood" exalted by MacArthur and the women occupiers. She began by triumphantly claiming that a new era had arrived. With the right to vote, Japanese women were finally liberated, gaining direct access to political decision making. This did not mean, however, that women as a group were to participate in politics; rather, women as part of the working masses now gained access to politics,[32] which would reflect the voices of the masses and contribute to the maintenance of "order and control" in everyday life.[33] Clearly

Katō was fulfilling her role as a spokesperson for the occupation, reiterating MacArthur's objection to a "women's block" as well as his understanding of Japanese women as a "stabilizing force" in postwar Japan.

Katō obviously saw her lecture as an important opportunity to articulate and disseminate dominant Cold War containment discourses, emphasizing home as the primary site of working women's political concerns and thereby attempting to domesticate female labor militancy that was increasingly salient at the time. Emphasizing working-class women's ignorance and political immaturity constituted an important part of her containment strategies. Many working women, she argued, were not ready to handle the new right, or to participate in politics in a sufficiently informed manner. Some women were even indifferent to politics. However, it would not take much for women to realize the deep connections between their lives and politics. A woman whose house had been burned during the war, for example, might wonder why it was taking so long for her to get a new house. Once she asked herself this question, it would become immediately obvious that her interest in housing involved her in politics. Similarly, a young, working woman could not help but notice issues that impacted her working conditions and wages, and the resulting family budget. Once again, she would immediately see the direct connection between her concerns and politics. Furthermore, unlike men, women were far more concerned with issues of marriage and divorce, children's education, food rations, and the availability of fuel—all obviously deeply affected by politics.[34]

Once they understand the close connections between their everyday lives and politics, Katō suggested, women should then take the next step, participating in politics as a way of obtaining "happiness," which cannot simply be given; one must strive for it. In the pursuit of one's happiness, knowledge of politics and an ability to assess political dynamics were vital. In Katō's vision of labor education, British and American women who well understood the connection between happiness and politics and who strove to educate themselves about political matters—either individually or through organizations—provided the models for Japanese women.[35]

Since Japanese women at present were not fully informed about politics, nor cognizant of their rights and duties, Katō argued, their political education was an urgent necessity. Predictably, she emphasized studying the new constitution. Disregarding the convoluted political dynamics that shaped the constitutional revision process, she pointed to the new constitution as evidence that Japan had been "reborn." It defined citizens' rights and duties, and specified gender equality and people's right to welfare, notions previously unthinkable in Japan. To become citizens truly qualified to vote in a democratic country, Katō argued, women should study this document carefully.[36] Then, as part of Japan's working mass, women's participation in politics would have significant consequences for the nation's future—not only the future of home life, but the very rise and fall of the nation.[37]

Katō's feminist nationalism, which was informed by the Cold War notion of female citizenry espoused by MacArthur and the CI&E reformers and which defined working-class women's role in relation to domestic and national duties and obligations, was directly contradicted by Nosaka Ryō. Women's suffrage and the new constitution did not for her signal the beginning of a new Japan or women's liberation. Neither did British and American women provide the models for Japanese women. Focused on Soviet women as exemplars and economic independence as the ticket to women's emancipation, Nosaka's lecture contrasted markedly with Katō's pedantic emphasis on Japanese working women's ignorance and indifference to politics. Despite her explicitly oppositional stance, however, Nosaka's discourse was never completely outside the existing parameters of power, either. Insisting on gender-sexual respectability of communist women in her otherwise oppositional discourse, she ended up espousing, rather than contesting, the containment narrative of heterosexual normativity.

At the time of the lecture, although she was head of the Japan Communist Party's women's section and a veteran activist who had successfully mobilized women of the left-labor front, Nosaka Ryō was overshadowed by her famous husband, Nosaka Sanzō, the leading figure of the Japan Communist Party. Born into a merchant family in 1896, and a graduate of a women teachers' college, Nosaka had married Sanzō in 1919. From 1920 to 1922, she had followed her husband to England, then to France, Switzerland, and Germany, learning English and studying women's movements in Europe. On her return to Japan in 1922, she joined the newly established Japan Communist Party and began organizing and educating women workers. In 1931, she once again followed Sanzō, this time to the Soviet Union, and spent the next sixteen years there, until after the end of World War II. With Sanzō frequently traveling to the United States, China, and so on, for Comintern activities, the couple had spent barely five years together during this period. On her return to Japan in 1947, Nosaka Ryō became a leading political figure and an advocate of the Soviet system, especially its treatment of women, as the model for postwar Japan.[38]

Nosaka began her lecture "Women's Issues Today" with a commentary on the remarkable changes taking place in postwar Japan. In prewar days, it had been extremely difficult to hold political meetings. Even if one had managed to start a gathering, police would immediately break it up and take people to jail. It was almost like a dream, Nosaka stated, that she could publicly give a talk as the head of the women's section of the Communist Party.[39] Nosaka corrected the common misunderstanding of the Japan Communist Party as a radical party that would cause chaos in Japan—an image produced by the propaganda of the Japanese ruling class. In fact, since its beginning a quarter-century before, the Japan Communist Party had been an advocate of popular sovereignty.[40]

Nosaka went on to explicitly counter Katō's argument, noting that the gender reform proclaimed in the new constitution did not actually bring gender equality to Japan. At work, women, not men, were still expected to stop and rush off whenever food rations were being distributed. Women were also expected to serve tea at lunch. According to Nosaka, these and other inequalities originated from women's lack of economic power. Currently, women did not have economic independence, and were unable to compete with men economically, not due to an innate inferiority, but because women had historically been deprived of opportunities. Thus allowing women access to educational and other opportunities was necessary for Japan to become a society truly based on gender equality.[41] Throughout her talk, Nosaka repeatedly emphasized the importance of economic independence for women. "Even after you get married," she admonished her audience, "please be determined not to retreat into the sphere of home." However, for women to continue working, the government needed to transform the existing social system, which was controlled by a ruling class—capitalists, landlords, and bureaucrats—that would not initiate any policy toward gender equality. More than anything else, she emphasized, large-scale social transformation was necessary.[42]

As if to further challenge Katō, Nosaka turned to the Soviet Union as the model society in which gender equality had been achieved. She stated explicitly that women's lives in the Soviet Union were a better model, for American and British women had been given only "superficial respect" but were never treated in a truly equal manner.[43] Relying on triangulated discourses of gender, race, and class, she provided a grand historical narrative about Soviet women and their struggles toward emancipation, tracing the remarkable transformation to the revolution in 1917. Under the reign of the czars, and under the control of capitalists and landlords, Russian and especially minority women had suffered from feudalistic oppressions far worse than those in Japan. Under Russia's imperial rule, for example, minority women in central Asia had been forced to wear "black veils," Nosaka claimed, and were given no freedom in their choice of marital partners. Following the revolution, however, these women's lives were "completely" transformed, as Vladimir Lenin and Joseph Stalin had made women's issues a priority. Without the emancipation of "enslaved women," the nation's leaders understood, there would be no liberation for the rest of the population. Important social institutions, including schools, factories, and stores, were nationalized, with particular efforts made toward improving conditions for women. Needless to say, women themselves strove to improve their status in society.

Now completely emancipated, women enjoyed the same rights as men. There were no "women's problems" in the Soviet Union, nor was there any need for women's groups or women's sections within labor unions or political parties. In postwar Japan, women should learn from the example of Soviet women and demand more than a constitution that only spoke about gender equality; they should demand government action.[44]

With her grand historical narrative of the Soviet Revolution, Nosaka clearly challenged the dominant discourses of gender and democracy, not only opposing Katō but also contending with MacArthur and American Cold War discourses. Gender, but also race, played crucial roles in her resistance strategy, figuring women of color as a focal site of Cold War rivalry. Just as MacArthur had deployed the image of "enslaved Eastern women" to emphasize the historic significance of the occupation's gender reform, Nosaka turned to a similarly gendered and racialized imagery—minority Asian women under black veils—to highlight the emancipatory consequences of the Soviet Revolution. Given the ultimate, slavelike subjugation they had endured in prerevolutionary Russia, a fate even worse than Japanese women's, their emancipation seemed all the more remarkable, and much more impressive, than MacArthur's gender reform in postwar Japan.

Nosaka's emphasis on the postrevolutionary state's role in emancipating the oppressed and subjugated explicitly challenged the Cold War constructions of "Soviet slavery" and "American freedom." At the time, anticommunist rhetoric frequently extolled the virtues of capitalist freedom and voluntarism in the United States and condemned the Soviet statist control that "enslaved" its citizens.[45] Nosaka's lecture explicitly disagreed. Far from being a totalitarian society, she argued, the Soviet Union granted its female citizens freedom and equality. Slavelike subjugation was a thing of the past, and the postrevolutionary state was indeed a protector of women's rights.

Despite its explicitly oppositional stance, Nosaka's lecture cannot be considered an instance of resistance performed completely outside the dominant structure of power, as it also participated in the hegemonic Cold War narratives. A double theme of resistance and complicity is especially noticeable in her discussions of Soviet women's femininity. In promoting the Soviet Union as the model for Japan, she emphasized that gender equality did not mean that Soviet women were "becoming like men." There was a prevalent misunderstanding, she stated, that women of the communist parties were "rugged like men," or that Soviet working women had "black" faces and wore men's clothes.[46] Simultaneously coded by gender, race, class, and sexuality, Soviet women, working outside the home, were perceived as deviant, abnormal, and even subhuman, in contrast to the "sexually attractive housewives and consumers under the American capitalist system."[47] Covered with soot and toiling in menial jobs under a totalitarian state, "mannish" Soviet women with "black" faces would be nothing but "beasts of burden,"[48] deviant not only sexually but also racially. Within the Cold War context where ideological subversion (communism) was always already associated with sexual subversion (homosexuality), the sexuality of Soviet women, who seemed to lack proper femininity, was clearly suspect.

Far from contesting Cold War heteronormativity, however, Nosaka insisted on the gender and sexual respectability of communist and leftist women in the Soviet Union and elsewhere. Gender equality did not mean that Soviet women were "acting like men" at home; they had retained their feminine virtues and strengths. Women were willing to cook, clean, and take care of children, as they knew that they were better at these domestic tasks. They would never force their men to mend their clothes or do their own laundry. Their femininity was also observed in their fashion as well, Nosaka continued. During the war, women in the Soviet Union wore trousers at work, but at home, they always changed into skirts. Even during air raids and in the midst of winter, she had never seen women in trousers. Women in the Soviet Union also followed fashion, as government-sponsored exhibits displayed clothes for all seasons, with varieties of colors and patterns. Their faces were never "black," and they used cosmetics and had their nails manicured and hair permed. How surprising it was for Nosaka to see, on returning to postwar Japan, Japanese women walking around in *monpe* (Japanese-style loose-fitting pants) and trousers! Japanese women should follow the examples of Soviet women; they too should retain their feminine virtues, beauties, and strength while also pursuing gender equality.[49] In effect, Nosaka reinforced rather than contested the dominant Cold War containment discourses of gender and sexuality, and with a rejection of "black face" even of race, and chastised Japanese working-class women for their neglect of proper performance of femininity.

Following her talk, audience members asked a number of questions. In their eyes, the contrasts between Nosaka's and Katō's position were obvious. While Katō's talk suggested that women's place was in the home, one attendee remarked, Nosaka argued that even after getting married, women should continue to work as a way of improving their status in society. Wasn't Nosaka contradicting Katō?[50] Nosaka agreed that there were indeed differences in their views. As far as she was concerned, women's access to economic autonomy was essential to achieving gender equality. While advocating continued participation in work, Nosaka was well aware of the enormous difficulties Japanese women faced. Juggling home and work life was by no means easy. She herself found it "painfully difficult" to balance the two, so much so that she often felt like retreating into the home and becoming a full-time housewife. Drawing on her own experiences, Nosaka characterized women's daily chores as extremely complex and never-ending. For example, in postwar Tokyo, due to a fuel shortage, gas was available only for a short period of time in the morning, when cooking needed to be done. Nosaka found herself waking up at five, and trying to cook several dishes with only one gas burner—it would usually be eight by the time the breakfast was on the table—while the men simply waited around, doing their work or reading the papers.[51]

Unlike Katō, Nosaka thus pointed to male domination at home as a problem for women in postwar Japan. Because of their burden of domestic labor, women never had time to read newspapers, go to lectures, or attend plays or concerts, making it impossible to raise their status. Men were responsible for the problem, as they had a stake in keeping women at home, since that was far more convenient for them. Such a sentiment was prevalent even among the men of her party, Nosaka pointed out. They frequently complained about their wives talking politics at home and not serving the meals on time. Some men even said that the women of the party were good to talk to or to have fun with, but were never cut out to be good wives.[52]

Nosaka's remarks about male domination at home and within the party prompted a comment from a union woman in the audience, who said she would like to continue her work even after getting married. Her union had made some effort in this regard; women union members were organizing lecture sessions to address the gender division of labor at home. However, the majority of the audience members at these lectures were women, and she was thinking about suggesting that men should also attend the lectures. However, she was afraid to do so—it was very likely that men would resent this. Indeed, not even a single book advocated equal sharing of domestic work. Was her idea about inviting men to the lectures somehow wrong, she asked. Nosaka reassured her that her approach was correct. One just cannot assume that men would understand on their own the importance of sharing domestic chores, she candidly remarked; young women needed to educate them.[53]

Equally or even more important than educating men, however, was working for institutional changes. Once again Nosaka emphasized the government's role, and especially its commitment to "rationalizing" domestic life, as the key to the improvement of women's status. Referring to her experiences in the Soviet Union, Nosaka talked at length about a social system that catered to women's needs. In the Soviet Union, she reported, women spent little time cooking. The staple food was bread, which could be readily purchased at stores. Cafeterias were also available where meals could be obtained and taken home. Each workplace had a laundry, where women could leave clothes to be washed and cleaned at reasonable prices. Even if done at home, washing was never a major chore, since hot water was abundantly available, thanks to the government's efforts to make natural gas available for the everyday use of citizens.[54]

Nosaka concluded her session by emphasizing the intersection of gender and class in women's struggles, a point often lost on the male leaders of the left-labor front and on the women occupiers alike. As she explained, in the Soviet Union, the leadership had made a commitment to raising women's status as part of the emancipation of the proletariat, successfully institutionalizing gender equality. In addition, women themselves had struggled fiercely to achieve gender equality, enduring not only their husbands' sarcasm or spite, but physical violence as well. However, they never gave in. Stressing the intersection of gender and class struggles, Nosaka described how women fought landowners as they also struggled against their fathers or husbands. As a result, they now enjoyed complete equality.[55]

Nosaka's lecture shows that in the Cold War context the meanings and consequences of resistance were never fixed but rather fluid and unpredictable. Just as Cold War American hegemony was incoherent and unstable, resulting in numerous unintended consequences, the stories of Japanese resistance constantly subverted themselves. On the one hand, Nosaka clearly challenged dominant discourses by introducing alternative visions of gender, class, and postwar democracy. She exposed the sexism prevalent among male members of the Japan Communist Party, bringing into the open issues of male domination within the left-labor front. By revealing her own struggles at home, she provided an implicit critique even of her husband. Furthermore, she contested the kind of femininity that the American occupiers, in collaboration with Katō and other Japanese middle-class women leaders, were disseminating. By drawing an explicit analogy between women's struggles against male authority at home and against the ruling class, she provided a radical vision of social transformation at the intersection of gender and class.

At the same time, Nosaka's contestatory politics often reinforced the existing parameters of power. Within the Cold War context where American, white, middle-class, and domestic femininity was overwhelmingly propagated as the ideal, Nosaka had to contend with anxieties surrounding the "black-faced" and "mannish" Soviet woman as the deviant other, anxieties often shared among Japanese women of the left-labor front as well. As Helen Mears documented, women unionists were indeed concerned with their self-image, and especially their lack of proper femininity, as a result of their political activism. They were "very anxious that their new political freedom and their new union activities shall not detract from their femininity."[56] Instead of criticizing the normative notions of gender, sexuality, and race that informed these anxieties, Nosaka chose to insist on and reinscribe these very notions. Despite gender equality at work and their involvement in class struggle, Soviet women, she argued, were never "rugged like men" nor "black," as shown by their (American-type) feminine practices: manicured nails, makeup, permed hair, a keen interest in fashion, and the willingness to take on the majority of domestic labor at home. Japanese women of the left-labor front were encouraged to emulate this model. In this sense, Nosaka's oppositional stance was limited, being compromised by and recuperated back into the Cold War containment narratives of gender, race, and sexuality.

Even the Women's Democratic Newspaper, which continued to publish articles by Nosaka and other women of the left-labor front that praised the lives of Soviet and Chinese women as the model for Japanese women, and critiqued American foreign policies in Japan and elsewhere as instances of postwar imperialism, could not ignore the widely disseminated desirability of American, and implicitly white and middle-class, femininity. The newspaper regularly published tips and essays about hair styles, makeup, and fashion associated with the West, and specifically with American femininity, even including sewing patterns for Western and American clothing. However, items explicitly associated with the Soviet Union or China rarely appeared. In the Cold War context where ideological subversion (i.e., communism) was closely associated with gender-sexual subversion (i.e., homosexuality), women of the left-labor were compelled to participate in the consumption and enactment of the American femininity, at least to a certain extent, to retain their own legitimacy.

Leftist Women, Jim Crow, and Discourses of Dangerous Others: Economic and Scientific Section and Cold War Containment

Nosaka's talk, as well as women unionists' active participation in labor struggles, did not go unnoticed by the American occupiers, especially by the Labor Division of the ESS, which viewed "labor education" as an important part of containment strategies. During the occupation, the Labor Division issued more than one hundred pamphlets, distributing them to the Japanese government, labor unions, and management sectors of industry. Similar to the CI&E's gender reform efforts, the ESS also used newspapers, radio, posters, lectures, films, plays, and so on to disseminate the occupiers' understanding of the place and function of labor.[57]

The ESS's containment strategy needs to be understood in relation to "reverse course" in occupation policies. SCAP interventions in labor movements between 1946 and 1952 illustrate the increasingly antilabor and anticommunist attitudes of the occupiers. As early as May 20, 1946, MacArthur spoke out against the relatively orderly and peaceful Food May Day that had taken place the day before, claiming that "the growing tendency toward mass violence and physical processes of intimidation, under organized leadership, present a grave menace to the future development of Japan." "Undisciplined elements," he declared, "constitute a menace not only to orderly government but to the basic purposes and security of the occupation itself." If the Japanese did not show "self-restraint," MacArthur warned, he "shall be forced to take the necessary steps to control and remedy such a deplorable situation."[58] MacArthur's statement was a sign of things to come. When union movements nationwide, in the process of converging as one, called a general strike for February 1, 1947, SCAP intervened, preventing it from occurring.

SCAP continued to tighten its grip on the left-labor front. In July 1948, it took away the rights of government workers and public employees—who constituted 40 percent of organized labor and were the most active faction in the labor movements—to strike and to bargain collectively. In 1949, the year of the Chinese revolution, SCAP issued the Dodge Line, a plan of economic retrenchment that immediately produced a massive number of layoffs. Government and industries used retrenchment policies to single out and fire active unionists and communist party members. Literally a million workers were laid off as a result. In 1950—the year the Korean War broke out and Cold War divisions became increasingly obvious—so too did SCAP's anticommunist and antilabor policies. In June, SCAP began a "Red Purge," expelling executive members of the Japan Communist Party and banning the publication of its official newspaper, *Akahata*. The Red Purge expanded to both the public and private sectors, driving communist party members and labor activists out of their work and unions.

SCAP's efforts at labor education reflect the containment contexts just described. *Minshushugi*, or *Primer of Democracy*, a two-part textbook published in 1948 and 1949 by the Education Ministry of Japan for secondary school students and adult education groups, was one instance of labor education. Before publication, it was carefully reviewed by various SCAP sections, including the CI&E and the ESS, with many of their suggestions incorporated into the final version.[59] It elaborates, among other things, a relation between labor and democracy that aimed to contain the left-labor front. Not only does it emphasize "industrial peace" and caution against "any collision of sentiments and political beliefs" between management and labor.[60] It defines communism as "dictatorship of the proletariat," even "absolutism," and therefore against "democracy."[61] Particularly salient in the *Primer*'s containment strategy is its construction of working-class population as immature and uneducated and thus in need of ideological guidance and protection. Labor unions should perform social and cultural functions so as to help its members "acquire culture and enlightenment which they could hardly hope to acquire individually" and to "prevent the atrophy of the intelligence and knowledge of laborers."[62] Education of workers is indeed crucial. Left alone, they would be manipulated by "undemocratic" forces:

If union members are not fully enlightened politically, a few persons with biased political thoughts and dictatorial methods are likely to gain control of the unions, exercise autocratic powers, and use the united power of the union to attain their own political ends. All of this is diametrically opposed to the basic aim of democratic labor unions. They should never permit themselves to be utilized as mere tools of a political party. Union members should constantly guard against these undemocratic tendencies.[63]

The theme of workers' ignorance is especially visible in the discussions of women. With women's increasing participation in work outside home, the *Primer* states, it is expected that women "participate in labor unions and improve their position by collective bargaining." However, at the moment, women tend to play minor roles in unions, primarily—echoing Katō Shizue's argument—because of their ignorance: "Generally speaking, utterances of women in labor unions tend to be extremely reserved, and few of them are selected as committee members or union officers. Presumably, this is partly due to the modest nature of Japanese women, and their insufficient consciousness as laborers, and partly due to the fact that they are unaccustomed to such activities." As soon as they "outgrow the past irrational traditions, become enlightened as human beings, and cultivate abilities and learning," the *Primer* continues, women would begin to play more significant parts. Women are to make distinct, even superior contributions to unions, the *Primer* argues, because women are inclined "to love peace and hate strife, and to value practical welfare and shun vain publicity."[64] Women are once again defined as the source of stability in postwar Japan.

Far from acknowledging the political agency of the working-class population in militant left-labor mobilization, the *Primer* presents working-class subjects as a whole as ignorant, irrational, and susceptible to communist propaganda, thereby justifying the need for their political (re)education. Working-class women are seen to be particularly uneducated, uninformed, and targets of communist manipulation. "Naturally" inclined to love peace and hate strife, women who behave radically and confrontationally in left-labor mobilizations are then not only incomprehensible, but unnatural and even deviant. Working-class women's reeducation then becomes absolutely necessary. They need to be taught not only the true meanings of labor and democracy, but should be disciplined to acquire proper femininity as well. Once (re)educated, working-class women, like their middle-class and elite counterparts, could contribute to the transformation of postwar Japan by applying their "natural" inclination to peace and harmony to the maintenance of industrial peace.

This understanding informed the ESS, especially Richard Deverall, the aggressively anticommunist chief of the Education Branch of the Labor

Section, in containment efforts vis-à-vis women of the left-labor front. Perceiving Japanese working women as lacking political agency, he promoted the kind of labor education that was simultaneously infantilizing and depoliticizing. Deverall's May 11, 1948 lecture, "Women and Labor Education," given to field representatives of the newly established Women's and Minor's Bureau (WMB) of the Labor Ministry, elaborated on the meanings and functions of labor unions for women, and suggested yet another set of educational "techniques" to be used to facilitate women's participation.[65] The lecture presents a fascinating case of the intersectionality of gender and class in Cold War containment, as it deploys discourses of indigenous male chauvinism and female oppressions to delegitimize and suppress the left-labor assertion for economic and class justice.

Deverall began his lecture with an anecdote about his visit to the home of a "liberal Japanese trade unionist." There he witnessed what he called a clear example of the continuing "feudalism" in postwar Japan. During dinner the conversation focused on labor and economic problems. However, the wife of the unionist did not speak a world. Concerned, Deverall turned to her and asked for her opinion. She simply blushed. Her husband explained that in Japan, women had no interest in labor or politics. To Deverall, the trade unionist's statement was nothing but "a grave manifestation of the feudalism of the Tokugawa Era" that continued to exist within the labor union movements: "Certainly it is a manifestation of the old-time feudalism when the men are happy to keep the women busy in their Women's Section learning about Tea Ceremony and Flower Arrangement." With this observation, Deverall went on to criticize women's sections within unions as yet another instance of Japanese male chauvinism. The existence of separate women's sections revealed the unacceptable "hypocrisy" of Japanese male unionists: "Many of the men who shout 'feudalistic' at their employer might well look in the mirror next time they say that, for they are to various degrees feudalistic in their thinking."[66]

Feudalism, Deverall continued, was found not only in Japan but also in the United States, for many American men were not free of "feudalistic understandings" of women, either. Thus, when Japanese women tried to obtain equality with men, they were "taking part in an international crusade," to which they were very likely to make a significant contribution. Women in Japan, to Deverall, "seem to be outstandingly democratic," as shown by their activities at home. He frequently "passed Japanese homes, late at night, and often heard the Okasan (mother) or the Obasan (grandmother) soundly chastising the husband for something he has done during the day." While "Japanese feudalism restricted women to the home, within the home there has been a good measure of democracy." Thus what women unionists should do is to "transfer the limited democracy of the home out onto the streets and

into the factory," and participate as "co-partners" in building a new democratic society.[67]

Yet Deverall noted a feeling of reservation or even indifference to union
movements among women workers: "How is this feeling (of indifference) to
be overcome? How can blushing girls in the factories be educated to the point
where they will appear at union meetings, argue with the men, and outvote
the men when the women know they are right?" The answer lay in transmitting the "techniques of democracy," a containment strategy widely used by
the CI&E women reformers in educating middle- and upper-class Japanese
women. As Deverall suggested, one way to facilitate women's participation
was "a discussion group"—"one of the finest devices developed through years
of democratic development in foreign countries." A small group of women,
not more than ten, would meet once a week, with one of them serving as the
chair. For each meeting, a topic could be chosen, studied, and presented, with
the chair asking each participant her opinions and thoughts. Held regularly,
this type of small group discussion "will in a few months train a small group
of women trade unionists."[68]

Another method Deverall espoused was "a small public speaking class."
Again, a group of women meeting regularly with the help of a manual of public
speech could learn this important skill. During the first several sessions, they
could discuss basic techniques: how to write a draft, how to stand and talk,
and so on. Then a topic would be assigned to each member, who would give
a three-minute practice talk in front of everybody else. Deverall gave a very
detailed scenario of such a session:

> Each girl must come prepared to make a three-minute speech
> on anything relating to the topic. Miss Sato is called upon by the
> Chairman, and after she has made her speech, the Chairman calls
> upon other members for criticism. One person says, "Miss Sato didn't
> look at us. She kept watching her notes." Another person says, "Why
> did Miss Sato keep twisting her fingers around her dress? It was very
> distracting." The next speaker is called upon, and after five or six
> speeches, followed by discussion, it is time to serve tea and assign
> topics for the next week.

Once women developed their skills, they could have a public speaking contest,
with each speaker given a topic several weeks in advance. It was important,
Deverall suggested, that "practical topics" were chosen, such as "What can we
do to kill the Black Market?" or "Does the Communist Party really represent
the workers of Japan?"[69]

Another equally useful technique, Deverall observed, would be "a labor
play": "The Japanese seem to have a genius for the dramatic art, and of the

sexes, the women seem to be better actors . . . and this in spite of the fact that Kabuki is strictly for men only!" Yet another technique "that should appeal to every Japanese woman for it involves painting and expressing ideas through pictures," was making posters. Since "Japanese women seem to have an especial flair for poster work," they could "make a valuable contribution by painting small educational posters for use within the plants," suggested Deverall. With such contributions, women would be appreciated as "good trade union members." These efforts would be further strengthened by a lecture series on "trade union problems," such as the Labor Standards Acts and unemployment compensation. Once again, Deverall provided specific instructions: "Each lecture should be given by a trade union official or a competent government official," and followed by discussions so that women would receive "further practice in speaking in public on trade union matters."[70]

Deverall's superficial understanding of gender issues, and his paternalistic and pedantic view of working women, ignored the active roles women were already playing in the left-labor movement. Importantly, his lecture began with the home—not the workplace, or marches and rallies, where women unionists joined in radical, even militant, actions. After figuratively putting women back to the domestic sphere, Deverall's talk simply followed the path set by the CI&E women reformers: Democracy meant discussion groups, small group speeches, and posters, not radical political action. His views on emancipating women by advocating their "equal participation" in unions went hand in hand with implicit efforts for their depoliticization and containment.

The triangulation of gender, race, and class was a distinctive feature in the ESS's containment narratives. The conflation of multiple categories of power is especially visible in the debates concerning women's sections, a working-class version of "women-only" sphere. As Gail Nomura documents, ESS personnel began to debate the meaning and function of women's sections as early as Fall 1947. In a memo dated October 3, Deverall presented his reasons for opposing the sections:

a. The position of women within the trade union movement is depressed because of the background of feudalism and repression of women's rights;

b. Male feudalism will continue unless something is done to shake the male society to its roots;

c. Women and men share the same rights and duties within the trade union. Therefore, I say that women and men should be united in their trade union work without any discrimination no matter how sweet-sounding the title.[71]

As far as he was concerned, maintaining a separate space for women within unions was "Jim Crowism."[72] Thus drawing an implicit connection between female and black others, both of whom were perceived as dangerous in Cold War culture, Deverall went on to accuse Weed and other women reformers in the CI&E of "speaking all over Japan endorsing indiscriminately anything with the label 'woman' or 'women's.'" Reform efforts that specifically focused on women, he argued, maintained the segregation of men and women and undermined democratization.[73]

Underneath the expressed concerns about "male feudalism" and "Jim Crow segregation" and implicit anxieties about female homosociality, however, was the far more pressing issue of political control. The women's sections

> operate on the local level to have youth meet in separate meetings, to have women meet in separate meetings and have the older men meet in their own meetings. With Communist infiltration into the Youth and/or Women Sections, and with this fractionalization of the local union, political control of the local level is made more difficult. . . . Any type of youth or women section which divides the membership on the local level should be condemned as feudalistic and anti-democratic.[74]

Many of the occupiers, including Deverall, believed that the youth and women's sections, both of which were very active in labor struggles, were filled with communists, and presented a serious problem to the occupation. Triply dangerous through the Cold War linking of leftist women, communist subversion, and sexual and racial anxieties, women's sections needed to be contained.

By using the term "Jim Crow" to highlight the feudalistic and anti-democratic nature of women's sections, however, Deverall inadvertently introduced an element of ambivalence to his anticommunist containment strategy. As pointed out by Penny Von Eschen and other scholars on the Cold War, Jim Crow was a salient, although extremely problematic, symbol in the postwar rivalry between the United States and the Soviet Union. Racial discrimination was the "Achilles heel in a propaganda battle with the Soviet Union for the allegiance of Africa and Asia"[75] for the United States. Indeed, racial inequalities in the United States were often cited by the communist nations "as an indication of the hypocrisy and failure of the American promise of freedom for all."[76] As a result, the U.S. government took limited steps to improve domestic race relations, including the dismantling of Jim Crow laws. "By ending 'Jim Crow,'" it was hoped, "the United States would improve its image in the world."[77] Yet, American leaders were never genuinely intent on eradicating racial discrimination, and inequalities persisted, making discrimination a salient issue domestically and internationally, as African American and other minority leaders continued to challenge the U.S. government's racist and undemocratic practices. In the Cold War United States, then, Jim Crow was both a symbol of the nation's racist past that had presumably been overcome, and also an uncomfortable reminder of continuing racial inequalities that undermined the U.S. claim to be the leader of the free world. Deverall's use of Jim Crow language as a Cold War containment strategy was therefore extremely precarious.

To control and depoliticize women of the left-labor front, the ESS Labor Division created a pamphlet titled "Women in Japanese Trade Unions," elaborating the changes believed necessary for the women's section. The pamphlet both critiqued existing practices of the women's section, and suggested new functions and roles. The women's sections "contain undemocratic features which tend to prevent or discourage women's participation in the general work of the union," including "constitutional provisions which make women's sections autonomous or semi-autonomous." Among women unionists, "autonomy has been wrongly identified with equality," leading to "objectionable practices" such as "separate voting for union leaders and on union issues, attendance only at separate meetings of women and non-attendance at general meetings of all union members, both at the local and national level."[78] Such practices needed to be eliminated, and the women's sections "should operate within the framework of the union as a whole."[79]

The "proper functions of women's section" involved "service to women," and the pamphlet specified four such functions. First and foremost was the "education of women for active and intelligent union participation." Echoing Deverall's lecture to the WMB representatives as well as the CI&E gender reform, the pamphlet noted the importance of providing women with information on parliamentary and bargaining procedures, and holding discussion and speech sessions.[80] Second, women's sections should "study the working conditions in their own plants and for women workers generally, and consider the special problems incidental to their employment," with the goal of the "improvement of working conditions for women." Male unionists should be included in these efforts so that men would understand the importance of taking women into consideration in union decision-making processes.[81] The third new function was "service with regard to 'off-the-job' problems." Juggling jobs and household duties was trying for working women. Thus women's sections "may sponsor classes and discussion groups on preparation of imported foods, how to vary food preparation (as in the case of green peas and sweet potatoes), how to utilize worn-out clothing for new purposes, how to care for children and similar practical problems." Finally, the women's sections should offer recreational activities, keeping "in mind what appeals to and reaches the largest number of its women unionists" and also that such activities should be "coordinated with the plans for the union as a whole." "If the women's sections do a good job in carrying out their service functions," the pamphlet concludes, "union women will be able to demonstrate their ability to union men in the meeting halls for all workers and prove the fact that they merit equal consideration."[82]

The timing of ESS interventions was significant. Disseminated to Japanese labor unions as part of the occupation's reverse course, ESS's "guidance" concerning the reform of women's sections coincided with massive layoffs that targeted women, and with antilabor and anticommunist policies pursued by SCAP and the Japanese government. This guidance—in actuality, an order— dealt a serious blow to women's sections. Many disappeared or reduced their status and functions to *Fujin Taisakubu*, or women's policy sections. Terribly shocked by the occupiers' interventions, women unionists were convinced that it was an attempt to curtail women's sections from becoming too active in the left-labor mobilization. Within the context of accelerating anticommunist and antilabor policies taken by Japanese and American authorities, the women's unionization rate began to decline. While more than half of working women were unionized in 1949, the percentage dropped to 37.9 percent in 1950, 37.4 percent in 1951, and 32.6 percent in 1952, leading to a political and economic displacement with serious consequences for working-class women's lives.[83]

Women's United Front and International Coalition Making

Japanese women of the left-labor front countered the occupiers' aggressive containment efforts by intensifying their own efforts to mobilize women, notably by attempting to create a women's united front. The formation of *Nihon Minshu Fujin Kyōgikai*, or *Minpukyō* (Japan Democratic Women's Council) in April 1948 was part of this effort. As I show in the next chapter, the council emerged from popular protest against indiscriminate round-ups of Japanese women conducted for the purpose of venereal disease control. A coalition of women's organizations including the Japan Communist Party, Sanbetsu and its affiliates, and Women's Democratic Club, among others, during its existence from 1948 to 1953, the council explicitly linked workplace and home. Not only working women, but housewives and mothers of working-class families were the target of the mobilization. Explicitly cross-ethnic and cross-national in its orientation, the council vehemently protested, for example, the treatment of Koreans in postwar Japan and the Korean War, and emphasized commonality and solidarity between Korean and Japanese women.[84] At its peak, forty-two organizations joined the women's council, pushing its membership to more than half a million. Reflecting the diverse nature of its constituencies, the council fought for a broad range of issues, from food prices, the distribution of rations, day care, and so on, to the economic rights of women and children, the Red Purge, war and peace, and international women's organizing efforts.

Fujinn Minshu Shinbun (Women's Democratic Newspaper), the official newspaper of the Women's Democratic Club, was particularly useful in the council's effort to build a women's united front. From Fall 1949 to Winter 1950, the newspaper functioned as the women's council's semiofficial organ, serving as a means of recruitment as well as communication. Both the council and the newspaper worked to forge connections with international women's organizations that were critical of postwar Western and especially U.S. international hegemony.

Despite their explicitly oppositional stance, however, neither the women's council nor the newspaper can be taken as the site of resistance performed completely outside the dominant apparatus of power, as they also participated in the hegemonic narratives of gender, sexuality, and nation. Born from protest mobilization against round-ups of Japanese women for venereal disease control, the council recirculated a gendered nationalist notion of "respectable" and "unrespectable" women. Insisting on the protection of respectable Japanese women, the council marginalized, and indeed stigmatized, poor working-class women who worked as prostitutes. Furthermore, the council's efforts to contest postwar U.S. imperial domination by building a coalition with other, especially Asian, women depended on a problematic assumption that Japanese women, having endured economic, political, and personal difficulties during and after the war, shared common experiences of oppression and victimization with other Asian women. Rarely were issues raised about Japanese women's direct and indirect involvement in Japan's colonial domination in Asia. Japanese leftist women's push for international commonality and solidarity as a way of resisting SCAP thus depended on the erasure of women's complicity in Japanese colonialism, the very same erasure American occupiers and Japanese middle-class women leaders were facilitating in their gender reform efforts.

The council's resistance strategies were often international in orientation as seen in its effort to reach out to the Women's International Democratic Federation (WIDF). The WIDF traced its origin to the Union des Femmes Françaises, a communist-dominated women's organization that had waged antifascist struggles during World War II. At a meeting in Paris shortly after the war, the union gave birth to the WIDF. Strongly procommunist, the WIDF claimed a membership of eight million women from fifty countries, and advocated fighting for democracy against fascism, and for gender equality and the welfare of mothers and children. A staunch supporter of anticolonial independence movements, it offered an explicit critique of Western, especially American, imperial domination. Japanese women of the left-labor front, and especially the women's council, quickly developed a relationship with the WIDF, with the Women's Democratic Newspaper informing the Japanese public about WIDF history, membership, and activities. The relationship developed between Japanese women of the left-labor front and the WIDF in explicit opposition to the U.S. occupiers' gender reform fits into the larger pattern of postwar international women's mobilization identified by Leila Rupp: "The cold war enveloped the world of international women's organization," and "rivalry between the two camps led to increased global organizing, especially as more and more countries fought for and won their independence from Western domination."[85] Occupied Japan became a major site for this rivalry. As discussed in Chapter 3, the WIDF's increasing influence among Japanese women alarmed the occupiers, prompting Weed to call the WIDF a "communist-backed" organization engaged in "undemocratic practices." During the Japanese women leaders' visit to the United States, Weed introduced the delegates to representatives at the UN as a way of countering the expanding WIDF influence.

The effect of Cold War international divisions on SCAP's policies toward women's organizations can be clearly observed in the controversy surrounding the annual International Women's Day celebration on March 8. Tracing its origin to socialist women's protest in the United States and Europe, and counting among its participants such notable figures as Clara Zetkin and Alexandra Kollontai, International Women's Day had had a historic association with the 1917 Russian Revolution. In postwar Japan, the International Women's Day celebration organized by a coalition of left-labor front women became an important site of resistance and protestation.[86] The Women's Democratic Newspaper reported on the history and significance of International Women's Day, especially its close association with socialist and working-class traditions. At the first postwar celebration in 1947, a thousand women showed up in front of the Imperial Palace, waving red flags, protesting existing economic and political conditions, condemning indiscriminate round-ups of women for venereal disease control, and calling for international women's solidarity.[87] At the second celebration, participants numbered more than five thousand.

Predictably, the annual celebration of International Women's Day soon met with objections from SCAP, and specifically from Weed. Under pressure from SCAP, the Japanese government tried to institute a Woman's Day on April 10, the day of women's enfranchisement granted by MacArthur. In protest, women of the left-labor front insisted on continuing to celebrate

International Women's Day on March 8. By the third celebration in 1949, SCAP interventions were explicit. Weed issued a statement calling the International Women's Day a "communist event," and discouraging women from participating.[88]

Leftist women's resistance strategy introduced a new figure into the gendered Cold War rivalry: Chinese women. The Women's Democratic Newspaper cast Chinese women as the model for Japanese women, challenging SCAP's gender reform that idealized American middle-class femininity. Yet, just as Nosaka's lecture on Soviet women held ambiguous implications, so did leftist women's deployment of Chinese women, as the very legitimacy and idealization of Chinese women hinged on their femininity and ability to speak in English as well as the adoration they inspired among Americans. The August 31, 1946, issue of the Women's Democratic Newspaper featured Chinese women. Since Japanese tended to imagine communists as "monsters," it was pointed out, highlighting these young Chinese women fighting for the causes of the Communist Party would help to dispel that myth. The young women were beautiful, cultured, and sophisticated, with excellent English-language skills. Although war conditions often forced them to hide in mountain caves, they never lost their femininity. Indeed, their refined self-presentations at one gathering were so impressive that an American reporter placed them on equal footing with New York socialites. While many of these women had originally been from "bourgeois" and "petit bourgeois" backgrounds, they had sacrificed their privileged lives for the sake of saving their nation during the war with Japan, and continued to be active "fighters" in the Communist Party.[89]

The communist revolution in China, and women's active participation in it, became important sources of inspiration for Japanese women of the left-labor front. The newspaper enthusiastically reported on major political changes in China, including conflicts between the Communist Party and the National People's Party,[90] the emancipation of Chinese women in the "liberated" (i.e., communist-controlled) areas,[91] a "nation-wide" women's meeting in the "liberated" area,[92] the birth of "New China,"[93] and the formation of a united women's front,[94] among others. Eyewitness accounts from Japanese women who had stayed on and continued to work in postwar and postrevolutionary China were also published.[95] Like Nosaka's portrayal of the Soviet Union, these accounts presented China as an ideal country where women had access to an abundance of food, clothes, and other materials, as well as various opportunities for work, education, culture, leisure, and politics. Gender equality was completely realized in postrevolutionary China, which was indeed a "ray of hope" in Asia where remilitarization and the possibilities of wars loomed large. In celebrating postrevolutionary China and Japanese women's "friendship" with Chinese people, however, these articles never mentioned the history of Japanese colonialism in China nor the problematic roles Japanese women had played during colonial rule.

Among the advocates of the New China, Miyamoto Yuriko—a well-known resistance writer, leading figure among women of the left-labor front, and wife of a leading Communist, Miyamoto Kenji—was a particularly subversive figure, not only because of her political and ideological opposition to the United States, but also because of her gender-sexual transgression. Born into an elite family in 1899, she had explicitly rejected her class privileges, becoming in her teens a writer for the poor and wretched.[96] After the dissolution of her first marriage, she had fallen in love with a woman, Yuasa Yoshiko, and in 1925 began to live with her. From 1927 to 1930, the two women stayed in the Soviet Union. Miyamoto's seven-year relation with Yuasa, a self-identified lesbian and scholar and translator of Russian literature, had been emotionally and intellectually intense. Not only had Yuasa introduced Miyamoto to Marxism, she had also "taught her uncompromisingly to reject bourgeois conventions, especially gender restrictions."[97] Upon their return to Japan in 1930, Miyamoto ended her relationship with Yuasa, and married Miyamoto Kenji. In prewar Japan, where the Communist Party was outlawed, her husband imprisoned, and literary expression severely censored, Miyamoto struggled to maintain her career as a Marxist resistance writer, until finally her publications were banned in 1941. With the end of the war, she reemerged as a vocal critic of the U.S. occupation, articulating alternative notions of gender and democracy, especially those found in China, until her untimely death in 1951.

Like Nosaka Ryō, Miyamoto Yuriko was often at loggerheads with Katō Shizue, particularly in their activities in the Women's Democratic Club. They flatly disagreed about the kind of "democracy" postwar Japan should pursue. Promoting the type found in the Soviet Union and among the Communist revolutionaries in China, Miyamoto castigated as anachronistic Katō's support of American-style democracy.[98]

The significance of China as a site of opposition, and of Miyamoto as a figure of resistance, became especially clear in the controversy surrounding an Asian Women's Conference organized by the WIDF in Beijing in 1949. The purpose of the conference was elaborated in the WIDF's invitation to Japanese women, the full text of which was published in two parts in the Women's Democratic Newspaper on July 16 and July 23, 1949. The impetus for the Conference came from the WIDF delegates' trip to South and Southeast Asia the year before, the invitation explained. The delegates witnessed Asian women's daily struggles against extreme poverty, and their lack of freedom under imperial domination. As an organization with a firm belief in the dignity of people regardless of their color, nationality, status, and creed, the WIDF proposed the Asian Women's Conference to support Asian women's struggles against the "slave like" conditions under which Asian women and children were forced to live. The meeting would address three major issues: (a) unity among Asian women, which in turn would lead to unity of women worldwide, in promoting democracy, freedom, and liberation from colonial subjugation; (b) women's rights; and (c) protection of children. The invitation called for forging an international alliance among women in the name of world peace.[99]

The Japan Democratic Women's Council immediately accepted the invitation, publishing its statement of acceptance. The council expressed a deep appreciation for the invitation; it provided great encouragement to the Japanese women, who were facing difficult struggles. In Japan, the reactionary government was driving workers out of their jobs, imposing low wages, and pushing the nation down the path toward war. The government was not fulfilling its obligation to provide decent education to children. With the legal guarantee of gender equality proving to be an empty promise, Japanese women were suffering enormously. Yet, they were determined to build a truly democratic country in postwar Japan. A massive labor offensive, led by the national union of railroad workers, was about to engulf Japan. People would surely overthrow the government and achieve "victory," and Japanese women were an indispensable part of this labor offensive, ready to fight for the cause of democracy. The WIDF's invitation to the Asian Women's Conference strengthened the resolve of the Japanese women.[100]

The conference began on December 10, 1949, in postrevolutionary Beijing. The 159 delegates attending the conference included representatives from fifteen Asian countries. However, SCAP and the Japanese government prevented Japanese women from attending. Ever defiant, Japanese women held their own conference in Tokyo on December 16 and 17, in solidarity with the women gathered in Beijing. A wireless message was sent to congratulate the women at the Beijing conference, and the WIDF sent a report to the council, providing detailed information about the conference proceedings. The Women's Democratic Newspaper not only printed this on January 27, 1950, but it also published several articles covering the conference.

The Asian Women's Conference was about creating an international solidarity among women against postwar American hegemony. The meanings of democracy, freedom, and women's liberation articulated by the conference organizers were explicitly opposed to American discourses. Far from being the leader of the free world, the United States was criticized as an imperial power, creating problems in women's lives everywhere. By reaching out to Chinese women, as well as the WIDF, Japanese leftist women were obviously challenging the American operations in Japan. Overt and covert protests by the women's council and newspaper did not stop there. On February 3, 1950, in the midst of an increasingly explicit anticommunist climate, the newspaper published on its front page an exchange of letters between Miyamoto Yuriko and Sung Qing Ling, a revolutionary leader, a widow of Sun Yat-Sen, and later the honorary chairwoman of the People's Republic of China. Characterized as "letters of friendship" that would build a bridge between China and Japan, the exchange was initiated by the newspaper, which had asked Miyamoto to write a letter of congratulations to Sung for the successful revolution in China. One of the topics discussed was the Asian Women's Conference.

Dated December 9, 1949, Miyamoto's letter began with a brief reflection on the significance of the twentieth century, a testament to the victory of "human rationality." In 1917, a revolution established the socialist regime in Russia; the Soviet Union was now the "leading force in human history" and "guardian of world peace." After being devastated by imperialism and fascism, Eastern European nations were building populist societies as well, based on the principles of ethnic autonomy and people's welfare. Finally, in 1950, with the birth of the People's Republic of China, a new chapter in the history of Asia opened, providing an inspiration for those fighting the forces of oppression. Calling Sung "*kakumei no haha* (the mother of revolution)," Miyamoto conveyed her sincere congratulations for the successful revolution in China, and shared her joy and anticipation for the coming year.

Miyamoto also reflected on the numerous sacrifices made by revolutionary leaders in China. Japanese imperialism, Miyamoto lamented, had been nothing but the worst kind of obstacle to the liberation of China. Yet, this allusion to Japan's colonial exploitation was immediately replaced by her concern over the difficult lives that the Japanese were now leading. She was sure that people in China would see that Japanese postwar imperialism was now destroying the lives of Japanese people themselves. Freedom of speech was suppressed, the working-class population oppressed, and democratic development obstructed. She was not even sure if the Japanese government would allow women delegates to attend the upcoming Asian Women's Conference in Beijing, which was scheduled to start in a few days. Despite these obstacles, Miyamoto assured Sung of the Japanese people's continuing commitment to world peace.

Sung's reply, dated January 5, 1950, was encouraging and sympathetic in its tone, never mentioning the Japanese colonial atrocities in China that Miyamoto had alluded to and Sung had known too well. Instead, she referred to the contributions "progressive" Japanese had made during the revolutionary struggles, which resulted in the establishment of the Republic of China in 1911. Sung assured Miyamoto that Chinese women were strong supporters of the Japanese who were fighting for democracy and liberation. Chinese women had a deep sympathy for the difficult circumstances the Japanese were facing, but at the same time were more than confident about the successful outcome of the Japanese struggles toward democracy.

Sung's belief in the eventual "victory of democracy"—in Japan and elsewhere—came from her observations at the Asian Women's Conference, which held international and historical significance, Sung reported to Miyamoto. The women delegates were able to engage in free, thoughtful, and thorough exchanges, and to encourage and learn from each other. As a result, a firm and unshakable unity emerged. All shared the will to oppose imperialist wars, bring eternal peace to the world, and emancipate colonized populations. With much enthusiasm, Sung stated that their efforts were casting a bright light on the future, guiding all to a complete victory.[101]

Following the exchange of letters between Sung and Miyamoto, the women's united front continued to issue a passionate call for the "victory of democracy," tenaciously reaching out to international women's organizing efforts. However, the front could not effectively counter such containment efforts by the American occupation forces as the dissolution of women's sections within the unions, mass layoffs of women workers, and the Red Purge. The anticommunist hysteria that swept through occupied Japan resulted in growing tension among members of the women's council, which severed its ties to the Women's Democratic Newspaper. To make matters worse, the women's united front also suffered the loss of its leaders. In 1951, a year after her exchange with Sung Qing Ling, Miyamoto Yuriko suddenly passed away, and Nosaya Ryō and other leaders were ousted in the Red Purge. The economic and political dispossession of working women pursued during the occupation had serious consequences. As discussed in the next chapter, disenfranchised poor women, with no means to support themselves, turned to prostitution for survival, leading to an epidemic of venereal disease. In this process, a new sexual regime emerged, rendering working-class women's bodies and sexuality as a focal site of Cold War containment politics.

This chapter's discussions provide a turbulent and unpredictable picture of domination and resistance in the Cold War politics of gender, race, class and sexuality. In postwar Japan, the conflation of multiple categories of power differently informed the occupiers' containment and the left-labor front's resistance discourses. Calling a woman's section in a union an instance of Jim Crow segregation and thereby marking leftist women as dangerous others, the ESS tried to contain and depoliticize the radical mobilization of women workers. Yet Jim Crow was at best an ambivalent symbol of American race relations, thus introducing instability to the occupiers' claim as democratic reformers. While the Cold War divisions sparked a radical mobilization of leftist women, their deployment of Soviet and Chinese women as the countericons to American femininity was equally ambiguous. Discourses of solidarity between Japanese and Chinese women depended on the erasure of racial and colonial hierarchies between the two nations, and the narratives of Soviet and Chinese women's emancipation often reinforced, rather than challenged, the Cold War heteronormativity. In the Cold War context, then, the meanings and consequences of resistance were less than fixed, blurring the boundary between domination and contestation in leftist women's politics.

5

Making the Body Respectable

Cold War Containment and Regulation of Sexuality

On December 4, 1948, Colonel D. D. Martin, together with several other colonels and a Signal Corps photographer, visited the Eighth Army Replacement Training Center in Atsugi. The purpose of the visit was to inspect a "medical museum" established to provide "venereal disease control instructions" to American soldiers, whose high infection rate had become a serious problem. At the museum, the visiting colonels were presented with the "venereal disease materials," including "a life size cardboard model of prostitutes," a "comic strip," "wax models" of infected bodies, "a chart showing the ABC's of VD control," and "a series of drawings for instruction in the use of preventive measures." Pictures and models were "not of the museum of horror type," Colonel Martin noted, and care was taken so that "the wax models show only infected areas . . . and the card board prostitute does not portray an alluring, romantic, or beautiful subject." The visiting colonels were quite impressed by the "ingenuity" shown by the officers who had created these materials. Equally impressive was the method of instruction. Captain J. Rutkin acted out "a step-by-step procedure to be followed by company officers in presenting venereal disease materials to enlisted men." Since the presentation was given to just five people, the instruction was "quite personal." Because the session took place "on the country fair principle," a maximum of twenty-five men could be instructed per hour. The men's access to the models was carefully monitored. They were instructed to "come forward and see details shown on the model," but "unsupervised examination" was to be avoided. The visiting colonels found the instructional materials and methods to be extremely useful, and Colonel Martin strongly recommended their duplication and distribution to all unit and detachment commanders in the Far East command.[1]

Venereal disease in occupied Japan posed an extremely serious problem. As soon as the occupation forces landed in 1945, sexual encounters took place between American soldiers and Japanese women, and the quick spread of venereal disease followed. "[F]irst, in the typhus epidemic and later by the appearance of cholera among Japanese repatriates," American forces faced an "extremely serious and potential health menace," but venereal disease was considered a far more serious and immediate threat.[2] The authorities' understandings of the problem were deeply informed by Cold War gender, sexual, and class dynamics: Japanese working-class women who were marked as "deviant" and "dangerous" due to their militant labor activism were considered the primary source of this "menace," as their allegedly unruly, uncontrollable sexuality threatened both American and Japanese authorities and jeopardized the success of the occupation. No less problematic were diseased American soldiers, whose bodies signified not simply medical conditions in need of treatment, but weakness, mental degeneracy, and the susceptibility to communist manipulation. In the course of the occupation, military, religious, and medical institutions, among others, were deployed to regulate, contain, and rehabilitate the sexuality of American soldiers and Japanese women.

This chapter examines the politics of sexuality that evolved in U.S.-occupied Japan. That venereal disease became such an urgent issue—an epidemic considered far more serious than any other health menace—had much to do with the Cold War understanding of venereal disease as not simply a public health issue but a threat to national security, the American way of life, and ultimately democracy.[3] Cold War historians have documented the postwar U.S. reliance on "a quasi-medical metaphor," especially a language of epidemic and disease, to express its fears and anxieties about communism, the containment of which was often analogized to the containment of disease. As early as 1946, containment policy was articulated in terms of "counter-epidemic" strategies. Communism was a "disease," a "dangerous pathology," and a "political virus." If unchecked, it would break out and endanger national security and democracy.[4] Venereal disease proved to be a particularly potent metaphor in anticommunist rhetoric. In a 1951 article in the *Journal of Social Hygiene*, Elaine Tyler May documents, Harvard physician Charles Walter Clarke described the social and moral chaos that would follow an atomic bomb explosion. An atomic attack would break down family and community life, leading to widespread moral chaos and sexual promiscuity, and to a thousand percent increase in venereal disease. To cope with this horrific scenario, Clarke called for "vigorous repression of prostitution," "measures to discourage promiscuity," and the stockpiling of penicillin.[5] The Cold War link among venereal disease, morality, and communism constituted a salient feature in U.S.-occupied Japan, mobilizing a wide range of discursive and material resources to control and contain sexuality. Despite the heavy-handed nature of sexual regulation imposed by the occupiers, however, sexual containment efforts constantly "leaked," leading to numerous conflicts and contradictions among the occupiers and resistance and subversion by the occupied.

The proliferation of sexual discourses and practices in occupied Japan supports Foucault's exposition of sexuality as generating "an institutional incitement to speak about it," and "a determination on the part of the agencies of power to hear it spoken about, and to cause it to speak through explicit articulation and endlessly accumulated details."[6] Sexuality mobilizes an array of institutions (medical, criminal justice, religious, psychiatric, etc.) and incites new practices and technologies to count, classify, manage, administer, and discipline sexualized bodies.[7] This productive aspect of sexuality is an obvious, although underexamined feature of the occupation, as concerns about venereal disease mobilized various sections of the occupation forces and set in motion a proliferation of endless and detailed talks about sexuality, body, and disease. Equally important, the controversy also generated a series of sexual discourses and practices among the Japanese. Japanese men vehemently opposed the indiscriminate round-ups of women for medical examination, protesting the occupiers' (i.e., foreign) control over female sexuality as a challenge to their (i.e., Japanese) patriarchal and national prerogative to own their women. Japanese women, especially feminist leaders, criticized the occupiers' sexual regulation in the name of women's rights, but they also condemned Japanese male inability to protect women. Together, Japanese male and female leaders demanded stricter control over "fallen" and "unrespectable" women as a way of rebuilding the new nation. In occupied Japan, the controversies over disease and sexuality constituted an iconic space where dynamic convergence of feminism and nationalism occurred within the context of Cold War.

More specifically, the controversy generated several competing discourses and practices concerning disease, sexuality, and democracy. Constructing infected Japanese women as "criminals," the American military command conducted indiscriminate round-ups and forced medical examinations, drawing strong protests not only from Japanese men and women, but also from SCAP's CI&E and GS. Sharply disagreeing with the military command, the Public Health and Welfare Section (PHW) framed the issue in medical terms, defining infected women as "patients," criticizing the lack of coordination among the agencies involved in venereal disease control, and accusing the military authorities of creating chaos through their indiscriminate round-ups. Expressing severe anxieties about American masculinity, the military chaplains' organization framed the issue in moral and religious terms. Venereal disease was "a symptom of character breakdown"; the soldiers' moral, spiritual, and physical degeneration was at the core of the problem. This lack of self-discipline, they argued, would lead to the failure of "democracy" in Japan and elsewhere. The chaplains suggested a series of disciplinary measures, or "character guidance," intended to rehabilitate American masculinity. More than any other aspect of the occupation examined in this book, the controversies surrounding venereal disease starkly reveal the incoherent and internally divided nature of American hegemony in postwar Japan.

The productive nature of sexuality is also seen in an extremely active form of feminist mobilization spurred by sexual controversies.[8] Often exceeding the American and Japanese authorities in zeal and intensity, Japanese women leaders debated the nature of sexuality, morality, and national identity. The intersection of gender, race, class, and nation informed women leaders' simultaneous resistance against and participation in sexual containment politics. Empowered under the guidance of the CI&E, Japanese middle-class women fiercely protested the indiscriminate round-up of "innocent" women, insisting on the racial and sexual purity and respectability of middle-class wives and mothers and criticizing the "undemocratic" nature of the occupiers' sexual regulation. Women of the left-labor front whose sexuality was often suspect in the Cold War context joined middle-class women leaders and insisted on their own respectability. Together they demanded that the occupiers observe a preexisting nationalist distinction between respectable and unrespectable women and called for stricter surveillance and regulation of "fallen women" as part of the effort to build the New Japan. Protest mobilization became a crucial political space where women leaders insisted on Japanese racial and national respectability in the emerging Cold War context and thereby articulated a vital link among postwar feminism, nationalism, and containment politics.

Throughout the occupation, sexual encounters between American soldiers and Japanese women constituted a source of disturbance and disorder that seriously challenged and destabilized American containment efforts.[9] Most important, the controversy calls into question a gendered understanding of the occupation as a heterosexual encounter between a masculine and dominant United States and a feminine and subordinate Japan, a notion widely shared by occupiers then and recirculated by scholars until now.[10] Rather than a stable symbol of postwar U.S. domination, I argue, American masculinity became a source of ambivalence and anxiety, and far from reflecting the subordinate status of a defeated nation, Japanese femininity—of those who were infected with venereal disease as well as those who challenged the occupiers' sexual regulation—became a "menace" that threatened the occupation's success. The occupation's sexual encounter thus urges us to go beyond the well-accepted binary framework of masculine domination and feminine subordination in analyzing imperialism and to examine the far more precarious and unpredictable process of imperial encounter in which the female or feminine functions as a source of instability and disorder.

Defending the National Body Against the Foreign Menace: Recreation and Amusement Association

From the outset of the occupation, sexuality, together with gender and race, informed the nature of U.S.–Japan encounters. For the Americans, the defeated country was often imagined as a playing field for sexual conquest and the possession of indigenous women of color. For the Japanese, the arrival of foreign soldiers was an immediate threat, certain to violate the purity of their daughters, wives, and mothers, who represented the racial and sexual purity and respectability of the national body. This concern led to a number of gendered and classed strategies aimed at nationalist defense, most famously the establishment of the Recreation and Amusement Association (RAA), which is well documented by historians of the occupation.[11] As the American occupation forces began to arrive, the Japanese were immediately concerned with the protection of respectable women from foreign male sexuality. Precautionary measures included demanding that women stay home and not go outside, avoid places where they would run into American soldiers, and stay with Japanese men so that they could be protected.

Japanese authorities wasted no time in instigating measures to protect respectable women from the "foreign menace." Only three days after the surrender, the Home Ministry sent a wireless message to prefectural authorities, directing them to set up "comfort facilities" that would provide sex, food, and other recreational services to American soldiers. At the Cabinet meeting on August 21, 1945, Vice Premier Prince Konoe insisted that Japanese women had to be protected from American soldiers. He sought out the Chief Commissioner of the Metropolitan Police, begging him to protect "Japanese daughters" at any cost. Collaboration between government authorities and the sex industries led to a plan to deploy women already in the sex and entertainment industries, along with new recruits. Advertisements for "New Japanese women" were placed on the streets and even in newspapers. The ads sought "female clerks," age 18 to 25, to provide comfort for American soldiers. In war-devastated Japan, with acute shortages of the most basic necessities, the material incentives were high: food, clothing, and shelter for women recruited into the RAA. Japanese women of lower class backgrounds, with no economic options, became "expendable women" who could be sacrificed for the protection of respectable women in the name of nationalism. The classed nature of this sexual mobilization is also seen in the medium of recruitment. Following a pre-1945 practice, "labor suppliers," with a free pass for transportation issued by the police, played a prominent role in recruiting women. Among them were young women—high school students—who had been working as the Women's Volunteer Corps at munition factories during the war.[12]

The inauguration of the government-sponsored brothel project, the RAA, took place on August 28, 1945, in front of the Imperial Palace. The inaugural statement was an example of "fantastic conflation" of multiple vectors of power that articulated the significancde of the RAA at the intersection of gender, race, class, sexuality and nation. The RAA's central mission was to protect the "*junketsu* (purity) of the Japanese race" and to "contribute to the maintenance of the national polity" by protecting respectable women. The protection of these women from the hands of foreign male sexuality was defined as a "postwar emergency measure of national significance." To protect these respectable women who embodied the pure national and racial body, women recruited for the RAA—those from precarious economic backgrounds—would be sacrificed as *bōhatei*, or a human breakwater.[13] In defining the mission of the RAA, a language of racial purity and national body, long nurtured in Japanese colonial modernity, was redeployed as a nationalist protest against foreign invaders as well as a justification for exploiting poor women's sexuality. Class, racial, sexual, and national politics were simultaneously etched onto these women's bodies.

Yet, Japanese efforts to contain the foreign menace were never successful. The confluence of gender, race, sexuality, class, and nation observed in the RAA project was only temporary, immediately followed by their dispersal and a series of chaotic and often uncontainable dynamics. Venereal disease began to spread quickly among the American soldiers, and alarmed by the rate of infection, in March 1946, the occupation authorities declared RAA brothels off-limits. The women workers were literally thrown out into the streets. Many became street-walkers, or *panpan*, a derogatory term coined for women who sold their bodies to foreign soldiers in occupied Japan. Far from disappearing with the shutdown of the RAA, fraternization between American soldiers and Japanese women continued to flourish, and so did the problem of venereal disease infection. As the occupiers' sexual surveillance began to target not only lower but middle- and upper-class women, Japanese men and women began to mobilize, protesting the new sexual regime imposed by the occupiers and insisting on the boundary between respectable and unrespectable women. Occupied Japan witnessed a proliferation—indeed an explosion—of sexual discourses and practices among the occupiers and the occupied. In the emerging Cold War context, sexuality came to constitute "an especially dense transfer point for relations of power"[14] where gender, sexual, racial, class, national, and imperial politics converged to set in motion a series of political dynamics in occupied Japan: Imperial hegemony was contested by indigenous nationalism; white masculine domination was challenged by sexual transgression of colored women; national, racial, and class boundaries embodied by women were violated by foreign sexual interventions; and feminists' demands for female protection reinforced, rather than challenged, national, racial, and class hierarchies.

Character Guidance and the Making of a Citizen Soldier: Military Chaplains and Rehabilitation of American Masculinity

The controversy surrounding sexuality and venereal disease consumed an extraordinary amount of the American authorities' time, energy, and resources. Unlike other reforms targeting women, many high-ranking male occupiers were involved in this controversy. As early as October 16, 1945, an ordinance was issued, directing the Japanese government to designate syphilis, gonorrhea, and chancroid as infectious diseases. Cases had to be identified by name, age, and sex, and the full address of infected individuals had to be obtained. Hospitals, clinics, and laboratory facilities, personnel and equipment were to be mobilized, and uniform technical and administrative standards were to be established for medical operations concerning venereal disease.[15]

This was just the first step. The occupation authority went on to officially end the existing system of licensed prostitution in Japan. It directed the Japanese government to "abrogate and annul all laws, ordinances and other enactments which directly or indirectly authorize or permit the existence of licensed prostitution," and "nullify all contracts and agreements which have for their object the binding or committing, directly or indirectly, of any women to the practices of prostitution." The ordinance further stated that "licensed prostitution was in contravention of the ideals of democracy and inconsistent with the development of individual freedom."[16] To the American occupiers, the existence of licensed prostitution was a sign of Japan's "moral backwardness." Unlike the West, where prostitution was morally condemned, the occupiers argued, the East had customarily accepted prostitution without any moral concerns. As the occupiers understood the issue, Japan was a nation with sexual mores based on essentially different traditions, and venereal disease became a problem because the Americans, with a different—and superior—set of medical, moral, and ethical standards, arrived.[17]

The American military command perceived the quick spread of venereal disease as a serious menace to the health of the occupation forces. How to contain the proliferation of infection and how to rehabilitate physically and morally degenerate bodies were constantly debated. The Army Chaplains' Association, the PHW, the Provost Marshal and Military Police, and other occupation sections generated their own understandings of body, sexuality, and disease, and proposed competing strategies for containment.

The military chaplains' organization brought moral and religious discourse to the debate. Focusing first and foremost on the American soldiers' moral, spiritual, and physical regeneration, the chaplains' proposed disciplinary measures included religious counseling and athletic training. On the one hand, this repeated familiar discourses and practices already in place. As Allan Brandt documents, numerous efforts had been made to control the sexuality of the American soldiers since the end of the nineteenth century, often using religious discourses and articulating the need for sexual control in relation to family, nation, and democracy.[18] Moral and spiritual education, combined with athletic training, had constituted a central method for rehabilitation. The arguments presented by the chaplains, and the methods taken in occupied Japan, echoed and sometimes literally repeated these preexisting discourses and practices.

At the same time, the postwar U.S. military faced a new set of medical, cultural, and political imperatives. The discovery of penicillin as an effective cure for venereal disease contributed to an increase in public concern about sexual morality. Once the danger of venereal disease abated, it was feared that "a moral debacle" would ensue, leading to the spread of sexual promiscuity. In response, a renewed emphasis was put on self-discipline among the soldiers, and "character guidance" became a primary method for venereal disease control.[19] In the emerging Cold War context, moreover, sexual and moral issues were understood in political terms, as containment narratives made a clear connection among venereal disease infection, sexual and moral laxity, communist menace, and American national (in)security. Providing proper discipline and guidance to the soldiers was nothing short of a security issue, since its failure would jeopardize American democracy.

In occupied Japan, the preexisting understandings of sexuality and morality were being reconfigured within the Cold War containment context, mobilizing diverse and otherwise unrelated discourses and knitting them together to produce hegemonic understanding that linked sexuality, body, religion, nation, and anticommunism. As early as December 1945, chaplains in the Tokyo-Yokohama area held a meeting to discuss strategies to deal with problems of "sexual promiscuity." In a memo submitted to MacArthur in January 1946, the chaplains expressed concern about the "moral degradation" caused by Japanese prostitutes, which was "exceptionally widespread and unusually ruinous to the character of American troops."[20] American masculinity was in crisis. How to regulate and rehabilitate it was the primary focus of the debate.

The chaplains made a number of recommendations. At the top of the list was "moral education": "In view of the present serious threat to the moral and spiritual well-being of the U.S. Occupation Forces, further attention to moral education should be given." "Sex Morality Lectures" were recommended. Chaplains were to lecture "not only against prostitution but also on the responsibilities and problems of marriage."[21] Also recommended was an increase in efforts to offer "an athletic and recreational program," since "the lack of decent diversion is in part responsible for the moral problem." The chaplains' involvement in sexual regulation of the soldiers was further articulated in relation to their mission to God. It was argued that "their responsibility to God, to the members of the armed forces and to the families of military personnel compel them to seek immediate and drastic action to reverse the trends to sexual promiscuity."[22]

The chaplains' arguments clearly reflected an important link among masculinity, marriage, sexual regulation, and national defense. As Elaine Tyler May suggests, this discursive connection was an important feature of the Cold War containment culture:

> National strength depended upon the ability of strong, manly men to stand up against communist threats. It was not simply a matter of general weakness leading to a soft foreign policy; rather sexual excess or degeneracy would make individuals an easy prey for communist tactics. According to the common wisdom of the time, "normal" heterosexual behavior culminating in marriage represented "maturity" and "responsibility"; therefore, those who were "deviant" were, by definition, irresponsible, immature, and weak. It followed that men who were slaves to their passions could easily be duped by seductive women who worked for the communists. Even worse were the "perverts" who, presumably, had no masculine backbone.[23]

Given this understanding, it is no surprise that disciplining American masculinity became an urgent security issue in occupied Japan.

The problem's urgency led to the establishment of the Venereal Disease Council in December 1946, and the General Headquarters Character Guidance Council in August 1948. The membership of these councils consisted of the Assistant Chief of Staff, the Surgeon, the Inspector General, the Special Service Officer, the Provost Martial, and the Chief of PHW, as well as chaplains who were given central roles. The council was to provide educational and religious activities as a way of containing venereal disease and rehabilitating immoral, deviant sexuality among the soldiers.

In his report, Chaplain (Captain) Primus Bennett propounded the meanings of the sexual and moral regulations of the soldiers and the roles the chaplains were to play. More than anything else, he emphasized the significance of male self-discipline and control as a method of Cold War containment. "Venereal disease control is ultimately a matter of character and life attitudes on the part of the individual," Bennett argued, so rather than imposing rules and regulations, it is more effective to draw on "the inner control within a man's heart," through "citizenship and morality lectures."[24] The ultimate objective was the internalization of discipline. "Self-discipline," the chaplain stated, "must always spring forth from a vast depth of self-respect and personal worth properly related and directed toward goals worthy of a man's best." Each soldier "should be treated as a man who can be trusted with the important task of managing himself honorably. He must be taught to understand the benefits to be derived from a life of self-discipline and proper control." One method of nurturing self-discipline was "an individual orientation interview" by chaplains with newly enlisted soldiers. In each interview, the chaplains "should discover the man's personal background, which contributed so much to the present life attitudes he maintains" and also "something of the man's present character, life attitudes and future hopes and goals."[25]

The chaplains' discourses of sexual and moral discipline were further articulated in relation to postwar male citizenry and anticommunism. The chaplains were responsible for exerting "the constructive influences of the home, the church, the school, and normal wholesome community influences," as a way of inculcating "democratic standards of character and morals" among the soldiers. The Cold War link among sexual morality, the responsibility of citizen soldiers, and democracy was obvious in the following statement by Bennett: "A citizen's greatest contribution to a democracy is himself in terms of good moral character, attitudes deeply concerned with aiding the common welfare. Since service in the army is a service to his country, the citizen soldier should render his service as an expression of his solemn citizenship obligation to his country." Within this context, the Army "must become the greatest *character building* organization and citizen-making institution in the world." Otherwise, "democracy will fail." Venereal disease, "a symptom of character breakdown, the absence of self-discipline and self control on the part of the citizen," was thus nothing less than a threat to democracy.[26]

Bennett proposed the establishment of "religious centers" where soldiers could be given moral and spiritual guidance. With such facilities, the Army would become "a school for the further training of its country's citizens in the responsibilities of citizenship" by offering help in developing "the inner man" and "vitally touch(ing) his spirit, attitudes and objectives." In other words, the Army "should be a training school in the arts of democracy." As he argued, defense of democracy had a particular urgency as the United States entered a new era: "There never was a more crucial time in the life of our nation for men grounded in character and strongly motivated for great living on the plane of high moral standards. The goal sought in the measures proclaimed above is one of training in the moral and ethical aspects of good citizenship."[27] By the time this memo was written in December 1947, occupied Japan had witnessed a failed February 1 general strike and other instances of massive mobilization of the left-labor front under communist leadership. Cold War conflicts were becoming increasingly visible, within and outside Japan. His call for morally grounded men who could cope with the "crucial time" faced by the nation cannot be read without considering such new geopolitical conditions.

Anxieties surrounding American masculinity were pervasive, leading to a further proliferation of sexual discourses and practices and creating an all-male sphere where issues of sex and sexuality were incessantly elaborated and where male bodies were constantly scrutinized. At the Eighth Army Replacement Training Center in Atsugi where the medical museum was established, enlisted men infected with venereal disease were encouraged to talk about sex as part of their "venereal disease training." Quarantined for treatment, venereal disease trainees were required to attend lectures on citizenship and morality and to engage in a personal interview with chaplains to provide detailed accounts of their sexuality. The fifteen-minute interview consisted of two parts. First, trainees were to respond to the chaplains' questions concerning drinking habits, first sexual experiences, sexual activities with Japanese women, use of prophylaxis, knowledge of sexuality, types and frequencies of infection, and record of court-martial, among other things. In the second part of the interview the chaplains offered religious and moral instructions.[28]

Sexual regulation demanded not only discursive but physical engagement of the soldiers. Similar to the CI&E's gender reform where Japanese middle-class women were required to enact the notion of democracy, Cold War sexual containment of American servicemen called for their bodily mobilization. One such effort, Special Services, aimed at (re)building the physical, mental, and moral health of the soldiers. Participation was voluntary, and the program was not defined as venereal disease control, pursuing instead "the more positive goal of providing wholesome leisure time activity." The program's primary concern was "providing a healthy, normal outlet for socially desirable basic urges," rather than "sublimat(ing) undesirable" ones.[29] Special Services' multifaceted activities were intended to "help the individual regenerate his wholesome instincts" by appealing to his "repentant nature."[30] For example, at craft shops, participants could make signs portraying a "typical American soldier, posted near the gate, with a motto emphasizing individual's responsibility as an ambassador of the U.S." or a "chart depicting unit disciplinary and venereal rates."[31] Craft shops could also be put to use for "beautification plans of units." Alternatively, an "advisory committee" could be formed to "take positive action in arranging or arousing wholesome interests in all unit personnel."[32] Athletics and other recreational programs were strongly recommended. Free time, especially after dark, was the soldiers' "bewitching time," "a vulnerable period for gratification of basic desires," and measures were needed to "guide their course toward wholesome terminals."[33] Athletic activities in which the entire command could partici-pate were particularly recommended. After all, "too many Army athletes are poorly conditioned." To provide incentives, "progress charts" were to be maintained, "indicating sports qualifications and progressive achievement in basic physical fitness tests such as chinning, high jumping, running, broad-jumping, push-ups, etc."[34]

The controversies surrounding venereal disease control indicate that American masculinity was never a stable symbol of postwar U.S. domination. In the context of Cold War containment where a healthy male body was a sign of national strength, the spread of venereal disease among the American soldiers was nothing short of a crisis in national security. The sexual panic led to programs intended to restore moral, spiritual, and physical health, which in the process placed the American soldiers under heavy regulation and surveillance designed to control body and mind and compelled the occu-piers' anxious reiterations of masculinity, morality, and nationhood. A Cold War containment strategy that intended to restore the normative sexuality and masculinity ironically resulted in a formation of all-male homosocial sphere where soldiers and chaplains engaged in incessant talks about male sexuality and constant observations of male body, thereby disturbing from within the heterosexual and familial order that was considered critical in the defense of American democracy against communism. Far from becoming a regenerative site of American masculinity in crisis, occupied (and feminized) Japan disturbed the meanings of white male body and sexuality and postwar US domination.

Military Commands, Indiscriminate Round-Ups, and the Politics of Respectability

In the course of sexual controversies, the U.S. military command focused on what it considered the "real" source of the problem: Japanese women. Headquarters, Eighth Army dispatched a letter, "Venereal Disease Control," to the Commanding General, 24th Division, on July 21, 1947, clearly stating that infected Japanese women who solicited or had sexual intercourse with American soldiers committed crimes that threatened the security of the American forces, and the round-up of these "criminals," followed by enforced medical examinations, was necessary to ensure the "security" of U.S. military forces.[35]

At one level, round-ups were a class-specific containment strategy simultaneously informed by gender and sexual politics. The round-up of Japanese prostitutes—most of whom were working-class women—took place in the context of extremely active left-labor mobilization involving the radicalization of working-class women. Women of the left-labor front were doubly transgressing the postwar social orders the occupiers were trying to construct—on the labor front, by becoming active participants in the anti-imperial labor mobilization, and on the gender and sexuality front, by defying Cold War domestic femininity and even creating "women's sections," that is, women-only sphere, within unions. American and Japanese authorities' extraordinarily coercive, indeed violent, strategies of regulation involving working-class women need to be understood within this context.

Which women would become the target of this containment effort was a slippery question, however. The American occupiers often perceived the Japanese population *as a whole* as "an extremely large and virulent reservoir of venereal disease" or a "health menace" that posed a danger to the U.S. military command.[36] Carried out on the streets of Japan, the round-ups and enforced medical examinations ended up targeting any Japanese woman—not only prostitutes, but also housewives, students, and even women of the Diet. In the eyes of the Japanese, this American practice violated the sexually and racially pure Japanese women (i.e., middle- and upper-class women) who embodied the national respectability. The American infringement on the boundary between respectable and unrespectable women amounted to desecration of the nation and unleashed virulent Japanese protests. The protection of respectable Japanese women from violation by the American occupiers was the rallying call that mobilized a diverse array of individuals and organizations, including American women reformers and Japanese women leaders.

One well-documented instance of the round-up at Ikebukuro Station in Tokyo on November 15, 1946, sheds light on how the occupiers' sexual regulation facilitated cross-class feminist mobilization. At approximately 7 p.m., American military police, Japanese policemen, and interpreters detained women who happened to be around the station, including female workers on their way home from a union meeting. They were taken to Itabashi Police Station and subjected to questioning and harassment, then loaded into a truck and taken to Yoshiwara Hospital for internal medical examinations, during which the women were subjected to another series of demeaning remarks by Japanese doctors and police. Military police were also present in the examination rooms, causing the women further humiliation.

On release, the women union members took action, sending representatives to Katō Shizue and other women of the Diet. By then, these woman members of the Diet had heard numerous complaints from middle- and working-class women about indiscriminate round-ups. They turned to Weed and other women occupiers in the CI&E, which immediately began investigation, contacting other sections within SCAP. From late 1946 to early 1947, numerous interviews were conducted with Japanese women who had been subject to indiscriminate round-ups and internal examinations; records and memoranda were created based on these interviews and circulated among different sections within SCAP.[37] The connection thus forged among union women, middle-class women leaders, and American women occupiers provided a crucial political space in which Japanese women would articulate protests against indiscriminate round-ups by drawing on nationalist discourses of respectability, purity, and femininity.

The indiscriminate round-ups greatly mobilized Japanese civilians. After a period of waiting that allowed the CI&E to examine the "advisability" of a Japanese protest meeting, on December 15, 1946, organizations across the political spectrum held a major demonstration, "Rally to Protect Women." The two thousand participants ranged from conservatives to radical leftists, and represented both middle- and working-class organizations, including the Japan Socialist Party, the Japan Communist Party, the All Japan Congress of Industrial Unions, the All Japan Federation of Labor, the Women's Democratic Club, the Women Workers Union, the National Farmers Association, the Japan WCTU, and the Youth Communist Federation.[38]

Following the opening remarks, a chair, vice-chair, and secretaries were appointed, and women representing political parties, labor unions, and women's clubs and organizations made speeches. The rally targeted first the Japanese government and economic system, and in a more subdued way, the occupation authorities. A woman from the Japan Communist Party decried the wrongful arrest of poor women out to get food. A woman unionist noted that the poor wages paid to women demonstrated disrespect for women's right to live. Yet another argued that even though women's equality and freedom were nominally declared, in reality women suffered from discrimination. Together these women denounced the Japanese government and the police for treating working women as if they were streetwalkers, forcing them to undergo confinement and medical examination. Each speech was followed by the protest cry, "Down with the Yoshida Cabinet."[39]

The rally was carefully observed and recorded by an unidentified occupier. Ironically, the rally presented an occasion for judging whether the CI&E's efforts to transfer "techniques of democracy" to Japanese women were producing the intended results. The place was "over-crowded with many of the audience kept to stand," the occupier reported, and the two chair women—one for the morning session and the other for the afternoon—were both "tactful," with a mostly young audience "very eager and active in their discussion." All the speeches were brief, no more than three minutes, which she found "very effective." Furthermore, "making motions" and "discussions" were well carried out by women at the rally. Despite the protestors' critique toward the occupation, the rally became an occasion, at least for this occupier, to confirm the successful nature of the occupation.[40]

At the rally, Japanese women protestors presented a petition addressed to General MacArthur. Compared to their strong denunciation of the Yoshida government, their appeal to MacArthur was subdued. The petition began with an expression of gratitude for the occupation's effort to democratize Japan and emancipate its women, who appreciated the occupiers' "humanitarian action" that tried "to improve this sorrowful situation in Japan where patients of venereal disease and tuberculosis are increasing due to the incompetence of the Japanese government to cope with the war and its results." Despite the humanitarian intentions, however, the protestors pointed out, a difficulty had arisen. Utilizing Orientalist discourses of Japan and its "peculiarity" to their own ends, these women attributed this "difficulty" to the unique nature of the Japanese language, which was "so different from any European language." "Too much standardization" and "action without explanation" had led to "unexpected misunderstandings of each other" in the process of venereal disease control.

As the protestors argued, such misunderstandings led to dire consequences for Japanese women. The protest statement was couched in the discourses of respectability:

> This matter is of serious concern to society. Please consider and judge for yourself. What would you say if your innocent sisters or loved ones were caught in a net spread for social health and denied explanation, refused the validity of their identification cards, and taken to a certain place? Please consider and judge further. What feelings would you have if you had heard that these detained innocent girls were compelled to submit to a medical examination at a special hospital built for venereal examination of prostitutes! Not all women who have to walk on Broadway are prostitutes. Not all women who have to walk on the streets of Tokyo are prostitutes. Haven't the appearances of simple and respectable "office girls" been more lovely and ladylike than those of prostitutes who are the concubine of the rich?

The petition went on to explain the damage inflicted on "respectable" Japanese women by the round-ups and medical examinations. Central to their complaint was the violation of the innocent, virgin body of the respectable Japanese woman, and its consequences for marriage:

In Japan, a mere "excuse me" will not end the results of such sacrifice caused by too standardized methods. Call it feudalistic and lacking in sex education, but to the pure, young women, they being suspected as being prostitutes is a great shame to them, and furthermore, they practically hold their life in contempt for being subjected to compulsory medical examination. It will be a hindrance to their marriage.

Then the petition appealed to MacArthur on behalf of "all" Japanese women:

We, the women of all Japan, appeal to your good senses so that appropriate methods will be devised for a proper objective. . . . We are appealing to the good senses of all citizens of democratic nations who have brought a new century to Japan. Please do not forget the sagacious advice of your mother, your wife, your sisters, your daughters, when a measure is devised for the unfortunate Japanese women.[41]

Contrary to the concerns frequently expressed by the American occupiers that Japanese women would not comprehend "modern" notions such as democracy or women's rights, these ideas, along with notions of Japanese nationalism, gender, race, class, and sexuality, clearly informed this protest that targeted both the American and Japanese authorities. Like the RAA project, this protest critically hinged on and reemphasized a nationalist boundary between respectable middle- and working-class women, and unrespectable women who fell to the path of prostitution. Clearly, the politics of nation and sexuality were not exclusively a male domain, as Japanese women became deeply involved as well. It is from this rally that a women's united front—*Minpukyō*, or the Japan Democratic Women's Council—emerged, which went on to play a central role in mobilizing women of the left-labor front and protesting postwar U.S. domination, with complex and often ironic consequences discussed in Chapter 4.

Not only Japanese women protested the indiscriminate round-ups and enforced medical examinations; Japanese male authorities also objected, deploying the occupiers' discourses of democracy and Cold War alliance making to articulate their protests. In a meeting with Alfred Hussey, Chief Tanikawa of the Metropolitan Police Bureau was asked who had given the Japanese police orders to carry out the round-ups. Tanikawa stated that first verbal, and later written instructions, came from Major Smith of the Provost Marshal's office. Avoiding direct criticism of the military police, Tanikawa nonetheless noted that "a trained (Japanese) policeman can easily recognize a prostitute but the M.P.'s prefer making indiscriminate round-ups to distinguishing between possible street walkers and respectable women." He related an incident in which Japanese police protested the indiscriminate round-ups, and were prohibited by the military police from accompanying the women to the hospital. During one round-up, he pointed out, a Japanese woman who was with an American soldier was not detained.[42] The indiscriminate round-ups by the foreign military occupiers denied the authority of Japanese police on two levels: as state apparatus and as masculine authority. Tanikawa's statement was the protest about his deprivation of that authority and prerogative to control women's bodies and sexuality.

Japanese male criticism of the round-ups was expressed more directly in a 1948 petition by S. Yamashita, the Chief of the Liaison and Coordination Office in Ōita prefecture, located in southern Japan. Yamashita pointed out that the continuing and indiscriminate round-ups by the military police were creating enormous anxiety among the residents in Beppu City: "Parents and husbands are in an uneasy mind over their daughters and their wives, for their loved ones may at any time be subjected to ignominy and humiliation. Girls are in constant fear while outdoors lest an MP jeep may swoop upon them." He provided a list of "innocent women" who were wrongly arrested, including "a bride on honeymoon," "a housewife," and "a former schoolmistress." Then, he drew on the discourse of Cold War alliance making to further critique the occupation forces' conduct. People in Ōita were "united in their efforts to cultivate and consolidate U.S. friendship, not out of selfish consideration but purely out of deep gratitude and love" for the benefits the occupation forces had brought to Japan. However, while "Japanese friendship toward America is now fairly deep-rooted and would not be undermined easily," if nothing was done about the indiscriminate round-ups, they might "leave scars on the good relations" between the two countries, damaging "the cause of democracy" and even "the future friendship between the U.S.A. and this country."

"The basis of a true democracy to which the Occupation Forces are guiding Japan is regard for individual's rights," Yamashita pointed out, but those very rights were being violated by the military police, and people were accepting those violations with the same resignation they had shown during the days of militaristic domination:

> I am fully aware that the present situation is against the wish of the authorities of the Occupation Forces, for you yourself have on many occasions warned through my office against violations of individual rights on the part of Japanese police. . . . The situation has only been brought about by MPs' overzeal in carrying out their duties and by the lamentable manner on the part of MPs' interpreters. The Japanese Police are not wholly unblamable, for they are not unable [sic] to advise MPs more strongly.

As a solution, Yamashita suggested that Japanese police should be primarily responsible for "locating, questioning, and arresting" women, with the military police simply "supervising" and the interpreters just interpreting.[43]

Like his female counterparts' appeal to MacArthur, Yamashita's criticism did not challenge the premises, legitimacy, and purposes of the American occupation, as his protest was explicitly couched in the language of "alliance making," a crucial Cold War goal. However, his critique, like Tanikawa's, challenged the American authority in other ways, as it insisted on the notion of indigenous male control over female bodies. In his protest, the central concern was no longer the violation of the women's rights in the course of the round-ups. Instead, he was contesting which men—Japanese or American—would ultimately control Japanese women. In exchange for a successful partnership between the two nations, he was demanding the reinstatement of Japanese men (husbands, fathers, as well as male state authorities) as the rightful owners of Japanese women.[44]

Yamashita's report also reveals the class dynamics at work in the Japanese protests. Despite working-class women's insistence at the protest rally on their own respectability, their ambiguous, indeed precarious, location is revealed in a memo attached to Yamashita's petition:

All the working girls employed at restaurants, dance-halls, hotels, and other places of similar nature are regarded wholesale as prostitutes. . . . It is conceded that many girls of this class are of loose morals and may well be regarded as habitual prostitutes. But the majority are honest workers. It is, however, extremely hard even for well-experienced Japanese detectives to separate goats from sheep. . . . It is believed that many girls of this class are holding unexpressed grudges (caused by indiscriminate round-ups and internal medical examination), for among them there are honest daughters, widows and common-law wives of good citizens.[45]

Not only was working-class women's sexuality suspect, the memo argues, but even those who were not sexually promiscuous were potential problems because of their latent discontent vis-à-vis the occupiers. The alliance between middle- and working-class women in the course of sexual controversies would therefore be an unstable one. Middle-class women enjoyed an essentially unquestioned respectability, while their working-class counterparts' respectability was constantly suspect. The ambivalence surrounding working-class sexuality would soon generate yet another set of discourses and practices, with American and Japanese medical and public health authorities playing a central role in regulating and rehabilitating prostitutes as part of "the building up of new Japan." Despite their oppositions to SCAP, Japanese women leaders

became active participants in the sexual regulation of economically disenfranchised women, articulating a problematic link among nationalism, feminism, and Cold War containment politics.

Producing Democratic Bodies: Public Health, Prostitutes, and Cold War Sexual Containment

The PHW of the occupation forces, especially its Venereal Disease Control
Branch, invented its own set of strategies for venereal disease control. In
contrast to the chaplains' religious, moral, and therapeutic construction, and
the military command's "criminal" approach, the PHW cast the problem
in medical terms, defining Japanese women as "patients." By producing a
massive amount of data, statistical charts, memoranda, and summaries on
venereal disease control, the PHW contributed to a further proliferation of
sexual discourses and practices in occupied Japan. Their obsessive record-
keeping—with memoranda and papers all numerically ordered, identified
by date and brief description, and sorted by year—provided "evidence" for
the PHW's claim to be a modern, scientific organization practicing up-to-
date medical and scientific technology, further enhancing the American self-
understanding as modern, civilized, and thus superior.

The PHW's strong disagreement with indiscriminate round-ups and
explicit criticism toward the agencies involved shed light on the internally
divided and incoherent nature of American domination: "The problem
of prostitution as related to venereal disease control has been a source of
constant conflict between the Occupation Force Commanders and Public
Health and Welfare Section, SCAP, resulting in a lack of cooperation and
coordination in venereal disease control activities between these agencies."
This caused much confusion, and "hampered the proper implementation
and execution of the venereal disease control program, both at the national
and local levels."[46] Furthermore, "[t]he indignities forced upon these women
and the injustice done to them have given the venereal disease program a
black eye in the eyes of the public." The venereal disease hospitals to which
innocent women were forcibly taken were "jails, complete with barbed wire
fences, bars over windows, and police guards." Given this, "it is no wonder
that our efforts to induce the general public to utilize the service of these
hospitals have failed."[47] In contrast to the military command's forcible and
even oppressive practices, the PHW considered its own practices beneficent,
offering to the Japanese public health measures to counter venereal disease
and bringing modern medical and scientific knowledge to postwar Japan.

Despite its self understandings, however, the PHW was never outside
the problematic operations of power. Its discourses were deeply informed by

the notions of American superiority and Japanese inferiority, and its practices were no less problematic than the measures pursued by the military command. The PHW repeatedly emphasized Japan's inability to understand and handle modern medical technology, and voiced exasperation, and often barely concealed contempt, at the "backward" medical-moral conditions in Japan. At a meeting with Japanese officials in November 1945, Lieutenant James Gordon, Chief of the Venereal Disease Control Branch of the PHW, argued that the disease control would be extremely difficult to enforce in Japan "because of the limited comprehension of the Japanese of the basic concepts of public health administration and the techniques involved."[48] Two years later, in February 1947, Gordon's successor, Oscar Elkins, MD, observed that the Japanese Ministry of Welfare was incapable of understanding "the desire of SCAP that a program of public health employing preventive and curative measures will be conducted for the people of Japan." The Japanese authorities were "reluctant" to deal with the disease, which Elkins interpreted not as a form of covert resistance, but as backwardness: "The underlying reason for this lack of cooperation is a remnant of former Japanese style thinking which gives no consideration to individual welfare and does not realize that the health and welfare of the people is the primary concern of the government."[49]

According to the PHW, Japanese democratization necessitated the transmission of modern medical and public health knowledge. Despite the seemingly benign nature of such argument, introduction of modernity and democracy often entailed violent methods in the context of foreign occupation. As Yoshikuni Igarashi documents, the PHW considered the production of healthy, sanitary, well-nourished bodies as the "prerequisite" for transforming Japanese society as well as a crucial avenue for disseminating "American democracy" in the Cold War context, and resorted to invasive and violent strategies, including the use of DDT sprayed from planes or administered to individual Japanese forcefully and without consent as a way of preventing infectious disease.[50] The venereal disease control pursued by the PHW sheds light on the occupiers' project to produce "democratic bodies" that involved extensive surveillance and disciplinary techniques particularly focused on working-class women's sexuality.

In the Cold War containment context where venereal disease control was a national security issue, the PHW's health reform called for nothing less than general mobilization, as elaborated in a "Summary Report of Venereal Disease Control Activities in Japan, October 1945–December 1949." Written by Isamu Nieda, MD, Japanese American occupier who served as the Chief of the Venereal Control Branch of Preventive Medicine Division of PHW, this detailed and carefully organized report included information about the "guideline" (in effect, an order) the PHW issued to the Ministry of

Welfare as part of the modernization efforts in Japanese public health and medical institutions. The Ministry of Welfare was to carry out a nationwide campaign regarding venereal disease, providing guidance to the prefectural health departments regarding venereal disease control, and analyzing and documenting local conditions. The ministry was also to "raise professional techniques and inculcate public health methods," "develop public health laboratories so that modern procedures of the diagnosis of venereal disease can be carried out," and "standardize diagnosis and therapeutic measures."[51] To regulate and sanitize Japanese bodies, the PHW introduced a new "contact tracing" technique to identify infected women, as well as many new drugs, diagnostic techniques, and methods of treatment, including "venereal disease education" targeting not only the medical profession but also the general public.[52]

For Japanese physicians, the PHW produced such materials as "The Principles of Venereal Disease Control" and "Venereal Disease Control Service in the Health Center."[53] For the prefectural health authorities, the PHW offered training courses in venereal disease control.[54] The general public was targeted through radio, magazines, journals, lectures, exhibitions, posters, and leaflets. Numerous Japanese-language films were made during 1948 with titles that echo the Cold War fear of contagion and degeneracy: "Body and Devil," "A Thing That Will Ruin Japan," "Flowers of the Poisonous Plant," and "Guard Against Venereal Disease Danger." The first week of September 1949 was designated Venereal Disease Prevention Week, involving an intense public education and information campaign.[55] These education indoctrination efforts were greatly aided by the CI&E that helped disseminate information.[56]

Far from being passive recipients of these initiatives, Japanese women and men were enthusiastic participants in the project of producing "democratic bodies," pressing the occupiers for resources and support and demanding increased intervention by Japanese state authorities. Often exceeding the occupiers in zeal and intensity, Japanese middle- and upper-class leaders pursued "regeneration" and "rehabilitation" of prostitutes, refitting the prewar discourses of nation and sexuality to the postwar containment politics targeting working-class women's sexuality. Established in March 1946, the Central Co-ordinating Committee for Women's Welfare was a body of Japanese government officials and civilians whose aim was to devise measures for the prevention and rehabilitation of prostitutes. Its membership included the WCTU, Salvation Army, Purity Society, and others.[57] These organizations had been prominent in prewar sexual and moral regulation, forming the National Purification Federation in 1935 to pursue with the full support of the state the sexual and moral purity of the nation.[58] In postwar Japan, the Central Co-ordinating Committee for Women's Welfare was chaired by

WCTU leader Gauntlet Tsuneko, one of the six women chosen by Katō Shizue to assist Weed in CI&E's gender reform.

Gauntlet's December 1947 report to the PHW, "Report of the Central Coordinating Committee for Women's Welfare," shows how Japanese women leaders' class-based nationalist discourses regarding "unrespectable women"—articulated in their petition to MacArthur concerning indiscriminate round-ups—drove the Japanese efforts to regulate and discipline economically and sexually marginalized women. The report articulated the committee's concern about the urgent problem of "street girls": "The social evil created by such fallen women" needed to be strictly regulated, and every attempt must be made to "regenerate" them as part of "the building up of New Japan." While acknowledging that the plight of these women was due to "economic distress" stemming from the war years, the report was not concerned with such causes, but instead focused on the women's moral and spiritual lack and the remedial measures needed to reform them. The committee suggested that the state officials in charge of regulating prostitutes be given more resources and authority. Specifically, the committee called for educational efforts for the "enlightenment of those fallen women," including moral-religious instruction "to build up their character," "purity and sex education," "natural and physical education," and "vocational training."[59] Despite its focus on "fallen women," the committee did not limit this education to prostitutes only. Reflecting the PHW discourses of medical mobilization, the CI&E emphasis on information dissemination, and the Cold War concern with sexual regulation as a means toward national security, it recommended a nationwide campaign to educate the general public about prostitutes through newspapers, magazines, radio broadcasts, and public lectures and discussions. Educational, religious, and other organizations should provide "purity and sex education" to the public at school and at home.[60]

The committee's proposed measure for the "control and protection of the fallen women" called for regulatory practices, including surveillance measures as invasive as those pursued by the U.S. military command. The committee suggested that state authorities be empowered to interrogate and arrest "suspicious characters," enforce "compulsory examinations," "enter and inspect those houses of doubtful reputation," and keep a surveillance device "on the residence and movements of confirmed street girls." As a "protection" measure, the committee suggested that women be institutionalized. Following a "mental test," these women should be given "moral" and "spiritual" help, as well as educational opportunities for "honest employment." Ironically and notwithstanding women leaders' protests against indiscriminate round-ups by the occupiers, the committee called for surveillance of a broader segment of the female population. To control and possibly prevent venereal disease, it argued, more thorough medical control of the general public would be necessary, including premarital and prenatal examinations. Reiterating the PHW's concerns regarding modernization of the public health services, the committee also suggested standardization of medical examinations, as well as training of health care practitioners.[61] Despite numerous tensions, conflicts, and disagreements, Japanese and American leaders tapped into the same discursive repertoires of medical and moral surveillance, jointly articulating the Cold War containment narratives.

Convergence between Japanese and American containment politics was especially obvious in a meeting between Satō Kimiji of Ginza Church in Tokyo, and Marta Green, Welfare Service Advisor in the PHW, which was initiated by Isamu Nieda. On September 20, 1949, Nieda introduced Satō to Green and urged her to read Satō's critical report on the American occupiers' behavior toward Japanese women. In the report, Satō insisted on pointing out the injustices imposed on Japanese women, including sexual violence and desertion committed by American military personnel, as well as the indiscriminate round-up of "innocent women." The report remained, however, squarely within the parameters of the Cold War discourses of containment. Reminiscent of the army chaplains' discourses, Satō's report articulated the need for sexual containment in relation to Christian morality and as a defense against communism. He observed that many of the prostitutes had once been innocent women who had "degenerated" into the "path of depravity" after being raped by the American occupiers. Rape was a crime before God: "a serious crime equivalent to murder if the victim was betrothed," and "if she is not betrothed, she shall be his wife because he hath humbled her." He proposed a plan to rescue these women: Christian ministers would salvage a raped woman before she became a prostitute, taking her to facilities to heal "her wounds of heart and body."[62] As for "Japanese wives" who tended to become prostitutes when deserted by their "American husbands," such desertion, according to Satō, was once again "a crime before God," and "therefore marriage should be allowed to those couples who have already been united by themselves." If American occupation policy would not permit marriage between an American man and a Japanese woman, such information should be widely publicized, and cohabitation strictly prohibited.[63]

Satō's concern for prostitutes was rehabilitative, emphasizing moral and spiritual repentance of fallen women. Some measure should be provided for those who had "repented." He made an "appeal in Jesus Christ's name that means may be provided so that repentant girls be helped to start a new life." Punitive measures would not be helpful; instead, "preventive measures and assistance to start a clean life should be given." Especially important was "Christian education" of the youth, as the majority of prostitutes taken to venereal disease hospitals were young girls "accustomed to the corruption of society" with no "spiritual ground upon which to stand," "no real faith at all" and "not equipped with the whole armor of God." Because of these deficiencies, Satō argued, these women were "easily captured by evil," and "with their subsequent depraved living they are constantly pouring poison into the society." Christian education would solve this horrific postwar condition of Japanese youths, and one place where such education could be disseminated was in the schools.[64]

Satō's advocacy of Christian education was inseparable from Cold War anticommunist discourse. In his eyes, Christian education was crucial not only as a means of sexual regulation, but to fend off communist threats as well. At schools, he observed, communists were "propagating their idea with almost no restrictions." They were aggressive in their activities, "converting" many students into communists—an alarming development to Satō. As he argued, the Allied forces' victory and occupation were the outcome of God's plan to preach the Gospel in Japan, and he was more than willing to help promote the occupation's objective: "I wish very much that assistance is given so that Christianity can be freely explained at off hours to the Japanese students and they are allowed to buy bibles in the school if they wish to."[65] Echoing the arguments of the American military chaplains, Satō insisted on religious teaching as a crucial component of Cold War containment, articulating the link among sexuality, religion, and anticommunism.

Given the significance of sexual regulation in anticommunist containment, it may be no coincidence that the Ministry of Education launched *Junketsu Kyōiku Undō*, or the Purity Education Movement, in 1947, the year that witnessed radical mobilization of Japanese left-labor front and the occupiers' heavy-handed counterstrategies to suppress such movements. Similar to its prewar counterpart, the National Purification Federation, the postwar Purity Education Movement emphasized the importance of sexual and moral education in the name of preserving national and racial purity. At the same time, its call for a nationwide educational campaign and sexual and moral surveillance reflected Cold War links among sexual containment, family, and national strength. Not limited to sex education alone, the Committee of Purity Education articulated the ambitious goals of the movement:

> Debasement of morality between men and women, delinquency of youth, and the spread of venereal disease are now not only great problems of society but also national problems which affect us, the Japanese in general. Such tendencies as these have much influence upon the lives of individuals, and finally ruin families, their offspring, and society at large, and once degenerating, its betterment will become hard . . . In order to establish a new wholesome country with fragrant culture, it is necessary to solve problems by suitable, and thorough propagation of Purity Education.

Demanding a nationwide general mobilization to be carried out "simultaneously and unitedly in cooperation with general moral education, public citizens' education, science education and art and other cultural education," the committee defined four major objectives of the national rebuilding campaign:

a. To make an effort to purify society and to firmly establish morality between men and women.
b. To propagate right scientific knowledge of sex, and to raise the standard of sexual morality.
c. To encourage recreation, and to make efforts for wholesome development of the mind and body.
d. To encourage people to refine their sentiment and taste through art, religion, and general culture.[66]

To realize these objectives, parents at home and especially teachers at school were to provide youth with scientific and moral guidance. It was considered critical to give "scientific" and "objective" knowledge about reproduction, starting with observations of reproduction in plants and animals and later moving on to medical and scientific studies of human sexuality. Youth would be taught sound social intercourse between men and women, the importance of chastity before marriage, the harm caused by drinking and smoking, the ills of venereal disease, and wholesome hobbies and recreation. The committee's guidance about courtship etiquette, one of the major objectives in this education campaign, reminds of "a proliferation of articles" in the 1950s United States that provided American youth with a foolproof guide to "the dos and don'ts" as a Cold War phenomenon.[67] The ultimate objective of such instruction, both in Japan and the United States, was to regulate the sexuality of youth and guide them to early marriage. In postwar Japan, the Purity Education Movement constituted a salient Cold War site where a multitude of discourses—not only sexuality but also morality, family, science, art, culture, and nation—were simultaneously mobilized and knitted together to articulate containment strategies for bodily and national rehabilitation.

Yet, Cold War sexual containment was never stable or static, constantly subverted by internal dissents and contradictions. An August 12, 1950, report by Marta Green, "Rehabilitation Homes for Women," based on her inspection trip from 1949 to 1950 to facilities in nine prefectures that dealt with rehabilitation of "fallen" women, epitomizes ironic dynamics of containment politics. Focusing on women's sexual and moral failure as the primary cause of the problem, the report could not avoid discussing the economic plight faced by working-class women, exposing, although never admitting, the failure of SCAP economic and labor policies. Criticizing rehabilitation facilities run by Japanese women leaders, moreover, it reveals the undemocratic nature of sexual regulation on the one hand and the ambivalent state of collaboration between American and Japanese women leaders on the other. Finally, advocating more humane treatment of former prostitutes, the report nevertheless constructs them as deviant and even retarded, contributing to further stigmatization and marginalization of the women. Simultaneously bolstering and destabilizing American hegemony, the report is an emblematic artifact of Cold War containment politics.

The report begins with Green's critical observations concerning postwar economic conditions in Japan. Like Gauntlet Tsuneko and other Japanese women leaders, Green correctly saw economic conditions as a major factor contributing to the working-class women's plight: "[T]he closing down of war industries and large scale manufacture, with its resultant unemployment of young women" led to the current problem, as young women, "due to unemployment or loss of family and resultant loss of security, had gone into the streets to practice prostitution for a livelihood."[68] Yet Green did not address the occupation's economic and labor policies that failed to address such conditions, nor did she critique the American and Japanese men who exploited those economically vulnerable women. Instead, her focus was overwhelmingly on the moral and physical regeneration and economic rehabilitation of the women.

According to the report, rehabilitation facilities were established in urban industrial areas such as Tokyo, Nagoya, Kyoto, Osaka, Kobe, and Fukuoka in 1947, with funding appropriated from the national and prefectural governments. By the beginning of 1950, 7,815 women were institutionalized in these facilities.[69] The homes were not to be "penal institutions," but rather places where women would gain access to "a home atmosphere" as well as "moral guidance" and "vocational training."[70] In reality, however, many of the rehabilitation facilities engaged in oppressive and exploitative practices. For example, Green criticized the *Jiai Ryō,* the Tokyo facility run by the Japan WCTU under the directorship of Gauntlet Tsuneko, the chair of the Central Coordinating Committee for Women's Welfare, for its poor, unsanitary conditions. Of the forty women institutionalized at the home, Green met ten, who were "spinning yarn and braiding rugs." They struck her as "apathetic" and "of low intelligence." Conditions were physically and morally "deplorable," and she called for "a definite program and professional supervision."[71] Green was equally displeased with another Catholic facility, the *Shiragiku Ryō* in Kanagawa prefecture. Run by the Catholic Sisters of the Order of the Sacrament of Worship, the facility kept women under "lock and key" and severely restricted their physical freedom. Women were required to attend an eight-hour vocational training course each day, which taught them embroidery and lace making. Green stated that "discipline and surveillance" needed to be considerably relaxed for "better development of individual character and personality," and "better lighting and more comfortable chairs and equipment" provided for the women at work, so that "the physical well-being of the girls is to be guarded."[72]

Green's report reveals the class-based exploitation these women who were from poor, working-class backgrounds and economically displaced by the occupation continued to endure even after their entry into the rehabilitation homes. In many of the facilities visited by Green, the women were used as a source of cheap labor, doing piecework in a manner reminiscent of sweat shops and providing additional income for the homes' operations. At the *Shisō En* in Kyoto run by a Buddhist temple, women were working eight hours a day, making toys, chopstick holders, and cigarette holders, among other items. They were physically confined, with exit doors "nailed shut" at the time of the inspection. The women complained to Green about insufficient food; the lack of vocational training and "recreational facilities" such as books, games, and music; and indifference on the part of the staff members concerning their "moral and emotional well-being."[73] A more blatant case of labor exploitation was found at the *Saibi Ryō* in Osaka, which was located next to a thread-spinning factory. The operation of this home was "a clear case of collusion between government officials and private enterprise to use and exploit unfortunate women and to use government funds for private gains," observed Green. Once sent there by the courts, the women were "immediately employed by the factories." The home was "nothing more than a dormitory to house employees of the factory." Strongly indignant, Green called for an investigation of the operation by the Ministry of Welfare and the prefectural government.[74]

Not all the facilities were condemned by Green. She found the *Fujin Ryō* run by the Japan WCTU in Kobe prefecture to be a model home. It was "located in a good residential section of Kobe," with excellent physical facilities. The staff members consisted of women who were "experienced, sympathetic and interested in the type of women and girls sent to them." A training program was given to women whereby they were taught sewing, knitting, as well as "domestic science." Furthermore, the staff members made "efforts to build up the women both morally and physically," and helped them "in making elevating contacts in the community." While Green saw the need for "a more strict segregation program" between the women with and without venereal disease, she still considered the facility to be "one of the best" she had visited.[75] Another facility, the *Asoka Gakuen* in Nagoya prefecture, also received a high mark from Green. In providing "excellent shelter and food to its inmates," the home "approximates a well supervised working girl's home." The staff members emphasized "finding outside employment, home placement, or marriage for the girls as soon as possible," and "many of the inmates

work at jobs outside of the home and return to domicile there." The operation of the home would be improved, Green noted, if "a program including
constructive leisure time and recreational pursuits be worked out which will
forward moral and physical rehabilitation as well as vocational."[76]

Despite her keen awareness of economic dimensions of the problem,
Green focused on disciplining the women with "deviant sexuality" for moral,
spiritual, and economic rehabilitation and reentry to postwar society, and
skirted around SCAP's labor and economic policies that deprived working-
class women of their livelihood to begin with. Commenting on the increased
awareness of venereal disease control in postwar Japan, she argued that the
Japanese now "recognize the evils attendant upon a life of prostitution and
the need for curtailing this vicious profession in the only possible way, by
providing the means whereby young women may be reeducated morally
and economically to their own lasting benefit." By providing a shelter to
"homeless and delinquent girls and women," the rehabilitation facilities were
providing not only "physical care" but were working toward "moral rehabilitation and placement" of the women "in a respectable environment upon
release from the home." These facilities were playing "a valuable part in the
VD program," where women with infections could receive "treatment, discipline and personal freedom."[77]

Improvements to rehabilitation facilities were urgently needed, Green
argued, because economic conditions in postwar Japan ensured that even
women with employable skills would be unable to find employment and that
the problem of prostitution and venereal disease would continue. However,
her discussions of economic conditions were immediately followed by a
demand for increased efforts to rehabilitate women. She called for a program
that would "provide rehabilitation homes for delinquent young women and
prostitutes who desire to change their way of life and become economically and socially acceptable, thereby becoming citizens on the credit side
rather than the debt side of the nation's ledger."[78] For this, the rehabilitation facilities provide "academic, moral, vocational, physical, and social
training" to restore "self-respect and self-reliance" as well as "emotional
and economic security." Rehabilitated women would "leave physically able,
and efficiently trained and equipped to take a normal competitive place in
the present economy."[79] The vocational training given to women who were
"desirous and able" should include instructions in "home nursing, sewing,
mending, remodeling of clothing, domestic sciences for home and institutions, simple clerical work, beauty culture, professional child care, sanitation
and hygiene for both small homes and institutions, business and industrial
facilities (trained janitor services)."[80] In effect, Green's argument was a Cold
War prescription for working-class femininity—repentant, sanitized, domesticated, and contained.

U.S.-Japanese efforts to contain and discipline working-class women's sexuality culminated in a report in February 1950, "Minimum Standard for the Girls' Rehabilitation Institution." Drafted by Ministry of Welfare officials, prefectural government officials, and the director of the rehabilitation facilities, the report reflected Green's vision of Cold War working-class femininity, with a focus on producing regulated and sanitized bodies. The report specified "daily routines" for the homes so that "scientific guidance and personal touch will be combined with humane and feminine generosity and charm."[81] The report also specified—in an extremely mundane and detailed manner—the locations and physical facilities of the homes, revealing an excessive concern with the "health" and "sanitation" of the women and the "cleanliness" of the physical space they were to occupy. First, "the girls" were to be fed properly according to a menu prescribed by a nurse, and "trained to cultivate a habit by means of cooking their own meals."[82] The women's "bodily cleanliness" should be maintained in every possible way. Their clothing and bedding should be kept absolutely clean. Their hair should be disinfected, as should their tableware. Baths should be taken more than twice a week, and a "cleaning-examination" conducted twice a month. Special measures for cleanliness and sanitation should be applied to those with venereal disease; not only should they be segregated, but their bodies and tableware should be subject to "strict disinfection."[83]

Furthermore, the report specified that the building that housed the rehabilitation facilities should be "pretty to look at" and "in sanitary conditions," with good ventilation and lighting, and protected against cold as well as hot weather.[84] A room where meals were prepared, for instance, should have a sterilizer on hand for disinfecting utensils and food items, and disposal of waste matter should be regularly attended to. Cooks should be without any infection, and must wear a "clean overall."[85] Lavatories should be built so that they would not face south, and arrangements should be made to keep them disinfected, clean, and free of bad odor. "Purified water" should be available for washing hands, and no common towels should be provided.[86] The report went on to specify in detail provisions for keeping the facilities as well as the inmates "sanitary" and "clean."

Obsessive concerns with disease and cleanliness clearly reflected the context of Cold War anticommunist containment, where regulating and rehabilitating infected bodies and minds became an important anticommunist strategy requiring a nationwide mobilization of occupiers and occupied alike. The political dynamics set in motion during the occupation did not simply cease to exist in 1952. They continued to shape postoccupation sexual politics in Japan. With heightened public awareness of sexuality, morality, and purity, prostitution was made illegal by the Prostitution Prevention Law in 1956. Although many, especially middle- and upper-class Japanese women, hailed the law as a victory for gender democratization, prostitutes opposed it as depriving them of their livelihood, and they bitterly resented and openly protested the middle-class moral discourse that the women members of the Diet used in stigmatizing prostitutes and arguing for the law.[87] The Cold War politics of sexual containment clearly produced uneven effects among Japanese women, protecting the respectable but marginalizing and even condemning those deemed unrespectable. While pursuing "democratization," Japanese middle- and working-class women leaders, including feminists, excluded poor, economically displaced women, implicitly and explicitly depriving them of candidacy for full citizenry and subjectivity.

6
Conclusion

This volume reinterprets the occupiers' gender reform as a case of Cold War mobilization of American and Japanese women with complex and contradictory results. During the occupation, American women reformers enthusiastically served as liberators of Japanese women and disseminators of Cold War femininity, domesticity, and heterosexuality, but their very involvement in a foreign occupation contradicted the tenet of domestic containment and their close bonds with Japanese women infringed on that of familial heterosexual normativity. Japanese middle-class women who were mobilized as the "poster girls" for MacArthur's democratization were more than willing to perform containment femininity, but were also ready to question the notion of America as the champion of freedom and democracy and to articulate their own, distinctly different visions of postwar womanhood. Working-class women whose economic and political rights were severely undermined under the occupation explicitly challenged American domination by turning to Chinese and Soviet women as their models, but their resistance frequently reinforced, rather than challenged, containment understandings of sexuality and respectability. Most disempowered of all, poor women who worked as prostitutes nonetheless became a major source of threat, indeed "menace," as their allegedly unruly and uncontainable sexuality challenged and destabilized American domination. The U.S. occupation of Japan is thus nothing less than a dynamic story of women's constant negotiations with power that sometimes reinforced but other times subverted American hegemony.

In illuminating the occupation's complex, contradictory, and disruptive dynamics, a multivector analysis of power proves to be crucial. The analytical framework that pays attention to the intersection of gender, race, class, and so on challenges essentialistic notions of women and men, occupiers and occupied, and white and colored, and reveals heterogeneity, difference, and hierarchy embedded within each category. The multivector analysis also avoids a pitfall of single-category analysis that "forecloses the possibility of ruptures and interventions when other forces are considered,"[1] and sheds light on how gender and other categories of power sometimes work together to reinforce, but other times against each other to destabilize and undermine, dominant orders of power. This volume applies this framework to reinterpret the occupiers' gender reform as a contentious site of Cold War politics where hegemony's ubiquity but also its instability were observed. Gender reform was an important strategy in American pursuit of postwar hegemony, as it reinforced a racialized notion of American superiority and Japanese inferiority and facilitated sexual and class containment of women. Yet, gender reform was also a source of instability in American domination, as it led to cross-class alliance of Japanese women that challenged the occupiers' sexual regulation on the one hand, and homosocial bonds between American and Japanese women that contradicted Cold War heteronormativity on the other. During the occupation, gender, race, class, and so on repeatedly converged and dispersed. The dynamic, uneven, and fractured nature of American Cold War hegemony becomes visible only when analytical attention is paid to the simultaneous working of multiple strands of power.

In reinterpreting the meanings and consequences of the occupation, this volume generates a multidisciplinary dialogue among occupation studies, Cold War cultural studies, and postcolonial feminist studies where assumptions of each discipline are challenged and altered. Occupation studies has long neglected the centrality of women and gender, and as a result, failed to understand the occupation as a deeply gendered (and also raced, classed, and sexualized) project where American and Japanese women played the centrally important roles in postwar U.S.–Japan negotiations. Drawing on insights from Cold War cultural studies and postcolonial feminist studies, the book urges occupation scholars to revisit Japanese women not as passive recipients of democratization, but as active participants in containment politics, and to reinterpret the occupation's gender reform not as a congratulatory moment of women's liberation, but as a complex instance of Cold War mobilization of women where Japanese and American racism, nationalism, and imperialism converged to enable a deeply problematic for feminism.

Cold War cultural studies has conventionally focused on domestic dynamics but not fully investigated the ways in which containment culture was also articulated abroad and even prior to its full realization in the United States, with significant involvement of non-American and nonwhite others. Furthermore, with an overwhelming focus on containment femininity and domesticity, existing scholarship has often overlooked the dynamic and unpredictable nature of women's agency whose discourses and practices frequently challenged and subverted the dominant culture's emphasis on gender, family, and heterosexual normativity. The occupation's gender reform suggests that the international feminist movement constituted a significant site in Cold War cultural formation where American and Japanese women played active roles in simultaneously bolstering and subverting the emerging orders of gender, race, sexuality, and nation. To gain a fuller understanding of the Cold War, it becomes necessary for scholars to cast their gaze beyond the national domestic context and examine transnational space, especially international feminist discourses and practices, as yet another site of historical and analytical significance, with critical attention to multitudes of tensions, dissonance, and incoherence in containment culture.

Postcolonial feminist studies has been generating increasingly critical and sophisticated understandings of Western feminism from which the book greatly benefits. Understanding Western feminism as deeply implicated in racism, nationalism, and imperialism leads to "not a search for a transparent or transcendent feminism but a need to examine the conditions of (its) possibility."[2] Applying this insight, the book reveals how feminist discourses and practices during the occupation were enabled by and in turn enabled Cold War racism, nationalism, and imperialism, facilitating American (re)assertion for racial and national superiority and contributing to its pursuit of postwar international hegemony. Clearly the occupation's gender reform was at one level an instance of Western imperial feminism where the politics of "women's emancipation" reinscribed and reinforced the conventional hierarchy between West and non-Western other. At the same time, the book's discussions suggest that the complex nature of the U.S.–Japan encounter requires a far more nuanced and multifaceted analysis. Far from powerless victims under U.S. domination, Japanese women engaged in a series of resistance, complicity, and subversion, not only challenging hegemonic orders imposed by the occupiers, but appropriating them to reassert Japan's racial and national superiority and to articulate their own version of postwar imperial feminism that was no less problematic than that of the Americans. The stories of American gender reform in Japan challenge the binary, oppositional notions of West and non-West, dominant and oppressed, or colonizers and colonized, and urge feminist scholars to critically reexamine the meanings and consequences of non-Western women's agency within the politics of race, nation, and empire.

Finally, this volume intervenes in American and Japanese postwar national memories and reveals a number of erasures, or incidents of historical amnesia, that have been enabled by the myth of American emancipation of Japanese women. The narrative of the occupation as successful emancipation and democratization of oppressed and subjugated people, especially women, has enabled America's self-understanding as the legitimate global leader in the post–World War II world, and has obscured the historical reality that the occupation was part of American pursuit of Cold War hegemony that entailed much domestic and international violence and oppressions. The occupation narrative has played an equally or even more problematic role in Japan's postwar self-understanding. Not only has the myth of Japan's rebirth as a democratic and peaceful nation under MacArthur concealed the nation's colonial past full of violence and atrocities; the narrative crucially depends on and sustains the understanding of Japanese women as helpless victims: Until the arrival of American women in 1945, Japanese women had been incapable of any action. This notion of Japanese women as victims without agency has erased from the nation's historical consciousness the problematic roles women played in prewar Japanese racism and imperialism in Asia. The two nations' continuing investment in the narrative of women's emancipation during the occupation thus needs to be interrogated and replaced by more critical understandings of women, nation, and empire in twentieth-century U.S.–Japan relations. This book is an effort toward that goal.

Notes

CHAPTER 1

1. Douglas MacArthur, "A Fourth of July Message," *Life* 23, no. 1 (1947): 34.

2. Florence Powdermaker, "Report of Dr. Florence B. Powdermaker," October 15, 1948, Folder 3, Box 112, Record Group 5, MacArthur Memorial, Archives and Library, Norfolk, VA (hereafter MMAL).

3. Ethel Weed, "Progress of Japanese Women, Prepared by the Women's Affairs Branch of the CI&E, for General Federation of Women's Clubs in Washington, D.C.," January 7, 1947, File "Weed, Ethel, Feature Stories," Box 5247, Record Group 331, National Records Center, Suitland, MD (hereafter NRC).

4. Douglas MacArthur, *Reminiscences* (New York: McGraw-Hill, 1964), 305.

5. "Women of Japan Lauded by General Douglas MacArthur, Extract of Press Release," June 21, 1946, Folder 21, Box 1, RG 25, MMAL.

6. *New York Times*, "Earnest Hoberecht, Popular Novelist in Occupied Japan, Is Dead at 81," September 26, 1999.

7. Raymond Higgins, *From Hiroshima with Love: The Allied Military Governor's Remarkable Story of the Rebuilding of Japan's Business and Industry after WWII* (Phoenix, AZ: VIA Press, 1995).

8. Susan Pharr, "The Politics of Women's Rights," in *Democratizing Japan: The Allied Occupation*, ed. Robert Ward and Yoshikazu Sakamoto (Honolulu: University of Hawai'i Press, 1987), 223.

9. Following the convention of occupation studies, I refer to the U.S. occupation of mainland Japan from 1945 to 1952 as the U.S. occupation of Japan. However, it is important to note that the U.S. occupation of Okinawa, the southernmost prefecture of Japan, lasted from 1945 to 1972.

10. John Dower, "Occupied Japan as History and Occupation History as Politics," *Journal of Asian Studies* 34, no. 2 (1975); Carol Gluck, "Entangling Illusions—Japanese and American Views of the Occupation," in *New Frontiers in American–East Asia Relations*, ed. Warren Cohen (New York: Columbia University Press, 1983).

11. Gluck, "Entangling Illusions," 177.

12. Yukiko Koshiro, *Transpacific Racisms and the U.S. Occupation of Japan* (New York: Columbia University Press, 1999), 16. In this study, Koshiro sheds important light on the genealogy of racism in the United States. As she documents, despite a shift in American academic discourse of race that moved away from the notion of physical and biological superiority versus inferiority based on skin color to the one of cultural and sociological differences and diversities in the 1940s, the physical and biological notion of race persisted in general. While the occupation authority increasingly adopted cultural and sociological discourse of race with the onset of "reverse course" to facilitate alliance making with Japan, the discourse of physical and biological racial differences continued at the grassroots level, informing everyday U.S.–Japan encounters in covert and overt ways.

13. John Dower, *War without Mercy: Race and Power in the Pacific War* (New York: Pantheon Books, 1986), 10. For another important study that provides a history of American constructions of "Orient" and "Orientals" (Asian Americans as well as Asians) within the context of Western colonial racism and culture, see Robert Lee, *Orientals: Asian Americans in Popular Culture* (Philadelphia: Temple University Press, 1999). Tracing the images of Asians and Asian Americans in American popular culture since the initial Asian immigration, Lee argues that despite changes in the images of the "Orientals" over time—the pollutant, the coolies, the deviant, the yellow peril, the model minority, and the gook—the same racist assumptions of Asians and Asian Americans as alien and dangerous run through all of them.

14. John Dower, *Embracing Defeat: Japan in the Wake of World War II* (New York: Norton/New Press, 1999), 211.

15. Pharr, "The Politics of Women's Rights," 222–223, 248.

16. For a study that characterizes the occupation as positive for Japanese women with personal accounts of Japanese women who were involved in gender reform, see Kiyoko Nishi, *Senryōka no nihon fujin seisaku: Sono rekishi to shōgen* (Tokyo: Domesu Shuppan, 1985), and Harumi Sakai, "GHQ de hataraita joseitachi," *Joseigaku Kenkyū* no. 3 (1994). For studies that focus on women's reform efforts carried out by Ethel Weed and other women occupiers, see, for instance, Megumi Itō, "CI&E kyōikuka no fujin kyōiku seisaku," in *GHQ no shakai kyōiku seisaku*, ed. Toshio Ogawa (Tokyo: Ōzorasha, 1990), and Chikako Uemura, "Nihon ni okeru senryō seisaku to josei kaihō" *Joseigaku Kenkyū* no. 2 (1992). For a study that focuses on constitutional revision as the occasion of Japanese women's liberation, see Kyōko Inoue, *MacArthur's Japanese Constitution: A Linguistic and Cultural Study of Its Making* (Chicago: University of Chicago Press, 1991).

17. Beate Sirota Gordon, *The Only Woman in the Room: A Memoir* (Tokyo: Kodansha International, 1997).

18. Beate Sirota Gordon, interview by Ted Koppel, "Nightline: The Only Woman In the Room," *ABC Nightline*, February 10, 1999, ABC Transcript #4620.

19. Beate Sirota Gordon, interview by Jackie Judd, *Morning Edition*, National Public Radio, February 18, 2002. Gordon is not alone in making an explicit connection between the U.S. occupation of Japan and the U.S. interventions in Afghanistan

a half-century later. In an article entitled "The Veiled Resource," *New York Times*, December 11, 2001, Nicholas D. Kristof writes, "During the United States' occupation of Japan after World War II, we wrote a constitution for Japan that guaranteed equal rights for women, and similar nudging by us in the coming years can help all Afghans, men and women alike."

20. See, for example, Yuki Fujime, "Reisen taisei keiseiki no josei undō," in *Nihon shakai to jendā*, ed. Yoshiko Miyake (Tokyo: Akashi Shoten, 2001); Yasuko Itō, *Sengo nihon joseishi* (Tokyo: Ōtsuki Shoten, 1974); Kinue Sakurai, *Bosei hogo undōshi* (Tokyo: Domesu Shuppan, 1991); Sayoko Yoneda, *Kindai nihon joseishi*, vol. 2 (Tokyo: Shin Nihon Shuppansha, 1973).

21. Seiichi Yoda, "Senryōki ni okeru fujin kaihō," in *Senryōki nihon no keizai to seiji*, ed. Takahide Nakamura (Tokyo: Tokyo Daigaku Shuppan, 1979).

22. Lisa Yoneyama, "Hihanteki feminizumu no keifu kara miru nihon senryō," *Shisō* no. 955 (2003). Carline Chung Simpson, *An Absent Presence: Japanese Americans in Postwar American Culture, 1945—1960* (Durham: Duke University Press, 2001); Naoko Shibusawa, *America's Geisha Ally: Reimagining the Japanese Enemy* (Cambridge, Massachusetts: Harvard University Press, 2006); Christina Klein, *Cold War Orientlaism: Asia in the Middlebrow Imagination, 1945—1961* (Berkeley and Los Angeles: University of California Press, 2003).

23. Joan Scott, *Gender and the Politics of History* (New York: Columbia University Press, 1988), 44–45.

24. Ibid., 46.

25. The critique of women's studies approaches that focus on gender as the sole category of analysis goes back several decades. Given space limitations, it is impossible to list all the scholars who have contributed to the debates or to summarize their arguments. For the purpose of this book, however, it is important to note that feminist scholars, such as Patricia Collins, Angela Davis, Inderpal Grewal, bell hooks, Ann McClintock, Chandra Mohanty, and Ann Stoler, have played crucial roles in illuminating the ethnocentric nature of feminist knowledge production that relies on and reinscribes racial and imperial hierarchies. To address the problem, they argue, feminist researchers need to do more than simply add race as another category of analysis or incorporate marginalized women as new research subjects. It is of fundamental importance to examine the ways in which feminism has informed and been informed by racialized imperial politics since its inception. Following this suggestion, I explore the intertwined relationship among feminism, racism, and imperialism as one of the major themes in this book.

Another aspect of the feminist paradigm shift concerns issues of sexuality. In analyzing the intersection of multiple categories of powers, it is crucial to recognize gender and sexuality as interrelated, but also distinctly different. As Gayle Rubin argues, sexuality has its own institutional dynamics and hierarchy. In the current system of sexual hierarchy, the normative sexuality is heterosexual, marital, monogamous, reproductive, and noncommercial sexuality. Other sexual activities and identities are defined as "bad," "abnormal," and "unnatural." These other forms of sexuality are further assigned hierarchical evaluations. For example, while promiscuous heterosexuality and longtime lesbian and gay partnerships are treated as *relatively* more permissible, sexual activities that take place outside the private and familial sphere are more strictly regulated, and sadomasochism and cross-generational sexual acts are condemned as "abnormal" and "sinful." Gayle Rubin, "Thinking Sex: Notes for a Radical Theory of the Politics of Sexuality," in *Pleasure Danger: Exploring Female Sexuality*, ed. Carole Vance (London: Pandra Press, 1989), 280–281.

26. Anne McClintock, *Imperial Leather: Race, Gender and Sexuality in the Colonial Contest* (New York: Routledge, 1995), 4–5.

27. Dorinne Kondo, *About Face: Performing Race in Fashion and Theater* (New York: Routledge, 1997), 149.

28. Amy Kaplan, "Left Alone with America: The Absence of Empire in the Study of American Cutulre," in *Cultures of United States Imperialism*, ed. Amy Kaplan and Donald Pease (Durham, NC: Duke University Press, 1993).

29. McClintock, *Imperial Leather*, 13.

30. See, for example, McClintock, *Imperial Leather*; Franz Fannon, *A Dying Colonialism* (New York: Grove Press, 1965); Ann Stoler, "Carnal Knowledge and Imperial Power: Gender, Race, and Morality in Colonial Asia," in *Gender at the Crossroads of Knowledge: Feminist Anthropology in the Postmodern Era*, ed. Micaela di Leonardo (Berkeley and Los Angeles: University of California Press, 1991); and Ann Stoler, "Rethinking Colonial Categories: European Communities and the Boundaries of Rule," in *Colonialism and Culture*, ed. Nicholas Dirks (Ann Arbor: University of Michigan Press, 1992).

31. See, for example, Kathy Ferguson and Phyllis Turnbull, *Oh, Say, Can You See? The Semiotics of the Military in Hawai'i* (Minneapolis: University of Minnesota Press, 1999); Robert Lee, *Orientals*; Haunani Kay Trask, *From a Native Daughter: Colonialism and Sovereignty in Hawai'i* (Monroe, ME: Common Courage Press, 1993).

32. For studies of European women's (especially feminists') complicity in and resistance against imperialism, see, for instance, Antoinette Burton, *Burdens of History: British Feminists, Indian Women, and Imperial Culture, 1865–1915* (Chapel Hill: University of North Carolina Press, 1994); Inderpal Grewal, *Home and Harem: Nation, Gender, Empire, and the Cultures of Travel* (Durham, NC: Duke University Press, 1996); Kumari Jayawardena, *The White Woman's Other Burden: Western Women and South Asia during British Colonial Rule* (New York: Routledge, 1990); Reina Lewis, *Gendering Orientalism: Race, Femininity and Representation* (London: Routledge, 1996); Susan Morgan, *Place Matters: Gendered Geography in Victorian Women's Travel Books about Southeast Asia* (New Brunswick, NJ: Rutgers University Press, 1996); Philippa Levine, ed., *Gender and Empire* (Oxford: Oxford University Press, 2004). For those concerning American imperialism and women (especially feminists), see, for instance, Tracey Jean Boisseau, *White Queen: May French-Sheldon and the Imperial Origins of American Feminist Identity* (Bloomington: Indiana University Press, 2004); Jane Hunter, *The Gospel of Gentility: American Women Missionaries in Turn of the Century China* (New Haven, CT: Yale University Press, 1984); Leila Rupp, *Worlds of Women: The Making of an International Women's Movement* (Princeton, NJ: Princeton University Press, 1997); Ian Tyrrell, *Woman's World, Woman's Empire: The Woman's Christian Temperance Union in International Perspective, 1880–1930* (Chapel Hill: University of North Carolina Press, 1991).

33. Tani Barlow, "Introduction: On 'Colonial Modernity,'" in *Formations of Colonial Modernity in East Asia*, ed. Tani Barlow (Durham, NC: Duke University Press, 1997), 10.

34. Mark Bradley, "Slouching toward Bethlehem: Culture, Diplomacy, and the Origins of the Cold War in Vietnam," in *Cold War Constructions: The Political Culture of United States Imperialism, 1945–1966*, ed. Christian Appy (Amherst: University of Massachusetts Press, 2000), 19. There are a number of excellent studies that examine

U.S. colonization of the Philippines at the end of the nineteenth century whose discourses and practices were to be often repeated in the U.S. occupation of Japan a half-century later. See, for example, Vicente Rafael, ed., *Discrepant Histories: Translocal Essay on Filipino Cultures* (Philadelphia: Temple University Press, 1995); Vicente Rafael, *White Love and Other Events in Filipino History* (Durham, NC: Duke University Press, 2000); and Kristin Hoganson, *Fighting for American Manhood: How Gender Politics Provoked the Spanish-American and Philippine-American Wars* (New Haven, CT: Yale University Press: 1998).

35. Inderpal Grewal, Akhil Gupta, and Aihwa Ong point out that the notion of "U.S. multiculturalism" is yet another cultural capital that is being circulated in a more recent transnational context and that generates desire for Americanness globally. See "Guest Editor's Introduction," *Positions: East Asia Cultures Critique* 7, no. 3 (1999).

36. For studies that focus on women and gender, see Elaine Tyler May, *Homeward Bound: American Families in the Cold War Era* (New York: Basic Books, 1999); Guy Oakes, *The Imaginary War: Civil Defense and American Cold War Culture* (New York: Oxford University Press, 1994); Laura McEnaney, *Civil Defense Begins at Home: Militarization Meets Everyday Life in the Fifties* (Princeton, NJ: Princeton University Press, 2000); and Joanne Meyerowitz, ed., *Not June Cleaver: Women and Gender in Postwar America, 1945–1960* (Philadelphia: Temple University Press, 1994). For studies that focus on race, see Peggy Von Eschen, *Race against Empire: Black Americans and Anticolonialism, 1937–1957* (Ithaca, NY: Cornell University Press, 1997); Mary Dudziak, *Cold War Civil Rights: Race and the Image of American Democracy* (Princeton, NJ: Princeton University Press, 2000). For studies that focus on sexuality, see Geoffrey Smith, "National Security and Personal Isolation: Sex, Gender, and Disease in the Cold War United States," *The International History Review* 14, no. 2 (1992); Frank Costigliola, "The Nuclear Family: Tropes of Gender and Pathology in the Western Alliance," *Diplomatic History* 21, no. 2 (1997); David Harley Serlin, "Christine Jorgensen and the Cold War Closet," *Radical History Review* 62 (1995); Lee, *Orientals*; Allan Berube, *Coming out under Fire: The History of Gay Men and Women in World War Two* (New York: Free Press, 1990); John D'Emilio, *Sexual Politics, Sexual Communities: The Making of Homosexual Minority in the United States, 1940–1970* (Chicago: University of Chicago Press, 1983); Rubin, "Thinking Sex." For studies that focus on American dissemination of Cold War containment culture abroad, see Robert Haddow, *Pavilions of Plenty: Exhibiting American Culture Abroad in the 1950s* (Washington, DC: Smithsonian Institution Press, 1997); Christina Klein, *Cold War Orientalism*. For studies that focus on the significant roles played by "others" such as Japanese and Japanese Americans in American Cold War cultural formation, see Simpson, *An Absent Presence*, and Shibusawa, *America's Geisha Ally*.

37. Oakes, *The Imaginary War*, 80.

38. Ibid., 8.

39. Meyerowitz, *Not June Cleaver*, 4.

40. McEnaney, *Civil Defense Begins at Home*, 121.

41. Ibid., 8.

42. Ibid., 121.

43. Robert Lee's analysis of the film, *Sayonara*, points to the significance of homoerotic tensions in Cold War imagining of American encounter with Japan, thus making a rare and critical intervention in existing gender studies of the occupation that

almost uniformly focus on the trope of heterosexual romance in analyzing the power relations between the U.S. and Japan. See Lee, *Orientals*, Chapter 5.

44. See Costigliola, "The Nuclear Family"; Serline, "Christine Jorgensen"; Steven Cohan, *Masked Men: Masculinity and the Movies in the Fifties* (Bloomington: Indiana University Press, 1997).

45. Gayatri Chakravorty Spivak, "Three Women's Texts and a Critique of Imperialism," in *"Race," Writing, and Difference*, ed. Henry Louis Gates, Jr. (Chicago: University of Chicago Press, 1986), 262.

46. Joyce Zonana, "The Sultan and the Slave: Feminist Orientalism and the Structure," *Signs: Journal of Women in Culture and Society* 18, no. 3 (1993): 594.

47. Chandra Mohanty, "Under Western Eyes: Feminist Scholarship and Colonial Discourse," in *Third World Women and the Politics of Feminism*, ed. Chandra Mohanty et al. (Bloomington: Indiana University Press, 1991).

48. Inderpal Grewal and Caren Kaplan, eds., *Scattered Hegemonies: Postmodernity and Transnational Feminist Practices* (Minneapolis: University of Minnesota Press, 1994), 2.

49. Grewal, *Home and Harem*, 11 emphasis added.

50. Ibid, 12.

CHAPTER 2

1. Gordon, *The Only Woman in the Room*, 9–10.

2. MacArthur, *Reminiscences*, 305.

3. "Potsdam Declaration: Proclamation by Heads of Governments, United States, United Kingdom, and China," July 26, 1945, reprinted in *Political Reorientation of Japan, September 1945 to September 1948: Report of Government Section, Supreme Commander for the Allied Powers*, vol. 2 (1949), 413.

4. "United States Initial Post-Surrender Policy for Japan," August 29, 1945, reprinted in *Political Reorientation of Japan*, 423, 425.

5. Kenzō Takayanagi et al., eds., *Nihonkoku kenpō seitei no katei*, vol. 2, *kaisetsu* (Tokyo: Yūhikaku, 1984), 4.

6. "Reform of the Japanese Government," reprinted in Takayanagi et al., eds., *Nihonkoku kenpō*, vol. 1, *genbun to honyaku*, 416.

7. *Civil Affairs Handbook, Japan* (Washington, DC: United States Army Service Forces, 1944), National Diet Library, Tokyo, Japan, 76. The content of the Handbook clearly reflects the American wartime project of "Japanese national character studies." For detailed discussions of the project's history, personnel, and findings, see Dower, *War without Mercy*, Chapter 6, and Simpson, *An Absent Presence*, Chapter 2.

8. Ibid., 77–78.

9. Ibid., 75–76.

10. Ibid., 68.

11. McClintock, *Imperial Leather*, 40. Simpson, *An Absent Presence*, 65.

12. McClintock, *Imperial Leather*, 4–5.

13. *Civil Affairs Handbook, Japan*, 73.

14. Ibid., 69.

15. This often-cited statement was made during the U.S. Senate hearings of MacArthur in 1951, and is quoted in Dower, *War without Mercy*, 303. For a fascinating

study that focuses on themes of gender and maturity in American postwar constructions of Japanese, see Shibusawa, *America's Geisha Ally*, Chapters 1 and 2.

16. Barlow, "Introduction: On 'Colonial Modernity,'" 10.

17. Nira Yuval-Davis and Floya Anthias, eds., *Women, Nation, State* (New York: St. Martin's Press, 1989), 7.

18. Kathleen Uno, *Passage to Modernity: Motherhood, Childhood, and Social Reform in Early Twentieth Century Japan* (Honolulu: University of Hawai'i Press, 1993), 296.

19. Mikiko Kōjiya, *Sensō o ikita onnatachi* (Kyoto, Japan: Mineruba Shobō, 1985).

20. For insightful discussions about the intersection of class and sexuality in Japan's modernization process with a focus on rural women, see Mariko Tamanoi, *Under the Shadow of Nationalism: Politics and Poetics of Rural Japanese Women* (Honolulu: University of Hawai'i Press, 1998).

21. Iris Chang, *The Rape of Nanking: The Forgotten Holocaust of World War II* (New York: Penguin, 1997); and Yuki Tanaka, *Japan's Comfort Women: Sexual Slavery and Prostitution during World War II and the U.S. Occupation of Japan* (London: Routledge, 2002).

22. Tyrrell, *Woman's World, Woman's Empire*, 4.

23. Sheldon Garon, "The World's Oldest Debate? Prostitution and the State in Imperial Japan, 1900–1945," *American Historical Review* 98, no. 3 (1993): 719–722. The Japanese state was not opposed to moral and sexual regulation itself, however. They perceived the licensed system as the means of regulating public morality and hygiene, as a way of keeping the Japanese family system intact and shielding daughters of respectable families from social vices.

24. Ibid., 729.

25. Noriko Hayakawa, "Nationalism, Colonialism and Women: The Case of the World Woman's Christian Temperance," in *Women's Rights and Human Rights: International Historical Perspective*, ed. Patricia Grimshaw et al. (New York: Palgrave, 2001), 22–25.

26. Fusae Ichikawa, *Ichikawa Fusae jiden, senzenhen* (Tokyo: Shinjuku Shobō, 1981), 117–118.

27. Sheldon Garon, "Women's Groups and the Japanese State: Contending Approaches to Political Integration, 1890–1945," *Journal of Japanese Studies* 19, no. 1 (1993): 32.

28. Yūko Suzuki, *Feminizumu to sensō* (Tokyo: Marujusha, 1986).

29. Katsuko Kodama, *Oboegaki: Sengo no Ichikawa Fusae* (Tokyo: Shinjuku Shobō, 1985), 13.

30. Ibid., 14.

31. Douglas MacArthur, "Statement to the Japanese Government Concerning Required Reforms," October 11, 1945, reprinted in *Political Reorientation of Japan*, 741. This was followed by four more reform items: the encouragement of the unionization of Labor, the opening of the schools to more liberal education, the abolition of systems that through secret inquisition and abuse had held the people in constant fear, and the democratization of Japanese economic institutions. As a separate item, MacArthur also demanded liberalization of the constitution.

32. Kodama, *Oboegaki*, 15.

33. "Shūgiin giin senkyohōchū kaisei hōritsuan shingi no keika," reprinted in *Nihon fujin mondai shiryō shūsei, Seiji*, ed. Fusae Ichikawa (Tokyo: Domesu Shuppan, 1977), 615–623.

34. "A Letter From Douglas MacArthur to Sally Butler, President of the National Federation of Business and Professional Women's Clubs," May 5, 1948, Folder "bus-buz," Box 12, RG 5, MMAL.

35. "Women of Japan Lauded by General Douglas MacArthur, extract of press release," June 21, 1946, Folder 21, Box 1, RG 25, MMAL.

36. Sonya Michel, "American Women and the Discourse of the Democratic Family in World War II," in *Behind the Lines: Gender and the Two World Wars*, ed. Margaret Higonnet et al. (New Haven, CT: Yale University Press, 1987), 154–155.

37. "Women of Japan Lauded by General MacArthur."

38. Dower, *Embracing Defeat*, 386.

39. There are a number of excellent studies that provide a chronological recounting of the constitutional revision in detail. See, for example, Dower, *Embracing Defeat*; Takayanagi et al., *Nihonkoku kenpō*; Dale Hellegers, *We the Japanese People: World War II and the Origins of the Japanese Constitution*, 2 vols. (Stanford, CA: Stanford University Press, 2001); Kyōko Inoue, *MacArthur's Japanese Constitution*; Shōichi Koseki, *The Birth of Japan's Postwar Constitution* (Boulder, CO: Westview Press, 1997); Akinori Suzuki, *Nihonkoku kenpō o unda misshitsu no kokonokakan* (Osaka, Japan: Sōgensha, 1995). For a brief but insightful discussion about Article 14 with a focus on race, see Koshiro, *Transpacific Racisms*. Gordon's autobiography is also useful for firsthand accounts of the constitutional revision process. The following summary of the chronological development of constitutional revision relies mainly on the studies by Koseki and Takayanagi, which are most frequently cited in studies on the topic.

40. Tatsuo Satō, *Nihonkoku kenpō seiritsushi*, vol. 2 (Tokyo: Yūhikaku, 1964), 662.

41. Robert Ward, "Pre-surrender Planning: Treatment of the Emperor and Constitutional Changes," in Ward and Sakamoto, ed., *Democratizing Japan*, 16.

42. Its members were the United States, Britain, the Soviet Union, China, France, Holland, Canada, Australia, New Zealand, the Philippines, and India. Pakistan and Burma joined in 1949.

43. The note reads:

I. The emperor is at the head of the state. His succession is dynastic. His duties and powers will be exercised in accordance with the Constitution and responsive to the basic will of the people as provided therein.

II. War as a sovereign right of the nation is abolished. Japan renounces it as an instrumentality for settling its disputes and even for preserving its own security. It relies upon the higher ideals which are now stirring the world for its defense and its protection. No Japanese Army, Navy or Air Force will ever be authorized and no rights of belligerency will ever be conferred upon any Japanese force.

III. The feudal system of Japan will cease. No rights of peerage except those of the Imperial Family will extend beyond the lines of those now existent. No patent of nobility will from this time forth embody within itself any National or Civil power of government. Pattern budget after British system.

Reprinted in Takayanagi et al., *Nihonkoku kenpō*, vol. 1, 98–100.

44. Gordon, *The Only Woman in the Room*, 106.

45. Ibid., 108.

46. Ibid., 110.
47. Ibid., 158.
48. Ibid., 108.
49. Ibid., 107.
50. Ibid., 108.
51. Ibid., 111–112.
52. Ibid., 109.
53. Ibid., 15.
54. Ibid., 115–116.
55. Ibid., 116.
56. Ibid., 118.
57. Takayanagi et al., *Nihonkoku kenpō*, vol. 1, 266–278.
58. Ibid., 322.
59. Ibid., 326–328.
60. Koseki, *The Birth*, 115.
61. Ibid., 123–124.
62. "General MacArthur's Announcement Concerning the Proposed New Constitution of Japan," March 6, 1946, reprinted in *Political Reorientation of Japan*, Appendix C, 657.
63. "Leftist Infiltration into SCAP," February 27/April 23, 1947, File 2, Box 18, RG 23, MMAL. Also see Hellegers, *We the Japanese People*, vol. 2, 581.
64. "Leftist Infiltration," 3.
65. Ibid., 16.
66. Dower, *Embracing Defeat*, 400.
67. Ibid., 389; Koseki, *The Birth*, 168.
68. Koseki, *The Birth*, 172.
69. Tatsuo Satō, *Nihonkoku kenpō seiritsushi*, vol. 3/4 (Tokyo: Yūhikaku, 1994), 462.
70. For discussions on gender issues in the House of Representatives during the Ninetieth Imperial Diet Sessions, see *Teikoku kenpō kaisei shingiroku*, vol. 6, *Kihonteki jinken hen (jo)* (Ōkurashō Insatsukyoku, 1959). Part of these discussions are also translated and reproduced in Inoue, *MacArthur's Japanese Constitution*.
71. Biographical information and a discussion of the political career of Katō are provided in the next chapter.
72. *Teikoku Kenpō*, 406–407. See also Inoue, *MacArthur's Japanese Constitution*, 241–242.
73. *Teikoku Kenpō*, 415–416.
74. Koseki, *The Birth*, 3.
75. *Teikoku Kenpō*, 417.
76. Ibid., 430–431.
77. Ibid., 433.
78. Ibid., 434–435.
79. Satō, *Nihonkoku kenpō*, 885.

CHAPTER 3

1. Carmen Johnson, *Wave-Rings in the Water: My Years with the Women of Postwar Japan* (Alexandria, VA: Charles River Press, 1996).

2. Ibid., 11.

3. See, for example, Tats Blain, *Mother-Sir!* (New York: Appleton-Century Crofts, 1953), and Margery Finn Brown, *Over a Bamboo Fence: An American Looks at Japan* (New York: Morrow, 1951).

4. Oakes, *The Imaginary War*, 80.

5. Feminist scholars of the Cold War, such as Elaine Tyler May, Joanne Meyerowitx, and Laura McEnaney, provide excellent analyses about gender and containment culture within the United States, but offer little on how they shaped, and in turn were shaped by, political dynamics abroad. See May, *Homeward Bound*; Meyerowitz, ed., *Not June Cleaver*; and McEnaney, *Civil Defense Begins at Home*. For the studies that demonstrate the importance of examining political and cultural dynamics abroad as contributing factors to U.S. Cold War cultural formation, see Koshiro, *Transpacific Racisms*; Haddow, *Pavilions of Plenty*; Simpson, *An Absent Presence*; Klein, *Cold War Orienatlism*, and Shibusawa, *America's Geisha Ally*.

6. May, *Homeward Bound*, especially Chapter 4.

7. McEnaney, *Civil Defense Begins at Home*, 121.

8. "Mission and Accomplishments of the Occupation in the CIE Fields," October 1, 1949, File: "Staff Studies," Box 5246, RG 331, NRC.

9. Marlene Mayo, "The War of Words Continues: American Radio Guidance in Occupied Japan," in *The Occupation of Japan: Arts and Culture*, ed. Thomas Burkman (Norfolk, VA: The General Douglas MacArthur Foundation, 1984), 46.

10. See, for instance, Haddow, *Pavilions of Plenty*; Maria Höhn, *GIs and Fräuleins: The German-American Encounter in 1950s West Germany* (Chapel Hill: University of North Carolina Press, 2002); and Reinhold Wagnleitner, "The Irony of American Culture Abroad: Austria and the Cold War," in *Recasting America: Culture and Politics in the Age of Cold War*, ed. Larry May (Chicago: University of Chicago Press, 1989).

11. "Mission and Accomplishments," NRC.

12. Chikako Uemura "Nihon ni okeru senryō"; and Susan Pharr, "Ethel Weed," in *Notable American Women, The Modern Period*, ed. Barbara Sicherman and Carol Hurd (Cambridge, MA: Harvard University Press, 1980), 721–723.

13. Lisa Meyer, *Creating GI Jane: Sexuality and Power in the Women's Army Corps during World War II* (New York: Columbia University Press, 1996), 7.

14. John D'Emilio, *Sexual Politics*, 24.

15. "Pat," interview by Peter Adair, in *Word Is Out: Stories of Some of Our Lives*, ed. Nancy Adair and Casey Adair (San Francisco: New Glide Publication/Delta, 1978), 60–61.

16. For the argument that it was simply about male conservative sentiment against women's rights movement, see for example Pharr, "The Politics of Women's Rights," 237; and Uemura, "Nihon ni okeru senryō," 7.

17. McEnaney, *Civil Defense Begins at Home*, especially Chapter 4.

18. For this information, see Meyerowitz, "Introduction: Women and Gender in Postwar America, 1945–1960," in Meyerowitz, ed., *Not June Cleaver*, 15; and McEnaney, *Civil Defense Begins at Home*, 102.

19. "Progress of Japanese Women, for General Federation of Women's Clubs," File "Weed, Ethel (Featured Stories)," Box 5247, RG 331, NRC.

20. Sara Whitehurst to Alben Barkley, January 14, 1948, Folder "Ban—Baro," Box 7, RG 5, MMAL.

21. Douglas MacArthur to Alben Barkley, February 18, 1948, Folder "Ban—Baro," Box 7, RG 5, MMAL.

22. Memorandum from CI&E to Commander in Chief, February 18, 1948, Folder "Ban—Baro," Box 7, RG 5, MMAL.

23. Sarah Whitehurst to Douglas MacArthur, March 22, 1948, Folder "Wo-Wood," Box 12, RG 5, MMAL.

24. Rupp, *Worlds of Women*; and Tyrrell, *Women's World, Women's Empire*.

25. J. L. Blair Buck to Douglas MacArthur, July 8, 1948, Folder "Wo—Wood," Box 12, RG 5, MMAL.

26. Douglas MacArthur to J. L. Blair Buck, July 26, 1948, Folder "Wo—Wood," Box 12, RG 5, MMAL.

27. Sally Butler to Douglas MacArthur, January 23, 1948, Folder "Bus—Bz," Box 12, RG 5, MMAL.

28. Sally Butler to Douglas MacArthur, May 5, 1948, Folder "Bus—Bz," Box 12, RG 5, MMAL.

29. Request for Interview with Commander in Chief—Doris Cochrane, August 11, 1948, Folder "Misc 201," Box 40, RG 5, MMAL.

30. Paul Boyer, *By the Bomb's Early Light: American Thought and Culture at the Dawn of the Atomic Age* (Chapel Hill: University of North Carolina Press, 1985), especially Chapter 18.

31. Aleta Jessup to Douglas MacArthur, November 21, 1949, Folder "Wo—Wood," Box 62, RG 5, MMAL.

32. Augusta Kent Hobbs to Douglas MacArthur, September 1, 1949, Folder "His—Hof," Box 28, RG 5, MMAL.

33. Cora Brunemeir to Douglas MacArthur, January 20, 1951, Folder "Wo—Wood," Box 62, RG 5. MMAL, emphasis original.

34. Uemura, "Nihon ni okeru senryō," 18–23.

35. Nancy Cott, *A Woman Making History: Mary Ritter Beard through Her Letters* (New Haven, CT: Yale University Press, 1991), 37.

36. Ibid., 52.

37. Ibid., 54.

38. Ann Lane, ed., *Mary Ritter Beard: A Source Book* (New York: Schocken Books, 1977), 8.

39. Ibid., 69.

40. Mary Beard to Ethel Weed, July 10, 1946, Mary Beard Collection, Sophia Smith Collection, Smith College, Northampton, MA (hereafter SSC).

41. Mary Beard to Ethel Weed, August 15, 1946, Mary Beard Collection, SSC.

42. "Request for Information for American Historian Mrs. Mary R. Beard," August 29, 1946, Folder "Bea—Bee," Box 7, RG 5, MMAL.

43. Memorandum from the Office of Commander in Chief to the CI&E, Colonel Nugent, September 17, 1946, Folder "Bea—Bee," Box 7, RG 5, MMAL. Also see Gail Nomura, "The Allied Occupation of Japan: Reform of Japanese Government Labor Policy on Women" (PhD dissertation, University of Hawai'i at Manoa, 1978), 57–58, where she argues that "public relations motives" notwithstanding, MacArthur's statement "made

clear his commitment to promoting the greater participation of Japanese women in the political life of a new peaceful and democratic Japan."

44. Mary Beard to Ethel Weed, October 31, 1946, Folder 5, Box 2, RG 5, MMAL.

45. Mary Beard to Ethel Weed, October 31, 1946, Mary Beard Collection, SSC.

46. Mary Beard to Ethel Weed, August 28, 1950, Mary Beard Collection, SSC.

47. Ethel Weed to Mary Beard, February 12, 1947, Mary Beard Collection, SSC.

48. Mary Beard to Ethel Weed. February 25, 1947. Mary Beard Collection, SSC.

49. Mary Beard to Ethel Weed, March 30, 1947, Mary Beard Collection, SSC.

50. Mary Beard to Ethel Weed, February 8, 1946, Mary Beard Collection, SSC.

51. Mary Beard to Ethel Weed, October 31, 1946, Mary Beard Collection, SSC.

52. Mary Beard to Ethel Weed, October 27, 1947, Mary Beard Collection, SSC.

53. Mary Beard to Ethel Weed, June 13, 1949, Mary Beard Collection, SSC.

54. "Emergence of Women," File "Publicity," Box 8495, RG 331, NRC.

55. For Katō's biography, see Helen Hopper, *A New Woman of Japan: A Political Biography of Katō Shidzue* (Boulder, CO: Westview Press, 1996).

56. Ibid., 157.

57. Ibid., 159. It will be recalled that Yamada Kōsaku, Gauntlett Tsuneko's brother, played an instrumental role in bringing Beate Sirota Gordon and her parents to prewar Japan, as discussed in Chapter 2.

58. See for example, File "Interviews 1947–1949," Box 5248, and File "Political Parties," Box 5250, RG 331, NRC.

59. Nobuko Takahashi, interview by Kiyoko Nishi, *Senryōka no nihon fujin seisaku*, 77.

60. Hopper, *A New Woman of Japan*, 196–198.

61. For the information on Frank Buchman and MRA, see Garth Lean, *Frank Buchman: A Life* (London: Constable, 1985).

62. Hopper, *A New Woman of Japan*, 257.

63. See, for example, Haddow, *Pavilions of Plenty*. In addition to Koshiro, a number of scholars document the significance of sending Japanese to the U.S. as part of Cold War containment strategy. For the case of Hiroshima maidens, a group of women who traveled to the U.S. to undergo reconstruction surgery for the injuries caused by the atomic bomb and stayed with American families to learn, among others, domestic skills from their "American mothers," see Simpson, *An Absent Presence*, Chapter 4, and Shibusawa, *America's Geisha Ally*, Chapter 6. For the case of a former kamikaze pilot who was sent to the U.S. to attend college, see Shibusawa, *America's Geisha Ally*, Chapter 5.

64. Koshiro, *Transpacific Racisms*, 74–75.

65. Ibid., 39–40.

66. May, *Homeward Bound*, xxi.

67. "Report on Japanese Women's Visit to U.S.A.," July 5, 1950, File "Report of Women Leaders Activities," Box 10126, RG 331, NRC.

68. "General MacArthur Greets Women Leaders Departing for US," Folder #1 "Review of Government and Politics in Japan, January 1950," Box 96, RG 5, MMAL, 8–10.

69. "Report on Japanese Women's Visit," 11.

70. Ibid., 12.

71. Ibid., 13.

72. Ibid., 10.

73. Mary Beard to Ethel Weed, August 28, 1950, Mary Beard Collection, SSC.

74. See, for example, Haddow, *Pavilions of Plenty*, 216–217; May, *Homeward Bound*, 10–12; Emily Rosenberg, "Consuming Women: Images of Americanization in the 'American Century,'" *Diplomatic History* 23, no. 3 (1999): 487; Simpson, *An Absent Presence*, 123; and Kristina Zarlengo, "Civilian Threat, the Suburban Citadel, and Atomic Age American Women," *Signs: Journal of Women in Culture and Society* 24, no. 4 (1999): 942.

75. Haddow, *Pavilions of Plenty*, especially see Chapter 6.

76. Yoshikuni Igarashi, *Bodies of Memory: Narratives of War in Postwar Japanese Culture, 1945–1970* (Princeton, NJ: Princeton University Press, 2000), 78.

77. "Report on Japanese Women's Visit," 17–18.

78. Ibid., 9.

79. "Fujin no mitekita amerika," *Kangyō rōdō* 4, no. 8 (1950): 29.

80. For the arguments that Cold War domestic containment primarily focused on women's identities as mothers, see, for example, May, *Homeward Bound*. For the arguments that characterize American women's relationship to Asians during the Cold War as that of adoptive mothers and orphaned children, see Klein, *Cold War Orientalism*, Chapter 4, and Shibusawa, *America's Geisha Ally*, Chapter 1. For the arguments that characterize American women's relationship to Japanese women as that of mothers and daughters, see Shibusawa, *America's Geisha Ally*, Chapter 6, and Simpson, *An Absent Presence*, Chapter 4. In her analysis of the Hiroshima Maiden Project and American women's role as white mothers, Simpson sheds important light on the disturbance caused by Japanese American women who were involved in the project as ethnic, non-white mothers.

81. "Fujin no mitekita amerika," 32.

82. Ibid., 35.

83. Ibid., 29.

84. Ibid., 35.

85. "A Tour Round America," June 1950, File "Japanese Women in Unions," Box 8495, RG 331, NRC, 5.

86. Ibid., 6.

87. Ibid., 7.

88. No title, File "Leadership Training Course," Box 5246, RG 331, NRC.

89. "Minshuteki na dantai to wa," reprinted in *Fujin mondai shiryō shūsei*, vol. 2, *Seiji*, 641–651.

90. McEnaney, *Civil Defense Begins at Home*; Oakes, *The Imaginary War*.

91. Oakes, *The Imaginary War*, 116.

92. McEnaney, *Civil Defense Begins at Home*, 83.

93. Johnson, *Wave-Rings in the Water*, 72.

94. Ibid., 29.

95. Ibid., 72.

96. Ibid., 73.

97. Ibid., 73.

98. Ibid., 74.

99. Ibid., 52.

100. Helen Hosp Seamans, "Occupationaire Observed," unpublished manuscript, n.d., MMAL, 23–24.

101. "Field Trip through Southern Honshu, Shikoku, and Kyushu," File "Field Trip, Kyushu, Shikoku," Box 5246, RG 331, NRC.

102. Seamans, "Occupationaire Observed," 30.

103. Ibid., 35.

104. "Report on Women's Training Course in Democratic Organizations, Tokai Hokuriku Military Government Region," File "Women's and Minors,'" Box 5961, RG 331, NRC.

105. For the details about the internal dynamics of "Women's Hours" during the occupation, see Akihito Iimori, "Senryōka ni okeru josei taishō bangumi no keifu," *Hōsō to kenkyū* 11 and 12 (1990).

106. Marlene Mayo's study indicates that radio broadcasts were under strict regulation of the "Radio Code" of SCAP, which determined what would go on the air. While SCAP criticized the Japanese government's censorship prior to the surrender as "undemocratic practice," the occupation forces instituted their own system of censorship. As a result, anything that would be deemed critical of the occupation or the Allies was banned. According to Mayo, Katō Shizue, who was on the advisory committee, "doubled as a SCAP informant on the inside politics of electing a new BCJ president." Mayo, "The War of Words," 62.

107. Egami was also a participant in the 1950 Women's Reorientation Program that was discussed earlier.

108. Iimori, "Senryōka ni okeru," no. 12, 12.

109. Ibid., 13.

110. Ibid., 7.

111. Ethel Weed to Mary Beard, October 15, 1946, Mary Beard Collection, SSC.

112. Mary Beard to Ethel Weed, October 31, 1946, Mary Beard Collection, SSC.

113. Mary Beard to Ethel Weed, May 19, 1948, Mary Beard Collection, SSC.

114. Johnson, *Wave-Rings in the Water*, 48.

115. Ibid., 58.

116. Ibid., 140.

117. Ibid., 141.

118. Donald Roden, "From 'Old Miss' to New Professional: A Portrait of Women Educators under the American Occupation of Japan, 1945–1952," *History of Education Quarterly* 23, no.4 (1983): 478.

119. Ibid., 483–484.

CHAPTER 4

1. "Nosaka fujin ni kiku, soren no jitsujō," *Fujin Minshu Shinbun*, February 6, 1947, reprinted in *Fujin minshu shinbun shukusatsuban, 1946–1953*, ed. Fujin Minshu Kurabu (Tokyo: Fujin Minshu Kurabu, 1982).

2. Needless to say, the existence of Japanese women active in the leftist movements predates the occupation. For biographical information of individual women active in the popular rights, anarchist, socialist, and communist movements in pre-1945 Japan, see Mikiso Hane, *Reflections on the Way to the Gallows: Rebel Women in Prewar Japan*

(Berkeley and Los Angeles: University of California Press, 1988). For analysis of prewar socialist women and their identity formations as workers, activists, wives, and mothers, see Vera Mackie, *Creating Socialist Women in Japan: Gender, Labour and Activism, 1900–1937* (Cambridge: Cambridge University Press, 1997). For a collection of writings by prewar socialist women, see Yūko Suzuki, *Josei, hangyaku to kakumei to teikō to* (Tokyo: Shakai Hyōronsha, 1990).

3. Kondo, *About Face*, 10.

4. For a general review of labor and economic conditions against which these policies took place, see, for example, Dower, *Embracing Defeat*; Joe Moore, *Japanese Workers and the Struggle for Power, 1945–1947* (Madison: University of Wisconsin Press, 1983); and Eiji Takemae, *Sengo rōdō kaikaku* (Tokyo: Tokyo Daigaku Shuppankai, 1982).

5. Kiyoshi Inoue, *Gendai nihon josei shi*, (Tokyo: Sannichi Shobō, 1976), 650.

6. Moore, *Japanese Workers and the Struggle for Power*, 61.

7. Ibid., 69.

8. Ibid., 69–70.

9. Ibid., 42.

10. Yūko Suzuki, *Onnatachi no sengo rōdō undōshi* (Tokyo: Miraisha, 1994), 30.

11. Moore, *Japanese Workers and the Struggle for Power*, 110.

12. Dower, *Embracing Defeat*, 260.

13. "Sōgi ni hana saku fujin kōdōtai," *Rōdō Sensen*, November 5, 1946, Tokyo-to Rōdō Shiryō Sentā, Tokyo, Japan.

14. "Handō kōchō osore iru," *Rōdō Sensen*, December 3, 1946.

15. "Onna wa naze son nano ka," *Rōdō Sensen*, January 21, 1947.

16. *Nikkyōso fujinbu sanjūnenshi* (Tokyo: Rōdō Kyōiku Sentā,1977), 60–61.

17. For witness accounts of women unionists themselves, see Suzuki, *Onnatachi no sengo rōdō undōshi*, part 2.

18. "Activities Women's Section, Communist Party, and International Women's Day," March 9, 1948, File "Political Parties, Communist Party," Box 5250, RG 331, NRC, 14.

19. Ibid., 15.

20. "Seisan fukkō sugoroku," *Rōdō Sensen*, January 1, 1947.

21. For instance, see "Organization, Membership, and Activities of Women in Major Labor Federation, Special Report Prepared by Public Opinion and Sociological Research," July 30, 1947, File "Labor Union," Box 5248, RG 331, NRC.

22. According to Gail Nomura, because of its critical nature, MacArthur banned the publication of Mears's book in occupied Japan. Nomura, "The Allied Occupation of Japan," 91.

23. "Women's Labor and Political Movements," June 28, 1946, File "Labor, Labor Relations," Box 5248, RG 331, NRC, 1.

24. Ibid., 3.

25. Ibid., 4.

26. Ibid., 5.

27. Ibid., 6.

28. Ibid., 9.

29. Ibid., 12.

30. Ibid., 15.

31. *Fujin Bunka Kōza*, vol. 2, ed. Nihon Minshushugi Bunka Renmei (Tokyo: Naukasha, 1949), Kanagawa Josei Sentā, Fujisawa, Japan.

32. Ibid., 83

33. Ibid., 88.

34. Ibid., 89–90.

35. Ibid., 90.

36. Ibid., 91–92.

37. Ibid., 95–96.

38. Nobuko Hiroi, *Josei kakumeikatachi no shōgai* (Tokyo: Shin Nihon Shuppan, 1989), 122–145.

39. *Fujin Bunka Kōza*, 99.

40. Ibid., 101.

41. Ibid., 102–104.

42. Ibid., 109.

43. Ibid., 124.

44. Ibid., 106–108.

45. See McEnaney, *Civil Defense Begins at Home*, 60–61; Joanne Meyerowitz, "Beyond the Feminine Mystique: A Reassessment of Postwar Mass Culture, 1946–1958," in *Not June Cleaver*, 241; and Von Eschen, *Race against Empire,*129–130, 132.

46. *Fujin Bunka Kōza*, 116.

47. May, *Homeward Bound*, 13.

48. Meyerowitz, "Beyond the Feminine Mystique," 241.

49. *Fujin Bunka Kōza*, 115–118.

50. Ibid., 131.

51. Ibid., 132–133.

52. Ibid., 133–134.

53. Ibid., 137–138.

54. Ibid., 138–140.

55. Ibid., 140–142.

56. Helen Mears, "Women's Labor and Political Movements," June 28, 1946, File "Labor, Labor Relations," Box 5248, RG 331, NRC, 10.

57. Eiji Takemae, *Amerika tainichi rōdō seisaku no kenkyū* (Tokyo: Nihon Hyōronsha, 1970), 334–338.

58. "Warning against Mob Disorder or Violence," May 20, 1946, reprinted in *Political Reorientation of Japan*, 750.

59. *Primer of Democracy*, 2 vols., Folder 1, Box 112, Record Group 5, MMAL. Chapters 10 and 11 of the version available at the archive do not have page numbers; as appearing here, a serial number is assigned, staring with the first page of each chapter. In 1995, reproduction of the original Japanese-language version was published with the same title, *Minshushugi* (Tokyo: Kei Shobō, 1995).

60. *Primer*, vol. 1, Chapter 10 "Democracy and Labor Union," 3.

61. Ibid., Chapter 11, "Democracy and Dictatorship," 8–9.

62. Ibid., Chapter 10, 2–3.

63. Ibid., Chapter 10, 7.

64. Ibid., vol. 2, Chapter 15, "The New Rights and Responsibilities of Japanese Women," 39.

65. "Women and Labour Education," May 1948, File "Labor Management Problems, Informational Material," Box 2955, RG 331, NRC.

66. Ibid., 1.

67. Ibid., 1–2.

68. Ibid., 3.

69. Ibid., 4.

70. Ibid., 5.

71. "Women's Role in the Labor Movement," October 3, 1947, File "Japanese Women in Unions," Box 8495, RG 331, NRC. See also Nomura, "The Allied Occupation of Japan," 198.

72. "Women's Sections and Women's Divisions," September 14, 1947, File "Japanese Women in Unions," Box 8495, RG 331, NRC. See also Nomura, "The Allied Occupation of Japan," 196.

73. "Women's Role in the Labor Movement." See also Nomura, "The Allied Occupation of Japan," 198.

74. "Women's Sections and Women's Divisions." See also Nomura, "The Allied Occupation of Japan," 195.

75. Von Eschen, *Race against Empire*, 126.

76. May, *Homeward Bound*, xix.

77. Koshiro, *Transpacific Racisms*, 33.

78. "Women in Japanese Trade Unions," File "Women Workers Section: August Campaign," Box 8494, RG 331, NRC, 1. While it does not identify its date or author, the Japanese-language pamphlet that contains exactly the same information indicates that it was written by Golda Standard and issued to Japanese women unionists in 1948. *Fujinbu no shiori* (Tokyo: Nihon Rōdō Kumiai Sōdōmei Shuppanbu, 1948).

79. "Women in Japanese Trade Unions," 2.

80. Ibid., 2–3.

81. Ibid., 3.

82. Ibid., 3–4.

83. Suzuki, *Onnatachi no sengo rōdō undōshi*, 31.

84. Yuki Fujime, "Reisen taisei keiseiki no josei undō," in *Nihon shakai to gendō*, ed. Yoshiko Miyake (Tokyo: Akashi Shoten, 2001), 163–176.

85. Rupp, *Worlds of Women*, 47.

86. "Activities Women's Section, Communist Party, and International Women's Day." 87. Kazuko Kawaguchi et al., *Kokusai Fujin Dē no rekishi* (Tokyo: Azekura Shobō, 1980), 268–271.

88. Ibid., 283.

89. *Fujin Minshu Shinbun*, "Sekai no shinjosei," August 31, 1946.

90. *Fujin Minshu Shinbun*, "Chūgoku wa doko e yukuka," November 20, 1947.

91. *Fujin Minshu Shinbun*, "Keibō kara gikai e shinshutsu," November 6, 1948.

92. *Fujin Minshu Shinbun*, "Zenchūgoku Fujin Kaigi semaru," January 22, 1949, and "Kaihō no yorokobi to tomo ni," March 26, 1949.

93. *Fujin Minshu Shinbun*, "Chūgoku no shinseiken wa," May 7, 1949.

94. *Fujin Minshu Shinbun*, "Zenchūgoku no fujin sensen tōitsu e," May 14, 1949.

95. *Fujin Minshu Shinbun*, "Harubin no nihon fujin kara futatsu no tayori," July 15, 1950, and "Akarui hi o okuru Chūgoku no Nihon fujin," February 18, 1951.

96. According to Masao Miyoshi, Miyamoto's choice of career as a proletarian writer as well as her rejection of class privileges had taken place "not so much out of necessity as from moral and intellectual compunction. Hers was an act of *noblesse oblige*, not of *ressentiment*, at least at the initial stage." Masao Miyoshi, *Off Center: Power and Culture Relations between Japan and the United States* (Cambridge, MA: Harvard University Press, 1991), 198.

97. Ibid., 199.

98. Hopper, *A New Woman of Japan*, 196–199.

99. *Fujin Minshu Shinbun*, "Ajia Fujin Kaigi wa maneku," July 16 and 23, 1949.

100. *Fujin Minshu Shinbun*, "Ajia Fujin Kaigi, Minpukyō susunde sanka o hyōmei," July 23, 1949.

101. *Fujin Minshu Shinbun*, "Chūgoku to Nihon o musubu yūjō no tegami," February 3, 1950.

CHAPTER 5

1. "Medical Museum, Eighth Army Replacement Training Center," December 4, 1948, File "VD Control—Character Guidance Council Meetings," Box 9370, RG 331, NRC.

2. "Venereal Disease Control in Army Air Force Personnel," November 21, 1946, File "VD Control, 47–48," Box 9370, RG 331, NRC.

3. The issues of sexuality during the occupation, especially those concerning the regulation of prostitutes, fraternization, as well as the Recreation and Amusement Association (RAA) which was the government-sponsored brothel system that catered to American soldiers, have attracted the attention not only of scholars, but also of journalists. For journalistic accounts, see, for example, Masayo Duus, *Haisha no okurimono* (Tokyo: Kōdansha, 1995); and Daijirō Kobayashi and Akira Murase, *Minna wa shiranai kokka baishun meirei* (Tokyo: Yūhikaku Shuppan, 1992). For scholarly analysis with varying focuses, see, for example, Michael Molasky, *The American Occupation of Japan and Okinawa: Literature and Memory* (New York: Routledge, 1999); Akiko Sugiyama, "Haisen to R.A.A.," *Joseigaku Nenpō* no. 9 (1988); Tanaka, *Japan's Comfort Women*; Igarashi, *Bodies of Memory*; Karen Kelsky, *Women on the Verge: Japanese Women, Western Dreams* (Durham, NC: Duke University Press, 2001); Sheila Johnson, *The Japanese through American Eyes* (Stanford, CA: Stanford University Press, 1988); Koshiro, *Transpacific Racisms*; Dower, *Embracing Defeat*; Simpson, *An Absent Presence*; and Shibusawa, *America's Geisha Ally*. A number of divergent interpretations have emerged out of this body of literature. The treatment of Japanese women's sexuality during the occupation is considered an example of the universal characteristics of military violence against women by Tanaka, of racism by Koshiro, of gendered nationalist dynamic by Molasky, and of Orientalist and colonial dynamics of masculine domination and feminine subordination by Johnson, Kelsky, Simpson, Shibusawa, and Igarashi, among others. In contrast to these arguments, this chapter considers the occupation-time sexual dynamics as symptomatic of the Cold War containment politics.

4. Smith, "National Security," 312.

5. May, *Homeward Bound*, 81.

6. Michel Foucault, *The History of Sexuality. Vol. I, An Introduction* (New York: Vintage Books, 1990), 12.

7. Ibid., 30.

8. Existing "feminist" analyses tend to simplify the occupation-time sexual politics as an instance of masculine or male domination over feminine or female subordination and thereby elide the active roles played by Japanese women. For instance, Yuki Tanaka argues that the postwar controversies over prostitution are examples of masculine-military violence that is part of the universal pattern of male domination, and thus constructs women as simply victims under patriarchal oppressions. Tanaka, *Japan's Comfort Women*, 6. Examining Japanese postwar nationalist literature, Michael Molasky also characterizes the sexual politics during the occupation as the male or masculine domain where a "distinctly male perspective" that utilizes "metaphors of linguistic and sexual subordination" of women as the narrative vehicle prevailed. As a result, he argues, women writers were "less deeply invested in the gendered rhetoric of Japanese nationalist identity" and avoided the trope of gendered nationalist narratives. Molasky, *The American Occupation of Japan and Okinawa*, 2, 132. In contrast to both arguments that place women outside the problematic operations of power, this chapter argues that Japanese women, especially middle-class women leaders, were deeply invested in a gendered and sexualized understanding of nation, national body, and women and played extremely active and problematic roles in sexual regulation and containment of "fallen women" during the occupation.

9. Some scholars argue, however, that the sexual encounters constituted a site of resolution. For the argument that fraternization between American soldiers and Japanese women and subsequent controversies surrounding biracial children provided an occasion where American racism collaborated with that of Japan and in the end cemented, rather than disrupted, the postwar U.S.–Japan relationship, see Koshiro, *Trans-Pacific Racisms*, especially Chapter 5. For the argument that Japanese war brides who immigrated to the postwar United States helped rehabilitate American white masculinity on the one hand and solidified the American myth of racial integration and democracy on the other, see Simpson, *An Absent Presence*, especially Chapter 5, and Shibusawa, *America's Geisha Ally*, especially Chapter 1.

10. See, for instance, Dower, *Embracing Defeat*; Igarashi, *Bodies of Memory*; Johnson, *The Japanese through American Eyes*; Kelsky, *Women on the Verge*; and Simpson, *An Absent Presence*.

11. See, for instance, Duus, *Haisha no okurimono*; Kobayashi and Murase, *Minna wa shiranai*; Molasky, *The American Occupation of Japan and Okinawa*; Sugiyama, "Haisen to R.A.A."; Tanaka, *Japan's Comfort Women*. The following recounting of the R.A.A. and other sexual dynamics in the earliest days of the occupation relies on these sources.

12. Tanaka, *Japan's Comfort Women*, 137–138.

13. "Tokushu ian shisetsu kyōkai teimeisho narabi ni shuisho," reprinted in *Fujin mondai shiryō shūsei*, vol. 1, *Jinken*, ed. Fusae Ichikawa (Tokyo: Domesu Shuppan, 1978), 535–536.

14. Foucault, *The History of Sexuality*, 103.

15. "SCAPIN 153, Control of Venereal Disease," October 16, 1945, File "Summary Report: VD Control, October 1945–December 1949," Box 9321, RG 331, NRC. Also see Duus, *Haisha no okurimono*, 124; and Tanaka, *Japan's Comfort Women*, 156.

16. "SCAPIN 642, Abolition of Licensed Prostitution in Japan," January 21, 1946, File "Summary Report: VD Control, October 1945–December 1949," Box 9321, RG 331. NRC. See also Duus, *Haisha no okurimono*, 177; and Tanaka, *Japan's Comfort Women*, 161.

17. In reality, venereal disease has historically been a major issue for U.S. military operations both domestically and internationally. See, for example, Allan Brandt, *No Magic Bullet: A Social History of Venereal Disease in the United States since 1880* (New York: Oxford University Press, 1985) for the account up to the end of World War II; Saundra Pollock Sturdevant and Branda Stoltzfus, eds., *Let the Good Times Roll: Prostitution and the U.S. Military in Asia* (New York: New Press, 1992) for the postwar account in Okinawa, Korea, and the Philippines; and Cynthia Enloe, *Bananas, Beaches and Bases: Making Feminist Sense of International Politics* (Berkeley and Los Angeles: University of California Press, 1989).

18. Brandt, *No Magic Bullet*, see especially Chapter 2.

19. Ibid., 172.

20. "Repression of Prostitution, Tokyo-Yokohama Chapter, Army-Navy Chaplains Association," January 11, 1946, File "VD Control 1945–1946," Box 9370, RG 331, NRC, 1. Also see Duus, *Haisha no okurimono*, 194; Tanaka, *Japan's Comfort Women*, 159–160.

21. "Repression of Prostitution," 3.

22. Ibid., 4.

23. May, *Homeward Bound*, 82.

24. "The Commanding Officer's use of his Chaplains to impress moral responsibility and self-disciplining in his command, in enforcing WD Cir. 227, Sect. IV, Par Ib (1) of 20 August 47," December 1947, File "VD Control, 1947–1948," Box 9370, RG 331, 1, NRC.

25. Ibid., 2.

26. Ibid., 3.

27. Ibid., 4.

28. "Venereal Disease Trainees, Eighth Army Replacement Training Center," July 2, 1948, File "VD Control—Character Guidance Council Meetings," Box 9370, RG 331, NRC.

29. "Venereal Disease Indoctrination Course, Special Services," December 1947, File: VD Control, 1947–1948, Box 9370, NRC, 2.

30. Ibid., 3.

31. Ibid., 2.

32. Ibid., 3.

33. Ibid., 4.

34. Ibid., 5.

35. Quoted in "Summary Report of Venereal Disease Control Activities in Japan, October 1945–December 1949," File "Summary Report, VD Control, October 1945 to December 1949," Box 9321, RG 331, NRC, 17.

36. "Venereal Disease Control in Army Air Force Personnel," November 21, 1946, File "VD Control 47–48," Box 9370, RG 331, NRC, 1.

37. "Round-up of Prostitutes," November 29, 1946, File, "Prostitution," Box 5250, RG 331; "Reports on Round-Up of Japanese Women," January 10, 1947, File "Solicitation of the Troops for the Purpose of Prostitution," Box 2191, RG 331, NRC. For an

account of the Ikebukuro case and especially uncritical descriptions of the roles played by Japanese Diet women, Ethel Weed, and other occupiers, see also Duus, *Haisha no okurimono*, 241–245.

38. "Rally to Protect Women," December 15, 1946, File "Prostitution," Box 5250, RG 331, NRC, 1.

39. Ibid., 4.

40. Ibid., 3–4.

41. "Petition to General MacArthur," December 15, 1946, 82 B, Reel 9, Hussey Papers, Microfilm, National Diet Library, Tokyo, Japan.

42. "Alleged Maladministration of V.D. Control by Japanese Police," January 23, 1947, File "Solicitation of the Troops for the Purpose of Prostitution," Box 2191, RG 331, NRC.

43. "Petition Concerning the Control of Prostitution, from Chief, Oita Liaison and Coordination Office, to the Commanding Officer, Oita Military Government Team," December 8, 1948, File "VD Control, Staff Visits," Box 9936, RG 331, NRC.

44. For an excellent discussion of the male-centered nature of anti-imperial nationalist politics, see Hyunah Yang, "Remembering the Korean Military Comfort Women: Nationalism, Sexuality, and Silencing," in *Dangerous Women: Gender and Korean Nationalism*, ed. Elaine Kim and Chungmoo Choi (New York: Routledge, 1998). Focusing on the postwar Korean politics, she reveals how Korean nationalist protests concerning "comfort women" are motivated by Korean men's insistence at "owning" their women and how such masculine nationalist discourses displace women from the position of subjects in the debates over Japanese colonial rule and its consequences. As she succinctly points out, Korean women simply become the "ground" on which the talks between Korean and Japanese men take place.

45. "Petition Concerning the Control of Prostitution." This memo was attached to the petition by Yamashita, but not signed by him. It is hard to discern whether Yamashita was the author.

46. "Summary Report of Venereal Disease Control Activities in Japan, October 1945–December 1949," 17.

47. Ibid., 18.

48. "Conference on V.D. Control," November 1, 1945, File "VD Control 1945–1946," Box 9370, RG 331, NRC.

49. "Non-cooperation of Ministry of Health and Welfare," February 6, 1947, File "VD Control 1947–1948," Box 9370, RG 331, NRC.

50. Igarashi, *Bodies of Memory*, 65–66.

51. "Summary Report of Venereal Disease Control Activities in Japan," 5.

52. Ibid., 11–12.

53. "The Principles of Venereal Disease Control," June 1947, and "Venereal Disease Control Service in the Health Center," October 3, 1949, File "Summary Report: VD Control—October 1945 to December 1949," Box 9321, RG 331, NRC.

54. "Summary Report of Venereal Disease Control Activities in Japan," 12.

55. Ibid. .

56. Ibid., 22.

57. Duus, *Haisha no okurimono*, 276.

58. Garon, "The World's Oldest Debate?" 729.

59. "Report of the Central Coordinating Committee for Women's Welfare," File "Protection of Women," Box 2851, RG 331, NRC, 1.

60. Ibid., 2.

61. Ibid., 2–3.

62. "Paper by Mr. Kimiji Sato Reporting His Findings Concerning Rape and Prostitution and the Handling of Female Delinquents by the Police and VD Control Officials," September 21, 1949, File "Rehabilitation of Prostitutes," Box 9370, RG 331, NRC, 1.

63. Ibid., 2.

64. Ibid., 4.

65. Ibid., 5.

66. "A Draft of Principles—Purity Education, by the Committee of Purity Education," File "Sex Education," Box 5247, RG 331, NRC.

67. May, *Homeward Bound*, 88.

68. "Rehabilitation Homes for Women," August 12, 1950, File "Rehabilitation of Prostitutes," Box 9370, RG 331, NRC, 3.

69. Ibid., 12.

70. Ibid., 3.

71. Ibid., 6.

72. Ibid., 7.

73. Ibid., 9.

74. Ibid., 10.

75. Ibid. .

76. Ibid., 8–9.

77. Ibid., 13.

78. Ibid., 14.

79. Ibid., 15.

80. Ibid., 16.

81. "Minimum Standard for the Girls' Rehabilitation Institution," File "Rehabilitation of Prostitutes," Box 9370, RG 331, NRC, 8.

82. Ibid., 4.

83. Ibid., 5.

84. Ibid., 9.

85. Ibid., 13.

86. Ibid., 14.

87. Yuki Fujime, "Akasen jūgyōin kumiai to baishun bōshihō," *Josei Shigaku*, vol. 1 (1991); *Sei no rekishigaku* (Tokyo: Fuji Shuppan, 1999), especially Chapter 9; and Masako Fukae, "Seidōtoku kara no kaihō," *Onna: Erosu* 9 (1977).

CHAPTER 6

1. Kondo, *About Face*, 149.

2. Grewal, *Home and Harem*, 11.

Bibliography

Adair, Nancy, and Chasey Adair. "Pat." In *Word Is Out: Stories of Some of Our Lives*. 55–65. New York: Delta, 1978.

Barlow, Tani. "Introduction: On 'Colonial Modernity.'" In *Formations of Colonial Modernity in East Asia,* edited by Tani Barlow. 1–20. Durham, NC: Duke University Press, 1997.

Beard, Mary. *America through Women's Eyes*. New York: Macmillan, 1933.

———. *Woman as Force in History: A Study in Traditions and Realities*. New York: Octagon Press, 1946.

———. *The Force of Women in Japanese History*. Washington, DC: Public Affairs Press, 1953.

Berube, Allan. *Coming out under Fire: The History of Gay Men and Women in World War Two*. New York: Free Press, 1990.

Blain, Tats. *Mother-Sir!*. New York: Appleton-Century Crofts, 1953.

Boisseau, Tracey Jean. *White Queen: May French-Sheldon and the Imperial Origins of American Feminist Identity*. Bloomington: Indiana University Press, 2004.

Boyer, Paul. *By the Bomb's Early Light: American Thought and Culture at the Dawn of the Atomic Age*. Chapel Hill: University of North Carolina Press, 1985.

Bradley, Mark. "Slouching toward Bethlehem: Culture, Diplomacy, and the Origins of the Cold War in Vietnam." In *Cold War Constructions: The Political Culture of United States Imperialism, 1945–1966,* edited by Christian G. Appy. 11–34. Amherst: The University of Massachusetts Press, 2000.

Brandt, Allan. *No Magic Bullet: A Social History of Venereal Disease in the United States since 1880*. New York: Oxford University Press, 1985.

Brown, Margery Finn. *Over a Bamboo Fence: An American Looks at Japan.* New York: Morrow, 1951.

Burton, Antoinette. *Burdens of History: British Feminists, Indian Women, and Imperial Culture, 1865–1915.* Chapel Hill: University of North Carolina Press, 1994.

Chang, Iris. *The Rape of Nanking: The Forgotten Holocaust of World War II.* New York: Penguin, 1997.

Chaudhuri, Nupur, and Margaret Strobel, eds. *Western Women and Imperialism: Complicity and Resistance.* Bloomington: Indiana University Press, 1992.

Cohan, Steven. *Masked Men: Masculinity and the Movies in the Fifties.* Bloomington: Indiana University Press, 1997.

Costigliola, Frank. "The Nuclear Family: Tropes of Gender and Pathology in the Western Alliance." *Diplomatic History* 21, no. 2 (1997): 163–183.

Cott, Nancy. *A Woman Making History: Mary Ritter Beard through Her Letters.* New Haven, CT: Yale University Press, 1991.

D'Emilio, John. *Sexual Politics, Sexual Communities: The Making of a Homosexual Minority in the United States, 1940–1970.* Chicago: University of Chicago Press, 1983.

Dower, John. "Occupied Japan and the American Lake, 1945–1950. In *America's Asia: Dissenting Essays on Asian American Relations,* edited by Edward Friedman and Mark Sheldon. 145–206. New York: Pantheon, 1971.

———. "Occupied Japan as History and Occupation History as Politics." *Journal of Asian Studies* 34, no. 2 (1975): 485–504.

———. *Empire and Aftermath: Yoshida Shigeru and the Japanese Experience, 1878–1954.* Cambridge, MA: Harvard University Press, 1979.

———. *War without Mercy: Race and Power in the Pacific War.* New York: Pantheon, 1986.

———. *Embracing Defeat: Japan in the Wake of World War II.* New York: Norton, 1999.

Dudziak, Mary. *Cold War Civil Rights: Race and the Image of American Democracy.* Princeton, NJ: Princeton University Press, 2000.

Duus, Masayo. *Haisha no okurimono.* Tokyo: Kōdansha Bunko, 1995.

Enloe, Cynthia. *Bananas, Beaches and Bases: Making Feminist Sense of International Politics.* Berkeley and Los Angeles: University of California Press, 1989.

Fanon, Frantz. *A Dying Colonialism.* New York: Grove Press, 1965.

Ferguson, Kathy, and Phyllis Turnbull. *Oh, Say, Can You See?: The Semiotics of the Military in Hawai'i.* Minneapolis: University of Minnesota Press, 1999.

Foucault, Michel. *The History of Sexuality, Volume I: An Introduction.* New York: Vintage Books, 1990.

Fujime, Yuki. "Akasen jūgyōin kumiai to baishun bōshihō." *Josei Shigaku* (1991): 16–36.

———. *Sei no rekishigaku.* Tokyo: Fuji Shuppan, 1999.

———. "Reisen taisei keiseiki no josei undō." In *Nihon Shakai To Jendā,* edited by Yoshiko Miyake. 159–186. Tokyo: Akashi Shoten, 2001.

Fujin Minshu Kubaru, ed. *Fujin minshu shinbun shukusatsuban, 1946–1953.* Tokyo: Fujin Minshu Kubaru, 1982.

Fukae, Masako. "Seidōtoku kara no kaihō." *Onna: Erosu* 9 (1977): 11–62.

Garon, Sheldon. "The World's Oldest Debate? Prostitution and the State in Imperial Japan, 1900–1945." *American Historical Review* 98, no. 3 (1993): 710–732.

———. "Women's Groups and the Japanese State: Contending Approaches to Political Integration, 1890–1945." *Journal of Japanese Studies* 19, no. 1 (1993): 5–41.

Gordon, Beate Sirota. *1945-nen no kurisumasu*. Tokyo: Kashiwa Shobō, 1995.

———. *The Only Woman in the Room: A Memoir*. Tokyo: Kōdansha International, 1997.

———. "Nightline: The Only Woman in the Room." Interview by Ted Koppel. *ABC Nightline*, February 10, 1999. ABC Transcript #4620.

———. "Morning Edition." Interview by Jackie Judd. National Public Radio, February 18, 2002.

Gluck, Carol. "Entangling Illusions: Japanese and American Views of the Occupation." In *New Frontiers in American–East Asian Relations*, edited by Warren Cohen. 169–236. New York: Columbia University Press, 1983.

Grewal, Inderpal. *Home and Harem: Nation, Gender, Empire, and the Cultures of Travel*. Durham, NC: Duke University Press, 1996.

Grewal, Inderpal, and Caren Kaplan, eds. *Scattered Hegemonies: Postmodernity and Transnational Feminist Practices*. Minneapolis: University of Minnesota Press, 1994.

Grewal, Inderpal, Akhil Gupta, and Aihwa Ong. "Guest Editors' Introduction." *Positions: East Asia Cultures Critique–Asian Transnationalities* 7, no. 3 (1999): 653–666.

Haddow, Robert. *Pavilions of Plenty: Exhibiting American Culture Abroad in the 1950s*. Washington, DC: Smithsonian Institution Press, 1997.

Hane, Mikiso. *Reflections on the Way to the Gallows*. Berkeley and Los Angeles: University of California Press, 1988.

Hayakawa, Noriko. "Nationalism, Colonialism and Women: The Case of the World Woman's Christian Temperance." In *Women's Rights and Human Rights: International Historical Perspectives*, edited by Patricia Grimshaw, Katie Holmes, and Marilyn Lake. 16–30. New York: Palgrave, 2001.

Helleger, Dale. *We, the Japanese People: World War II and the Origins of the Japanese Constitution*. 2 vols. Stanford, CA: Stanford University Press, 2001.

Higgins, Raymond. *From Hiroshima with Love: The Allied Military Governor's Remarkable Story of the Rebuilding of Japan's Business and Industry after WWII*. Phoenix, AZ: VIA Press, 1995.

Hiroi, Nobuko. *Josei kakumeika tachi no shōgai*. Tokyo: Shin Nihon Shuppan Sha, 1989.

Hoganson, Kristin. *Fighting for American Manhood: How Gender Politics Provoked the Spanish–American and Philippine–American Wars*. New haven, CT: Yale University Press, 1998.

Höhn, Maria. *GIs and Fräuleins: The German–American Encounter in 1950s West Germany*. Chapel Hill: University of North Carolina Press, 2002.

Hopper, Helen. *A New Woman of Japan: A Political Biography of Kato Shidzue*. Boulder, CO: Westview Press, 1996.

Hunter, Jane. *The Gospel of Gentility: American Women Missionaries in Turn of the Century China*. New Haven, CT: Yale University Press, 1984.

Hussey Papers. Microfilm. National Diet Library, Tokyo, Japan.

Ichikawa, Fusae. *Ichikawa Fusae jiden, senzenhen*. Tokyo: Shinjuku Shobō, 1981.

———, ed. *Nihon fujin mondai shiryōshūsei*. Vol. 1, *Jinken*. Tokyo Domesu Shuppan, 1978.

————, ed. *Nihon fujin mondai shiryō shūsei*. Vol. 2, *Seiji*. Tokyo: Domesu Shuppan, 1978.

Igarashi, Yoshikuni. *Bodies of Memory: Narratives of War in Postwar Japanese Culture, 1945–1970*. Princeton, NJ: Princeton University Press, 2000.

Iimori, Akihiko. "Senryōka ni okeru josei taishō bangumi no keifu, 1: 'Fujin no Jikan' no fukkatsu." *Hōsō to Kenkyū* 11 (1990): 2–19.

————. "Senryōka ni okeru josei taishō bangumi no keifu, 2: 'Fujinka' no Tanjō" *Hōsō to Kenkyū* 12 (1990): 2–19.

Inoue, Kiyoshi. *Gendai nihon joseishi*. Tokyo: Sannichi Shobō, 1976.

Inoue, Kyōko. *MacArthur's Japanese Constitution: A Linguistic and Cultural Study of Its Making*. Chicago: University of Chicago Press, 1991.

Ishimoto, Shizue. *Facing Two Ways: The Story of My Life*. New York: Farrar and Rinehart, 1935.

Itō, Megumi. "CI&E kyōikuka no fujin kyōiku seisaku." In *GHQ no shakai kyōiku seisaku*, edited by Toshio Ogawa. 209–233. Tokyo: Ōzorasha, 1990.

Itō, Yasuko. *Sengo niohon josei shi*. Tokyo: Ōtsuki Shoten, 1974.

Jayawardena, Kumari. *The White Woman's Other Burden: Western Women and South Asia during British Colonial Rule*. New York: Routledge, 1995.

Johnson, Carmen. *Wave-Rings in the Water: My Years with the Women of Postwar Japan*. Alexandria, VA: Charles River Press, 1996.

Johnson, Sheila. *The Japanese through American Eyes*. Stanford, CA: Stanford University Press, 1988.

Kangyō Rodō. "Fujin no mitekita amerika." *Kangyō rōdō* 4, no. 8 (1950): 28–35.

Kaplan, Amy. "Left Alone with America: The Absence of Empire in the Study of American Culture." In *Cultures of United States Imperialism*, edited by Amy Kaplan and Donald Pease. 3–21. Durham, NC: Duke University Press, 1993.

Kawaguchi, Kazuko, Oyama Itoko, and Itō Setsu, eds. *Kokusai Fujin Dē no rekishi*. Tokyo: Azekura Shobō, 1980.

Kelskey, Karen. *Women on the Verge: Japanese Women, Western Dreams*. Durham, NC: Duke University Press, 2001.

Kenpō Chōsakai Jimukyoku. *Teikoku kenpō kaisei shigiroku*. Vol. 6, *Kihonteki jinken (jō)*, and Vol. 7, *Kihonteki jinken (ge)*. Tokyo: Kenpō Chōsakai Jimu Kyoku, 1959.

Klein, Christina. *Cold War Orienatlism: Asia in the Middlebrow Imagination, 1945–1961*. Berkeley and Los Angeles: University of California Press, 2003.

Kobayashi, Daijiro, and Akira Murase. *Minnawa shiranai kokka baishun meirei*. Tokyo: Yūhikaku, 1992.

Kodama, Katsuko. *Oboegaki: sengo no Ichikawa Fusae*. Tokyo: Shinjuku Shobō, 1985.

Koikari, Mire. "Rethinking Gender and Power in the US Occupation of Japan, 1945–1952." *Gender and History* 11, no. 2 (1999): 313–335.

————. "Exporting Democracy? American Women, 'Feminist Reforms,' and Politics of Imperialism in the U.S. Occupation of Japan, 1945–1952." *Frontiers: A Journal of Women Studies* 23, no. 1 (2002): 23–45.

Kōjiya, Mikiko. *Sensō o ikita onnatachi*. Kyoto, Japan: Mineruba Shobō, 1985.

Kondo, Dorinne. *About Face: Performing Race in Fashion and Theater*. New York: Routledge, 1997.

Koseki, Shōichi. *The Birth of Japan's Postwar Constitution*. Translated by Ray A. Moore. Boulder, CO: Westview Press, 1997.

Koshiro, Yukiko. *Transpacific Racisms and the U.S. Occupation of Japan*. New York: Columbia University Press, 1999.

Kristof, Nicholas. "The Veiled Resources." *New York Times*, December 11, 2001.

Lane, Ann, ed. *Mary Beard: A Source Book*. New York: Schocken Books, 1977.

Lean, Garth. *Frank Buchman: A Life*. London: Constable, 1985.

Lee, Robert. *Orientals: Asian Americans in Popular Culture*. Philadelphia: Temple University Press, 1999.

Levine, Philippa, ed. *Gender and Empire*. Oxford: Oxford University Press, 2004.

Lewis, Reina. *Gendering Orientalism: Race, Femininity and Representation*. London: Routledge, 1996.

Lipsitz, George. *Class and Culture in Cold War America: "A Rainbow at Midnight."* New York: Prager, 1981.

MacArthur, Douglas. 1947. "A Fourth of July Message from General Douglas MacArthur." *Life* 23, no. 1 (1947): 34.

———. *Reminiscences*. New York: McGraw-Hill, 1964.

MacArthur Memorial, Archives and Library. The Records of the US Occupation of Japan. MacArthur Memorial, Archives, and Library, Norfolk, VA.

Mackie, Vera. *Creating Socialist Women in Japan: Gender, Labour and Activism, 1900–1937*. Cambridge: Cambridge University Press, 1997.

Mary Beard Collection. Sophia Smith Collection. Smith College. Northampton, MA.

May, Elaine Tyler. *Homeward Bound: American Families in the Cold War Era*. New York: Basic Books, 1999.

Mayo, Marlene. "The War of Words Continues: American Radio Guidance in Occupied Japan." In *The Occupation of Japan: Arts and Culture*, edited by Thomas Burkman. 45–83. Norfolk, VA: The General Douglas MacArthur Foundation, 1984.

McClintock, Anne. *Imperial Leather: Race, Gender and Sexuality in the Colonial Context*. New York: Routledge, 1995.

McEnaney, Laura. *Civil Defense Begins at Home: Militarization Meets Everyday Life in the Fifties*. Princeton, NJ: Princeton University Press, 2000.

Mears, Helen. *Mirror for Americans, Japan*. Boston: Houghton Mifflin, 1948.

Meyer, Lisa. *Creating GI Jane: Sexuality and Power in the Women's Army Corps during World War II*. New York: Columbia University Press, 1996.

Meyerowitz, Joanne, ed. *Not June Cleaver: Women and Gender in Postwar America, 1945–1960*. Philadelphia: Temple University Press, 1994.

Michel, Sonya. "American Women and the Discourse of the Democratic Family in World War II." In *Behind the Lines: Gender and the Two World Wars*, edited by Margaret Higonnet, Jane Jenson, Sonya Michel, and Margaret Weitz. 154–167. New Haven, CT: Yale University Press, 1987.

Michener, James. *Sayonara*. New York: Random House, 1953.

Miyoshi, Masao. *Off Center: Power and Culture Relations between Japan and the United States*. Cambridge, MA: Harvard University Press, 1991.

Mohanty, Chandra. "Under Western Eyes: Feminist Scholarship and Colonial Discourse." In *Third World Women and the Politics of Feminism*, edited by Chandra Mohanty, Ann Russo, and Lourdes Torres. Bloomington: Indiana University Press, 1991.

Molasky, Michael. *The American Occupation of Japan and Okinawa: Literature and Memory*. New York: Routledge, 1999.

Monbushō. *Minshushugi*. Tokyo: Kei Shobō, 1996.

Moore, Joe. *Japanese Workers and the Struggle for Power, 1945–1947*. Madison: University of Wisconsin Press, 1983.

Morgan, Susan. *Place Matters: Gendered Geography in Victorian Women's Travel Books about Southeast Asia*. New Brunswick, NJ: Rutgers University Press, 1996.

New York Times. "Earnest Hoberecht, Popular Novelist in Occupied Japan, Is Dead at 81," September 26, 1999.

Nihon Minshushugi Bunka Renmei, ed. *Fujin Bunka Kōza (gekan)*. Tokyo: Nauka Sha, 1949.

Nihon Rōdō Kumiai Sōdōmei Honbu Fujin Taisaku Bu, ed. 1948. *Fujinbu no shiori*. Tokyo: Nihon Rōdōkumiai Sōdōmei Shuppanbu, 1948.

Nikkyōso Fujin Bu, ed. *Nikkyōso fujinbu sanjūnen shi*. Tokyo: Rōdō Kyōiku Sentār, 1977.

Nishi, Kiyoko. *Senryō ka no nihon fujin seisaku: sono rekishi to shōgen*. Tokyo: Domesu Shuppan, 1985.

Nomura, Gail. "The Allied Occupation of Japan: Reform of Japanese Government Labor Policy on Women." PhD diss., University of Hawai'i at Manoa, 1978.

Oakes, Guy. *The Imaginary War: Civil Defense and American Cold War Culture*. New York: Oxford University Press, 1994.

Ōkurashō Insatsukyoku. *Teikoku kenpō kaisei shingiroku*. Vol. 6, *Kihonteki jinken hen (jō)*. Tokyo: Ōkurashō Insatsukyoku, 1959.

Pharr, Susan. "Ethel Weed." In *Notable American Women, the Modern Period*, edited by Barbara Sicherman and Carol Hurd. 721–723. Cambridge, MA: Harvard University Press, 1980.

———. "The Politics of Women's Rights." In *Democratizing Japan: The Allied Occupation*, edited by Robert Ward and Yoshikazu Sakamoto. 221–252. Honolulu: University of Hawai'i Press, 1987.

Rafael, Vicente. *White Love and Other Events in Filipino History*. Durham, NC: Duke University Press, 2000.

———, ed. *Discrepant Histories: Translocal Essays on Filipino Cultures*. Philadelphia: Temple University Press, 1995.

Roden, Donald. "From 'Old Miss' to New Professional: A Portrait of Women Educators under the American Occupation of Japan, 1945–1952." *History of Education Quarterly* 23, no.4 (1983): 469–489.

Rōdō Sensen Henshūkyoku. *Rōdō Sensen: zen nihon sangyōbetsu rōdō kumiai kaigi kikanshi. 1946–1949*. Tokyo: Tokyo-to Rōdō Shiryō Sentā.

Rosenberg, Emily. "Consuming Women: Images of Americanization in the 'American Century.'" *Diplomatic History* 23, no. 3 (1999): 479–497.

Rubin, Gayle. "Thinking Sex: Notes for a Radical Theory of the Politics of Sexuality." In *Pleasure and Danger: Exploring Female Sexuality*, edited by Carole Vance. 267–319. New York: Pandra Press, 1989.

Rupp, Leila. *Worlds of Women: The Making of an International Women's Movement*. Princeton, NJ: Princeton University Press, 1997.

Rupp, Leila, and Verta Taylor. *Survival in the Doldrums: The American Women's Rights Movement, 1945 to 1960*. Columbus: Ohio State University Press, 1990.

Sakai, Harumi. "GHQ de hataraita joseitachi." *Joseigaku Kenkyū* no. 3 (1992): 30–43.

Sakurai, Kinue. *Bosei hogo undōshi*. Tokyo: Domesu Shuppan, 1991.

Satō, Tatsuo. *Nihonkoku kenpō seiritsushi*. 4 vols. Tokyo: Yūhikaku, 1967–1994.

SCAP Records. Record Group #331. National Records Center, Suitland, MD.

Scott, Joan. *Gender and the Politics of History*. New York: Columbia University Press, 1988.

Seamans, Helen Hosp. "Occupationaire Observes." MacArthur Memorial, Archives and Library. n.d.

Serlin, David. "Christin Jorgensen and the Cold War Closet." *Radical History Review* 62 (1995): 136–165.

Shibusawa, Naoko. *America's Geisha Ally: Reimagining the Japanese Enemy*. Cambridge, Massachusetts: Harvard University Press, 2006.

Shikoku Military Government Region. "Techniques of Democracy: A Guide to Procedure for Japanese Organizations." n.d. Author's collection.

Simpson, Caroline. *An Absent Presence: Japanese Americans in Postwar American Culture, 1945–1960*. Durham, NC: Duke University Press, 2001.

Smith, Geoffrey. "National Security and Personal Isolation: Sex, Gender, and Disease in the Cold War United States." *International History Review* 14, no. 2 (1992): 307–337.

Spivak, Gayatri Chakravorty. "Three Women's Texts and a Critique of Imperialism." In *"Race," Writing, and Difference,* edited by Henry Louis Gates, Jr. 262–280. Chicago: University of Chicago Press, 1986.

Stoler, Ann. "Carnal Knowledge and Imperial Power: Gender, Race, and Morality in Colonial Asia." In *Gender at the Crossroads of Knowledge: Feminist Anthropology in the Postmodern Era*, edited by Micaela di Leonardo. 51–101. Berkeley and Los Angeles: University of California Press, 1991.

———. "Rethinking Colonial Categories: European Communities and the Boundaries of Rule." In *Colonialism and Culture*, edited by Nicholas Dirks. 319–352. Ann Arbor: University of Michigan Press, 1992.

Sturdevant, Saundra Pollock, and Brenda Stoltzfus, eds. *Let the Good Times Roll: Prostitution and the U.S. Military in Asia*. New York: New Press, 1992.

Sugiyama, Akiko. "Haisen to R.A.A." *Joseigaku Nenpō* no. 9 (1988): 34–46.

Supreme Commander for Allied Powers. *Political Reorientation of Japan, September 1945 to September 1948: Report of Government Section, Supreme Commander for Allied Powers*. 2 vols. Hamilton Library, University of Hawai'i at Manoa, Honolulu, Hawai'i.

Suzuki, Akinori. *Nihonkoku kenpō o unda misshitsu no kokonokakan*. Osaka, Japan: Sōgensha, 1995.

Suzuki, Yūko. *Feminizumu to sensō*. Tokyo: Marujusha, 1988.

———. *Josei, hangyaku to kakumei to teikō to*. Tokyo: Shakai Hyōronsha, 1990.

———. *Onnatachi no sengo rōdō undōshi*. Tokyo: Miraisha, 1994.

Takayanagi, Kenzō, Ichirō Ōtomo, and Hideo Tanaka, eds. *Nihonkoku kenpō seitei no katei*. 2 vols. Tokyo: Yūhikaku, 1972.

Takemae, Eiji. *Amerika tainichi rōdō seisaku no kenkyū*. Tokyo: Nihon Hyōron Sha, 1970.

———. *Sengo rōdō kaikaku*. Tokyo: Tokyo Daigaku Shuppan Kai, 1982.

Tamanoi, Mariko. *Under the Shadow of Nationalism: Politics and Poetics of Rural Japanese Women*. Honolulu: University of Hawai'i Press, 1998.

Tanaka, Yuki. *Japan's Comfort Women: Sexual Slavery and Prostitution during World War II and the U.S. Occupation.* New York: Routledge, 2002.

Trask, Haunani Kay. *From a Native Daughter: Colonialism and Sovereignty in Hawai'i.* Monroe, ME: Common Courage Press, 1993.

Tyrrell, Ian. *Woman's World, Woman's Empire: The Woman's Christian Temperance Union in International Perspective, 1880–1930.* Chapel Hill: University of North Carolina Press, 1991.

Uemura, Chikako. "Nihon ni okeru senryō seisaku to josei kaihō." *Joseigaku Kenkyū* no. 2 (1993): 5–28.

United States Army Service Forces Headquarters. *Civil Affairs Handbook, Japan.* Washington, DC: United States Army Service Forces, 1944.

Uno, Kathleen. *Passages to Modernity: Motherhood, Childhood, and Social Reform in Early Twentieth Century Japan.* Honolulu: University of Hawai'i Press, 1999.

Von Eschen, Penny. *Race against Empire: Black Americans and Anticolonialism, 1937–1957.* Ithaca, NY: Cornell University Press, 1997.

Wagnleitner, Reinhold. "The Irony of American Culture Abroad: Austria and the Cold War." In *Recasting America: Culture and Politics in the Age of Cold War*, edited by Larry May. 285–301. Chicago: University of Chicago Press, 1989.

Ward, Robert. "Presurrender Planning: Treatment of the Emperor and Constitutional Changes." In *Democratizing Japan: The Allied Occupation*, edited by Robert Ward and Yoshikazu Sakamoto. 1–41. Honolulu: University of Hawai'i Press, 1987.

Yang, Hyunah. "Remembering the Korean Military Comfort Women: Nationalism, Sexuality, and Silencing." In *Dangerous Women: Gender and Korean Nationalism*, edited by Elaine Kim and Chungmoo Choi. 123–140. New York: Routledge, 1998.

Yoda, Seiichi. "Senryō ki ni okeru fujin kaihō." In *Senryō ki nihon no keizai to seiji*, edited by Takahide Nakamura. 267–300. Tokyo: Tokyo Daigaku Shuppan, 1979.

Yoneda, Sayoko. *Kindai nihon joseishi.* Vol. 2. Tokyo: Shin Nihon Shuppansha, 1973.

Yoneyama, Lisa. "Hihanteki feminizumu no keifu kara miru nihon senryō." *Shisō* no. 955 (2003): 60–84.

Yuval-Davis, Nira, and Floya Anthias. *Women, Nation, State.* New York: St. Martin's Press, 1989.

Zarlengo, Kristina. "Civilian Threat, the Suburban Citadel, and Atomic Age American Women." *Signs: Journal of Women in Culture and Society* 24, no. 4 (1999): 925–958.

Zonana, Joyce. "The Sultan and the Slave: Feminist Orientalism and the Structure." *Signs: Journal of Women in Culture and Society* 18, no. 3 (1993): 592–617.

Index